THE GR5 TRAIL – THROUGH THE FRENCH ALPS

FROM LAKE GENEVA TO NICE, INCLUDING GR52 TO MENTON

by Paddy Dillon

CICERONE

JUNIPER HOUSE, MURLEY MOSS,
OXENHOLME ROAD, KENDAL, CUMBRIA LA9 7RL
www.cicerone.co.uk

© Paddy Dillon 2025
Fourth edition 2025
ISBN: 978 1 85284 860 6
eISBN: 978 1 78765 196 8
Third edition 2016
Second edition 2013
First edition 2008

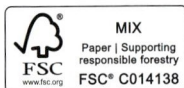

Printed in Czechia on behalf of Latitude Press Ltd on responsibly sourced paper.
A catalogue record for this book is available from the British Library.
All photographs are by the author unless otherwise stated.

Cicerone's EU representative for GPSR compliance is Easy Access System
Europe, Mustamäe tee 50, 10621 Tallinn, Estonia.
Email gpsr.requests@easproject.com.

lovelljohns.com

Route mapping by Lovell Johns www.lovelljohns.com
Contains OpenStreetMap.org data © OpenStreetMap con-
tributors, CC-BY-SA. NASA relief data courtesy of ESRI

FFRandonnée
www.ffrandonnee.fr

The routes of the GR®, PR® and GRP® paths in this
guide have been reproduced with the permission of the
Fédération Française de la Randonnée Pédestre holder of
the exclusive rights of the routes. The names GR®, PR® and GRP® are registered
trademarks.
© FFRP 2025 for all GR®, PR® and GRP® paths appearing in this work

Front cover: The view back to Col de Bise on the way down to the Chalets de
Bise (Stage 1)

CONTENTS

Updates to this guide

While every effort is made by our authors to ensure the accuracy of guidebooks as they go to print, changes can occur during the lifetime of an edition. Any updates that we know of for this guide will be on the Cicerone website (www.cicerone.co.uk/860/updates), so please check before planning your trip. We also advise that you check information about such things as transport, accommodation and shops locally. Even rights of way can be altered over time.

The route maps in this guide are derived from publicly available data, databases and crowd-sourced data. As such they have not been through the detailed checking procedures that would generally be applied to a published map from an official mapping agency, although naturally we have reviewed them closely in the light of local knowledge as part of the preparation of this guide.

We are always grateful for information about any discrepancies between a guidebook and the facts on the ground, sent by email to updates@cicerone.co.uk.

Register your book: To sign up to receive free updates, special offers and GPX files where available, create a Cicerone account and register your purchase via the 'My Account' tab at www.cicerone.co.uk.

Symbols used on route maps

Symbol	Description		Symbol	Description
Ⓢ	start point			main route
Ⓕ	finish point			variant route
Ⓢ	alternative start point			alternate stage
Ⓕ	alternative finish point			alternate stage variant
	woodland			route direction
	urban areas
	international border
	station/railway
	bus stop/station
	cable car station
▲	peak
	manned/unmanned refuge
■	building
	church/cross
	pass/bridge
	cave
•	water feature
·	other feature
	hotel
	home stay
	campsite
✳	bivouac
	restaurant/refreshments
	shop/groceries
	ATM
ⓘ	information

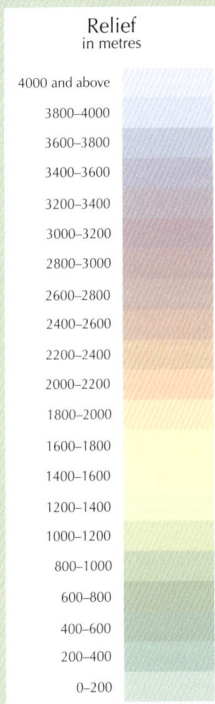

Relief
in metres

4000 and above
3800–4000
3600–3800
3400–3600
3200–3400
3000–3200
2800–3000
2600–2800
2400–2600
2200–2400
2000–2200
1800–2000
1600–1800
1400–1600
1200–1400
1000–1200
800–1000
600–800
400–600
200–400
0–200

SCALE: 1:100,000

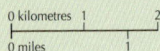

0 kilometres 1 2
0 miles 1

Contour lines are drawn at 50m intervals and highlighted at 200m intervals.

GPX files for all routes can be downloaded free at www.cicerone.co.uk/860/GPX.

Mountain safety

Every mountain walk has its dangers, and those described in this guidebook are no exception. All who walk or climb in the mountains should recognise this and take responsibility for themselves and their companions along the way. The author and publisher have made every effort to ensure that the information contained in this guide was correct when it went to press, but, except for any liability that cannot be excluded by law, they cannot accept responsibility for any loss, injury or inconvenience sustained by any person using this book.

International distress signal *(emergency only)*
Six blasts on a whistle (and flashes with a torch after dark) spaced evenly for one minute, followed by a minute's pause. Repeat until an answer is received. The response is three signals per minute followed by a minute's pause.

Helicopter rescue
The following signals are used to communicate with a helicopter:

Help needed: raise both arms above head to form a 'Y'

Help not needed: raise one arm above head, extend other arm downward

Emergency telephone numbers
For general emergency services, tel 112, but if using this service to call for mountain rescue, be sure to make that obvious to the operator. Specific telephone numbers for *PGHM (Peloton de Gendarmerie de Haute Montagne)* mountain rescue services depend on your location and are as follows:
PGHM Haute-Savoie, Chamonix-Mont Blanc, tel 04 50 53 16 89.
PGHM Savoie (Tarentaise), Bourg-St-Maurice, tel 04 79 07 01 10.
PGHM Savoie (Maurienne), Modane, tel 04 79 05 18 04.
PGHM Hautes-Alpes, Briançon, tel 04 92 22 22 22.
PGHM Alpes-de-Haute-Provence, Jausiers, tel 04 92 81 07 60.
PGHM Alpes-Maritimes, St-Sauveur sur Tinée, tel 04 93 02 01 17.

Mountain rescue can be very expensive – be adequately insured.

ROUTE SUMMARY TABLES

Stage	Start	Finish	Distance (km)	Ascent (m)	Descent (m)	Time	Page
Section 1							
1	St-Gingolph	La Chapelle-d'Abondance	17.5	1855	1210	8hr 45min	60
1a	Thonon-les-Bains	Vinzier	22	910	370	6hr 15min	65
1b	Vinzier	La Chapelle-d'Abondance	23.5	1920	1810	10hr 30min	70
2	La Chapelle-d'Abondance	Refuge de Chésery	19	1435	470	8hr 15min	75
3	Refuge de Chésery	Samoëns	23	725	2005	7hr	80
4	Samoëns	Refuge Moéde Anterne	21	1820	530	8hr	85
5	Refuge Moéde Anterne	Les Houches	19	975	1965	7hr	90
Section 2							
6	Les Houches	Les Contamines	17	975	820	5hr 45min	100
6a	Les Houches	Les Contamines	19	1455	1300	7hr 45min	105
7	Les Contamines	Plan de la Lai	20	1470	815	8hr 15min	109
8	Plan de la Lai	Landry	28	1040	2080	9hr 30min	114
Section 3							
9	Landry	Refuge d'Entre le Lac	19	1590	210	6hr 45min	128
10	Refuge d'Entre le Lac	Val d'Isère	18.5	725	1060	6hr	134
11	Val d'Isère	Bessans	22.5	1365	1485	8hr	139
11a	Val d'Isère	Bessans	26.5	1600	1720	9hr 15min	144
12	Bessans	Refuge du Plan du Lac	25.5	1415	755	10hr	149
13	Refuge du Plan du Lac	Le Montana	29	1290	1475	10hr 15min	153
14	Le Montana	Modane/Fourneaux	18	645	1745	7hr 25min	158

Stage	Start	Finish	Distance (km)	Ascent (m)	Descent (m)	Time	Page
Section 4							
15	Modane/Fourneaux	Refuge du Mont Thabor	15	1520	70	5hr 30min	196
16	Refuge du Mont Thabor	Roubion	17.5	440	1350	5hr 30min	201
17	Roubion	Briançon	24.5	1160	1550	8hr 15min	205
18	Briançon	Brunissard	18.5	1295	740	6hr	210
19	Brunissard	Ceillac	23	1335	1430	8hr 15min	214
Section 5							
20	Ceillac	La Barge/Maljasset	14	1060	800	6hr 45min	224
21	La Barge/Maljasset	Larche	25.5	1245	1475	8hr 15min	228
22	Larche	Bousieyas	20.5	1205	1005	7hr 45min	233
23	Bousieyas	Auron	22	1200	1480	9hr	237
24	Auron	Refuge de Longon	27	1775	1500	11hr 15min	242
25	Refuge de Longon	St-Dalmas	24.5	1065	1660	9hr 45min	247
Section 6							
26	St-Dalmas	Utelle	26	1160	1630	10hr	260
27	Utelle	Aspremont	24	870	1190	8hr 45min	265
28	Aspremont	Nice	13.5	220	720	4hr 15min	270

9

GR55

Stage	Start	Finish	Distance (km)	Ascent (m)	Descent (m)	Time	Page
1	Refuge d'Entre le Lac	Refuge d'Entre Deux Eaux	27	1200	1235	9hr 15min	163
2	Refuge d'Entre Deux Eaux	Refuge du Roc de la Pêche	21	1020	1230	7hr 15min	169
3	Refuge du Roc de la Pêche	Modane/Fourneaux	19	900	1730	7hr 10min	174

GR5E

Stage	Start	Finish	Distance (km)	Ascent (m)	Descent (m)	Time	Page
1	Bonneval-sur-Arc	Termignon	27	370	880	6hr 45min	179
2	Termignon	Modane/Fourneaux	21.5	425	670	5hr 45min	185

GR52

Stage	Start	Finish	Distance (km)	Ascent (m)	Descent (m)	Time	Page
1	St-Dalmas	Le Boréon	21	1365	1150	9hr 15min	275
2	Le Boréon	Refuge de Nice	18.5	1765	1040	11hr	280
3	Refuge de Nice	Refuge des Merveilles	9.5	620	720	6hr	285
4	Refuge des Merveilles	Camp d'Argent	13	595	975	6hr	288
5	Camp d'Argent	Sospel	22	470	1870	9hr	291
6	Sospel	Garavan/Menton	17.5	1130	1470	9hr 45min	296

Looking from France across the valley of La Morge to the peak of Miette in Switzerland (Stage 1)

OVERVIEW PROFILE/STAGING OPTIONS

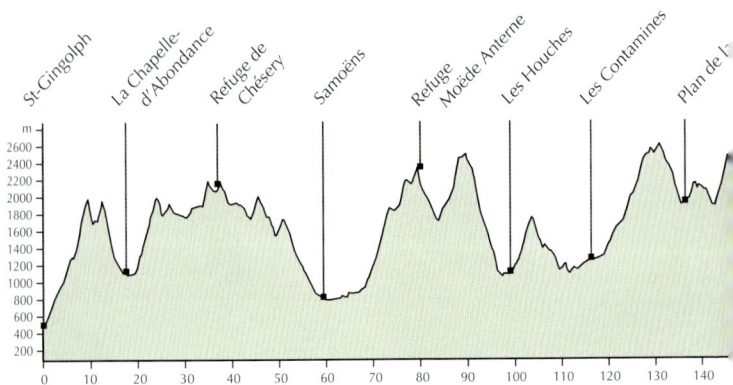

28 DAYS	St-Gingolph to La Chapelle-d'Abondance 17.5km 8hr 45min	La Chapelle-d'Abondance to Refuge de Chésery 19km 8hr 15min	Refuge de Chésery to Samoëns 23km 7hr	Samoëns to Refuge Moëde Anterne 21km 8hr	Refuge Moëde Anterne to Les Houches 19km 7hr	Les Houches to Les Contamines 17km 5hr 45min	Les Contamines to Plan de la Lai 20km 8hr 15min	Pl

31 DAYS	St-Gingolph to La Chapelle-d'Abondance 17.5km 8hr 45min	La Chapelle-d'Abondance to Refuge de Chésery 19km 8hr 15min	Refuge de Chésery to Samoëns 23km 7hr	Samoëns to Refuge Moëde Anterne 21km 8hr	Refuge Moëde Anterne to Les Houches 19km 7hr	Les Houches to Les Contamines 17km 5hr 45min	Les Contamines to Refuge du Col de la Croix du Bonhomme 17km 6hr	Refuge du la Croi du Bonho to Refuge da la 19.5km 7hr 45m

40 DAYS	St-Gingolph to Refuge de Bise 12km 5hr 45min	Refuge de Bise to Refuge de Trébentaz 12.5km 6hr 45min	Refuge de Trébentaz to Refuge de Chésery 13.5km 5hr 15min	Refuge de Chésery to Col de Golèse 14.5km 4hr 30min	Col de Golèse to Samoëns 8.5km 2hr 30min	Samoëns to Chalets d'Anterne 16km 6hr	Chalets d'Anterne to Refuge Bellachat 17km 6hr 30min	Refuge Bellachat to Col de Voza 13km 4hr 45min	Col de Voza to Le Pontet 13.5km 4hr 15min	Le Pontet to Refuge du Col de la Croix du Bonhomme 13.5km 5hr 15min	Refuge du de la Croi Bonhom to Refuge da la 19.5km 7hr 45m

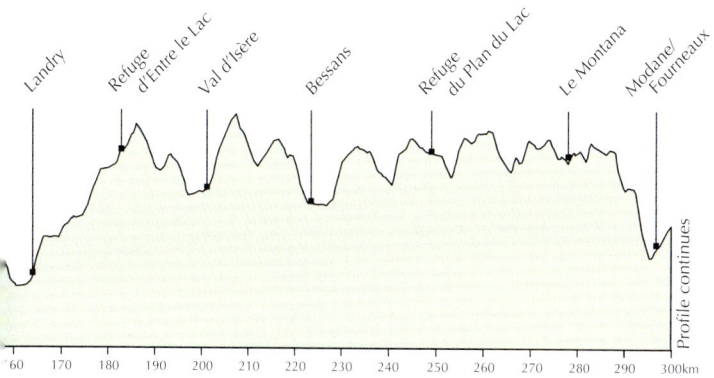

Profile labels (left to right): Landry · Refuge d'Entre le Lac · Val d'Isère · Bessans · Refuge du Plan du Lac · Le Montana · Modane/Fourneaux

Axis (km): 160 · 170 · 180 · 190 · 200 · 210 · 220 · 230 · 240 · 250 · 260 · 270 · 280 · 290 · 300km

Profile continues

Green option

Stage	Distance	Time
Landry to Refuge d'Entre le Lac	19km	6hr 45min
Refuge d'Entre le Lac to Val d'Isère	18.5km	6hr
Val d'Isère to Bessans	22.5km	8hr
Bessans to Refuge du Plan du Lac	25.5km	10hr
Refuge du Plan du Lac to Le Montana	29km	10hr 15min
Le Montana to Modane/Fourneaux	18km	7hr 45min

AVERAGE DAY – 21km / 7hr 45min

Blue option

Stage	Distance	Time
...ge da la Balme to ...ey-Nancroix	20.5km	5hr 45min
Peisey-Nancroix to Refuge du Col du Palet	17.5km	6hr 30min
Refuge du Col du Palet to Val d'Isère	14.5km	4hr 30min
Val d'Isère to Bessans	22.5km	8hr
Bessans to Bellecombe	23.5km	9hr 30min
Bellecombe to Refuge de l'Arpont	15.5km	5hr
Refuge de l'Arpont to Refuge de Plan Sec	17km	6hr 5min
Refuge de Plan Sec to Modane/Fourneaux	17.5km	7hr 25min

Profile continues

AVERAGE DAY – 19km / 7hr

Orange option

Stage	Distance	Time
...ge de Balme to ...ndry	5km	7hr
Landry to Chalet-Refuge de Rosuel	11km	3hr 45min
Chalet-Refuge de Rosuel to Refuge Col du Palet	12km	4hr 30min
Refuge Col du Palet to Val d'Isère	14.5km	4hr 30min
Val d'Isère to Bonneval-sur-Arc	14km	5hr 30min
Bonneval-sur-Arc to Refuge de Vallonbrun	16km	5hr 15min
Refuge de Vallonbrun to Bellecombe	16km	6hr 15min
Bellecombe to Refuge de l'Arpont	15.5km	5hr
Refuge de l'Arpont to Le Montana	15.5km	5hr 45min
Le Montana to Refuge de l'Orgère	13.5km	5hr 30min

AVERAGE DAY – 15km / 5hr 20min

13

Profile continued

Refuge du Mont Thabor · Roubion · Briançon · Brunissard · Ceillac · Maljasset · Larche

m
2600
2400
2200
2000
1800
1600
1400
1200
1000
800
600
400
200
0

300 310 320 330 340 350 360 370 380 390 400 410 420 430 44

28 DAYS

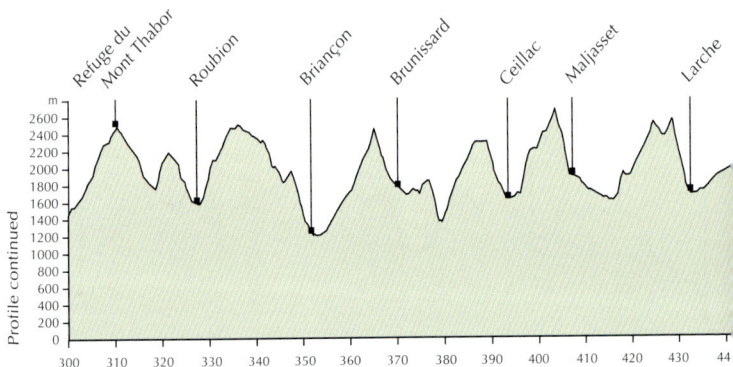

| Modane/Fourneaux to Refuge du Mont Thabor 15km 5hr | Refuge du Mont Thabor to Roubion 18.5km 5hr 30min | Roubion to Briançon 23.5km 8hr 15min | Briançon to Brunissard 18.5km 6hr | Brunissard to Ceillac 23km 8hr 15min | Ceillac to Maljasset 14km 6hr 45min | Maljasset to Larche 25.5km 8hr 15min | Bo… 2… 7hr |

31 DAYS

| Modane/Fourneaux to Les Granges de la Vallée Étroite 20.5km 7hr 15min | Les Granges de la Vallée Étroite to Cité Vauban 33km 11hr | Cité Vauban to Brunissard 20km 6hr 30min | Brunissard to Ceillac 23km 8hr 15min | Ceillac to Maljasset 14km 6hr 45min | Maljasset to Larche 25.5km 8hr 15min | Bo… 2… 7hr |

40 DAYS

| Valfréjus to Les Granges de la Vallée Étroite 16.5km 5hr 45min | Les Granges de la Vallée Étroite to Roubion 10km 3hr 15min | Roubion to Cité Vauban 23km 7hr 45min | Cité Vauban to Brunissard 20km 6hr 30min | Brunissard to Ceillac 23km 8hr 15min | Ceillac to Maljasset 14km 6hr 45min | Maljasset to Larche 25.5km 8hr 15min | Bo… 2… 7hr |

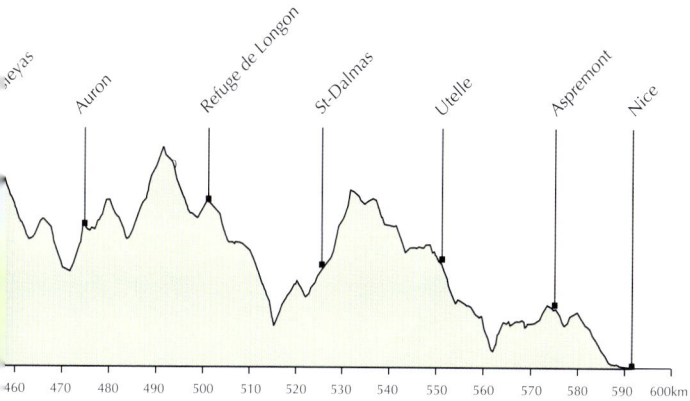

Green option — AVERAGE DAY – 21km / 7hr 45min

Bousieyas to Auron	Auron to Refuge de Longon	Refuge de Longon to St-Dalmas	St-Dalmas to Utelle	Utelle to Aspremont	Aspremont to Nice
22km	27km	24.5km	26km	24km	13.5km
9hr	11hr 15min	9hr 45min	10hr	8hr 45min	4hr 15min

Blue option — AVERAGE DAY – 19km / 7hr

Bousieyas to St-Étienne de Tinée	St-Étienne de Tinée to Roya	Roya to Refuge de Longon	Refuge de Longon to Rimplas	Rimplas to Les Granges de la Brasque	Les Granges de la Brasque to Utelle	Utelle to Les Grands Prés	Les Grands Prés to Nice
16.5km	13.5km	19km	17.5km	19km	14km	14km	23.5km
5hr 15min	6hr 15min	7hr 45min	7hr 15min	7hr	5hr 30min	5hr 30min	7hr 30min

Orange option — AVERAGE DAY – 15km / 5hr 20min

Bousieyas to St-Étienne de Tinée	St-Étienne de Tinée to Roya	Roya to Refuge de Longon	Refuge de Longon to St-Sauveur sur Tinée	St-Sauveur sur Tinée to La Bolline	La Bolline to Les Granges de la Brasque	Les Granges de la Brasque to Utelle	Utelle to Les Grands Prés	Les Grands Prés to Aire St-Michel	Aire St-Michel to Nice
16.5km	13.5km	19km	13km	8.5km	15km	14km	14km	16.5km	7km
5hr 15min	6hr 15min	7hr 45min	4hr 45min	4hr	5hr 30min	5hr 30min	5hr 30min	5hr 15min	2hr 15min

15

After passing the Chapelle St-Antoine, a metal stairway has been bolted onto a sheer cliff (Stage 27)

INTRODUCTION

Looking back down to Lac Ste-Anne from the high and stony slopes of Col Girardin (Stage 20)

Trekking across the French Alps between Geneva and Nice sounds like a daunting task even for experienced long-distance walkers, but let's start by taking a step back to look at the even bigger picture. The GR5 actually starts on the North Sea coast at Hoek van Holland in the Netherlands and heads southwards through Belgium, Luxembourg and France to finish in Nice. This guidebook is concerned only with the celebrated final part of the route, the walkers' 'Grand Traverse of the Alps' from Lac Léman (Lake Geneva) to the Mediterranean coast.

Every summer, thousands of walkers embark on this trek, either in full or in part, and complete the journey without any problems. Well-graded paths and tracks, the judicious use of strategic cols between the high peaks, and the availability of refuge and *gîte d'étape* accommodation ensure that the route is simply a long walk and one that can be completed by averagely fit, experienced hill-walkers.

People have been crossing the Alps for many centuries, as hunters, traders and warriors, and more recently, as travellers and tourists, racers and record-breakers. Your journey should prove much easier than those of many who have gone before, and with some advance thought and planning, coupled with a willingness to adapt and amend those plans on a day-by-day basis, a walk along the GR5 should present a fine challenge, without being too arduous.

It is primarily a summer trek, and a typical Alpine summer will be blessed with plenty of warm, sunny days, tempered by cool breezes on high cols, with views of dazzling snow-capped peaks rising above colourful, flowery slopes. Lodgings, food and drink are available at regular intervals; there is good signposting and waymarking, and the chance to get close to a variety of wildlife – all ensuring that a walk along the GR5 will provide memories that will last for a lifetime.

WALKING THE GR5

As there are a good many variant and alternative routes available (see 'Route outline' in this introduction), the GR5 can measure anything from 591 to 625km, and depending how walkers structure their route, in excess of 36,500m could be climbed. Yet despite its length, and despite the fact that it crosses the mighty Alps, the GR5 is still no more than a long walk.

Paths and tracks are usually well graded, and if they have to climb steep slopes, they do so by means of zigzags, so overall gradients are

seldom severe. However, there are some rough and rocky parts, and a few places where walkers who suffer from vertigo might experience problems, but only on very few occasions is it necessary to use hands to scramble up or down a rocky stretch. Also, bear in mind that a sudden snowfall (and it can snow on any day in the summer, although it usually clears very quickly) or ice-crusted rock could hamper progress. Unusually, the start of the 2024 summer season saw many high cols buried beneath snow, along with days of heavy rain.

Walkers with previous experience of the Alps, and of walking long-distance routes, will find a trek along the GR5 well within their ability, and no specialist equipment is required beyond your usual hill-walking kit. Those who have never walked in the Alps, nor ever attempted a long-distance walk before, should proceed with caution and preferably gain some experience before tackling the GR5.

Not everyone will wish to walk the whole route in a single trip. Some will be happy to cover a week here and a week there, over a period of a few years, or to split the route into two two-week trips, and since access by public transport is available at many points along the way, it is easy to do this.

In this guidebook, the schedule of six sections, taking around a month to complete, and the breakdown of timings within each day's walk, assumes

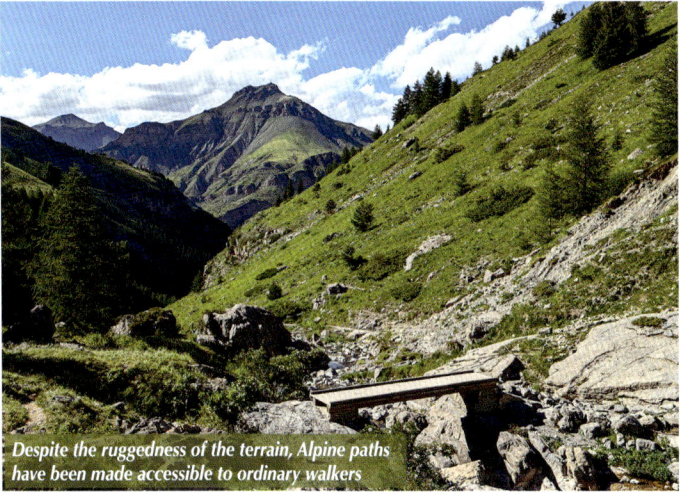

Despite the ruggedness of the terrain, Alpine paths have been made accessible to ordinary walkers

that the walker is fit, in good health, and has some long-distance walking experience. The GR5 can be covered in three weeks, so a trek of one month would comfortably suit most people. If you would prefer to take six weeks, just alter the schedule to suit your needs. The record for running the GR5 was set in the summer of 2021 by Sébastien Raichon: he ran the route in 150 hours and 27 minutes, from Thonon-les-Bains to Nice.

The author has taken careful note of the daily distances covered by other walkers along the GR5, and the stages recommended are achievable by someone who is used to long-distance walking, although these timings are easily adapted to match individual requirements. (See also 'Timings', in this introduction.)

The GR5 is not simply a linear walk but bristles with the alternatives and variants described in this guidebook. To begin with, there are two starting points on Lac Léman – at Thonon-les-Bains and St-Gingolph. Then there are two finishing points on the Mediterranean – at Nice and Menton. The GR5 sometimes splits, offering alternative options such as the GR55 and GR5E (Section 3). These routes may cover several days, as in the case of the GR55 (Section 3) through the Vanoise and the GR52 through the Parc National du Mercantour (Section 6). All of these alternatives are described in full, with maps, and are included on the maps for each section. (The French *grandes randonnées*, or GR long-distance routes, are administered by the

Fédération Française de la Randonnée Pédestre, or FFRP www.ffrandonnee.fr.)

ALPINE TRAVERSES

People have been crossing the Alps for thousands of years, hunting in the post-glacial forests, herding animals and clearing areas for cultivation. Routes from one valley to another, crossing cols between the peaks, have long been exploited. Perhaps the most famous early mountaineer was 'Otzi', whose mummified corpse was hacked from ice on the border between Austria and Italy in 1991. He lived around 3300BC, wore clothes of leather and woven grass, and was killed and left on the mountainside, to be buried by snow.

The Alps have a bloody history and are shared between countries that were often at war with each other. Celtic tribes once occupied many parts, and Roman armies stamped their authority on them. Hannibal famously crossed the Alps to fight the Romans on their own territory. Christianity became the dominant religion (today, the French Alps are overwhelmingly Roman Catholic), although Saracens often raided into the southern Alps.

There was great trade between Alpine valleys, with meat and cheese produced in the mountains finding eager consumers in towns and cities. To assist in the preservation of food-stuffs, mule trains carried salt from the Mediterranean into the mountain valleys, across high cols, to every village,

An abundance of lingering snow between Col des Fours and Col de l'Iseran (Stage 11a)

town and city. The backbone trade route was known as the Route du Sel (or Salt Route) and was important throughout medieval times.

Comte Amédée VII of Savoie was known as Le Comte Rouge, or the Red Count, as his armour was stained with the blood of his enemies. In the 14th century, he annexed Geneva and Nice to Savoie, and so must be credited with making an early bid for the ownership of the GR5, since he took possession of its terminal points! Walkers following the GR5 walk through several former fiefdoms and not only walk close to Switzerland and Italy but may actually enter those countries briefly. Massive fortifications are seen from time to time in the areas that experienced the most strife, and some roads were built by Napoleonic forces. These days, international frontiers around Europe are very casual, and in the Alps, it is possible to pass from one country to another without even realising.

The notion of making a 'Grand Traverse of the Alps' has appealed not only to walkers but also to cyclists and motorists, and routes are available for all. The GR5 used to be called La Grande Traversée des Alpes, or GTA, but that title is more often used for the motoring and cycling routes from Thonon-les-Bains to Menton.

WHO WALKS THE GR5?

You might think that a trek across the Alps would attract only the hardest of 'he-men', shouldering huge packs and gritting their teeth in the face of adversity, but you would be very wrong. There are indeed plenty of fit walkers on the route, but there are plenty more who are simply average types, and some who are unfit, or carrying injuries, yet they plod on regardless. The author has seen a blind man being led along the route, seen entire family groups with an amazing age range, and seen a family leading a donkey along the trail. The GR5 attracts all types, and providing they pitch in at a pace that suits them, they manage fine.

You may meet some of the typical characters along the route. The Flying Dutchman (or Belgian) will scoff at your short walk over the Alps and tell you that you are doing it all wrong, as you should have started from Holland. The Super-Fit Walker will be trekking solo across the Alps in three weeks or less, and won't have a bead of sweat on them, nor will they be out of breath. They'll pass you with ease, carrying hardly any gear, treating the whole thing as a stroll in the park, being well acquainted with the Alps. The Grossly Overburdened Walker will tell you that they've already posted their excess gear ahead to Nice. The Wild Camper objects to spending money, even begrudging paying for food, and camps in areas where it's forbidden, believing that anyone spending a night indoors is a softy. The Retired Couple will be taking twice as long as everyone else, having promised themselves this trip for decades and intending to enjoy every minute. The 'Last of the Summer Wine' English party are a threesome, are also retired, and generally have previous Alpine experience, even if they haven't mastered French yet. The Family Group, with mum, dad, the children, and maybe the odd aunt or uncle, will be tackling the GR5 over a period of years. The children are beginning to wonder if a beach holiday would be better, but mum and dad say they can have that when they get to the Mediterranean.

You'll be in good company on this trek!

ROUTE OUTLINE

Walking a route as long and as high as the GR5 might appear too difficult for an ordinary walker, but step back and put it into perspective. On a clear day, for example, a half-hour flight between Geneva and Nice reveals the whole route, with its long valleys and convenient passes between high mountains. Some walkers might prefer to drive along the signposted Grande Traversée des Alpes (GTA) motoring route first, between Thonon-les-Bains and Menton, which occasionally crosses the GR5, allowing an easy appreciation of the terrain it covers.

It is important to remember that if the whole distance seems too long to contemplate, the GR5 can easily be broken into short sections.

Public transport to and from a dozen points along the route is excellent, and many other points also have a reasonably good level of service. In addition, remember that the GR5 isn't simply a linear walk but has two different starting points, two different finishing points, and on most of the six sections, there are various alternative routes in between. It is entirely up to the individual walker to decide how much of the path is going to be covered and which alternative routes are to be followed when choices arise.

Read the route outline with reference to the overview map and the maps at the beginning of each of the six sections.

Section 1, Stages 1–5

Starting on the shore of Lac Léman, walkers must decide whether to trek from St-Gingolph to La Chapelle-d'Abondance in a day (Stage 1, direct) or to start from Thonon-les-Bains and take two days to cover the distance (Stages 1a and 1b). During this first section, the GR5 wanders through the Chablais region, where the pre-Alps give way to the Alps themselves. Start too early in the season and you run the risk of snow being a serious obstacle to progress on some of the high cols, or on the flanks of Le Brévent. As the mountains increase in height, many peaks carrying permanent snow and ice will be seen, culminating in magnificent views of the glaciated summit and flanks of Mont Blanc.

Those who don't want to complete the whole of the GR5 in a single journey could walk for a week and break at Les Houches (Stage 5). If a few more days are available, the Chamonix area could be explored before heading home, and if enough of the GR5 has been seen to want to return, it is easy to pick up the route and continue at a later date.

Section 2, Stages 6–8

Leaving Les Houches in tandem with the Tour du Mont Blanc, a steep climb onto Col de Voza reveals a choice of routes. The main route (Stage 6) simply descends to Bionnassay and Les Contamines, while the alternative route (Stage 6a) climbs higher to cross Col de Tricot before dropping to Les Contamines.

Either way, the route then runs up through a long valley on Stage 7, with a likelihood of finding snow towards the top of Col du Bonhomme. Always keep an eye on the weather, since very strong winds, or snow and ice on the path, will render the walk along Crête des Gittes dangerous, requiring the abandonment of the GR5 and a descent to Les Chapieux. (See 'Alpine weather', below, for information on how to obtain forecasts). Normally, there will be no problem continuing across the lush green mountainsides of the Beaufortain region.

Think ahead when accommodation options become sparse,

Approaching the Refuge du Col de la Croix du Bonhomme for food, drink and accommodation (Stage 7)

such as around Plan de la Lai (end of Stage 7) and over Col du Bresson to Valezan (Stage 8), and if camping and carrying all supplies, take careful note of the distance between shops where restocking is possible. A bit of advance planning could save a lot of wasted time and frustration. Again, those who wish to walk just this section of the GR5 will be looking for options to leave the route easily, and to assist with this approach, Landry (end of Stage 8) has a railway station.

Section 3, Stages 9–14 – three possible routes: GR5, GR55 and GR5E

One area that needs a good deal of advance planning is the Parc National de la Vanoise, where the GR5 itself (Stages 9–14) takes a very meandering route, while alternatives pursue remarkably different courses. The GR55 high-level route (GR55 Stages 1–3), for example, runs straight through the heart of the mountains, while the GR5E low-level route (GR5E Stages 1–2) stays down in the valley of the Arc. Ultimately, all three routes meet in Modane/Fourneaux but only after being apart for several days. Be sure before leaving Landry on Stage 9 and climbing up through a long valley to Col du Palet (Stage 10) that you are aware of your choices.

On the descent from Col du Palet to Tignes le Lac, the GR5 and GR55 part company. The GR5 runs over to Val d'Isère (Stage 10) then climbs over the Col de l'Iseran (Stage 11), which is 'officially' the highest point

on the route at 2770m (however, a variant route climbs to 2976m on Col des Fours). The route then descends towards the valley of the Arc, where, at Bonneval-sur-Arc (Stage 12), there is an option to take the easy, low-level GR5E to Mondane. Take stock of the time at your disposal, your fitness and energy levels, and the prevailing weather, while juggling these options.

The GR5, after descending to Bessans (Stage 11), makes a high-level traverse across the flanks of the mountains overlooking the Arc valley. In doing so, it has to traverse round the rugged gorge of the Doron (Stages 12 and 13), which pushes into the heart of the Vanoise. Fine *balcon* paths, literally like walking along a balcony, offer splendid views before a descent to Modane/Fourneaux (Stage 14).

The high-level GR55, meanwhile, runs through the heart of the Vanoise, crossing the broad Col de la Leisse and Col de la Vanoise to reach the village of Pralognan (GR55 Stage 2). In clear weather, the scenery is outstanding, but snow has a habit of lying late into summer on the passes. The Col de Chavière (GR55 Stage 3) is crossed at 2796m, higher than the main GR5 route though not as high as the variant route over Col des Fours, before descending to Modane/Fourneaux (GR55 Stage 3).

The low-level GR5E, in complete contrast, simply wanders from Bonneval-sur-Arc (GR5E Stage 1) down through the valley of the Arc to join the other two routes at Modane/

Fourneaux (GR5E Stage 2). Feel free to use this easy village-to-village route if lacking the energy for the higher routes, or if foul weather is forecast.

Section 4, Stages 15–19

Fourneaux has excellent transport links and so is a fine place to break the journey if covering the GR5 in sections. Beyond this point, subtle changes in the landscape and weather will make some walkers begin to feel that the Mediterranean is drawing near, but in fact the journey isn't even half completed!

There are two ways out of Modane. One is an old pilgrim route from the town, while the other is a steep, forested ascent from the railway station at Fourneaux. The routes reunite at the ski village of Valfréjus to continue towards the Refuge du Mont

Thabor near Col de la Vallée Étroite at the end of Stage 15.

In the Vallée Étroite, you could be forgiven for thinking that you have strayed into Italy. Signs are in Italian, other walkers are speaking Italian, and when a little settlement is reached, the food is Italian too. The Vallée Étroite was indeed part of Italy until after World War II, when it was annexed by France, and the nearest big town is Bardonecchia in Italy.

After crossing over Col des Thures on Stage 16, the route reaches the Vallée de la Clarée. There used to be a couple of variant routes here, but the original GR5 to Montgenèvre has been 'demoted' and a route originally designated as the GR5C is now the preferred route to Briançon on Stage 17. This route used to follow the rough and rocky crest of Crête

Walking through a grassy, flowery pasture high above Modane and Valfréjus (Stage 15)

de Peyrolle but it was later rerouted onto easier paths on the forested mountainside.

Briançon is the largest town along the course of the GR5 and is rich in military history. The area abounds in fortifications and was a garrison town. Naturally, because of its size, it has excellent transport links, and those walking the route in sections can easily break their journey at this point.

Beyond Briançon, the GR5 climbs over Col des Ayes on Stage 18 then enters the well-wooded Parc Naturel Régional du Queyras, traditionally a woodworking and timber-harvesting area, with Ceillac (end of Stage 19) at its heart.

Section 5, Stages 20–25

Section 5 begins at Ceillac, and once over Col Girardin, the route enters the Ubaye region, where it runs concurrent with the GR56 from Fouillouse, passing a series of high-level fortifications on its way to Larche at the end of Stage 21.

The northernmost part of the Parc National du Mercantour is entered, where wildlife is given special protection. The scenery is particularly grand on the crossing of Pas de la Cavale, although this is a remote area and walkers must rely on tiny hamlets, such as Bousieyas at the end of Stage 22, or small villages, such as St-Dalmas le Selvage on Stage 23, to provide food, drink and shelter.

The GR5 continues through the vast Vallée de la Tinée, but there are still mighty mountains to cross and occasional descents into the valley.

St-Étienne de Tinée and Auron, at the end of Stage 23, both have regular and exceptionally cheap daily bus services to and from Nice, and are therefore ideal start or finish points for those walking the GR5 in sections.

Beyond Auron and Roya (Stage 24) lie the sprawling slopes of Mont Mounier, where at last, the distant sheen of the Mediterranean catches the eye. The route makes a long traverse across the deep, forested Vallée de la Tinée, climbing to St-Dalmas on Stage 25.

Section 6, Stages 26–28 and GR52

At St-Dalmas there is a major decision to be made. At this point, the main GR5 can be followed straight to Nice or the GR52 offers a longer and much more rugged alternative, finishing on the Mediterranean coast at Menton.

Walkers choosing to stick with the GR5 follow an elevated crest, part forested but also rocky and arid, with food, drink and accommodation available at Granges de la Brasque. At the end of the long Stage 26 is the hilltop village of Utelle, sited defensively against Saracen raiders. Rugged mule tracks cross the deep, forested Gorges de la Vésubie, then easier walking leads from Levens to Aspremont (Stage 27), both villages sitting on hilltops. The final stage of the GR5 crosses the arid slopes of Mont Chauve d'Aspremont on Stage 28, finally descending from the mountains, before urban walking leads to the shore of the Mediterranean.

The GR52 provides a remarkable alternative ending to this long trek and is a really splendid route in its own right, allowing the southernmost parts of the Parc National du Mercantour to be explored. Leaving St-Dalmas, it heads northwards to cross the Col du Barn then continues through forested valleys, swinging southwards to Le Boréon at the end of GR52 Stage 1. Some steep, rough and rocky ascents and descents cross boulder-strewn slopes, passing little lakes and passing through the amazing Vallée des Merveilles on GR52 Stage 3.

There was originally a long day's walk from the Vallée des Merveilles to Sospel, completely lacking facilities, but this was diverted to hotels at Camp d'Argent, now at the end of GR52 Stage 4, continuing to Sospel, now at the end of GR52 Stage 5. The final stretch from Sospel to Menton stays high, so that the final descent is steep and rugged, landing suddenly on the shore of the Mediterranean at Menton, where this long trek through the Alps clearly reaches its end on GR52 Stage 6.

NORTH–SOUTH OR SOUTH–NORTH?

The vast majority of walkers follow the GR5 trek from north to south, from Lac Léman to the Mediterranean. There is

A route over the mountains past Col du Granon was only made part of the main GR5 in recent years (Stage 17)

no reason why the route shouldn't be followed from south to north, but fewer trekkers go in that direction. Walking north to south means you are likely to meet the same walkers during your journey. Coming the other way, you will probably walk on your own for most of the time, meeting other GR5 walkers around midday each day, maybe passing with only a nod of the head or a brief '*Bonjour*'.

Starting in the north invariably means there will still be snow lying on the high cols, while starting in the south might mean the trek can commence a couple of weeks earlier. While snow doesn't fall along the Mediterranean shore, it can be a problem further inland if you start too early. Walking southwards does not necessarily mean you will be squinting into the sun, as the sun rides high at these latitudes, and in any case, the route is very convoluted in places and takes in every point of the compass. The GR52 alternative (Section 6), for example, spends a whole morning heading northwards, even though its ultimate destination lies to the south.

The only real difference between walking southwards and walking northwards is the way other people are likely to view your progress. Walking southwards, people understand what you are doing and where you are heading. Walking northwards, it seems to take people longer to register what you are doing, and you get the distinct impression that they think you are going the 'wrong' way.

From a practical point of view, the waymarks and signposts usually work just as well in both directions, as do all the services and facilities along the route. However, users of this guidebook would find it tedious and occasionally frustrating to have to reverse all the route directions, as well as all the ascents and descents, while following the text.

TIMINGS

In the information box that precedes the route description for each stage, a total time for walking that stage is given, and the route description for each stage is further broken down into sections with timings.

In some ways, these timings are meaningless: some walkers go faster than others, and no one is ever going to match every given time for a whole month! Giving precise timings on a route where all kinds of things can affect onward progress is bound to invite criticism, but throughout the Alps people rely on such timings and they are frequently given on signposts.

Although most walkers trek from north to south, those who go the other way will naturally expect their timings to be different – when a long descent heading southwards becomes a long ascent heading northwards, and vice versa, for example.

Don't expect to match any of the timings given, but do take note of them and use them as a guide while assessing your progress. If you keep beating

The first marker for the GR5 at St-Gingolph on the shore of Lac Léman (Stage 1)

the stated times then you probably always will, and you might safely plan to walk longer and further each day as a result. If you keep falling well short then you probably always will, and you should take careful note and be prepared to split a long day into two shorter days. Some walkers might start quite slowly on the GR5 but pick up speed after a week or so, and if they spot this happening then they will find it useful when planning ahead.

The timings are purely walking times and do not take into account time spent resting, stopping for lunch, or taking more than a few snaps with the camera along the way. Any time spent motionless must be added to the time given for each stage. Walkers

who like to stop for a few minutes every hour or so, or stop for a couple of beers at every bar, or who take long lunch breaks, might need to allow an extra three or more hours per day!

Occasionally, the timings given in this guidebook will vary from those given on signposts along the GR5. In some instances, the author may consider the information on signs to be wrong and therefore offer an alternative timing. In other cases, information is clearly wrong and has been corrected.

WAYMARKING

Waymarking on French GR (or *grande randonnée*) routes is fairly standard. Horizontal red and white paint stripes are used along these routes, with the white stripe always appearing above the red one. Sometimes, little red/white plaques or stickers are screwed or glued to posts, rocks, buildings and other immovable objects. The same stripes might appear on signposts after a particular placename, indicating that the GR route runs there and, by inference, does not run to any other place that might be indicated. The system is easy to understand but not entirely foolproof.

The red/white flashes should appear at intervals, either to confirm that the route is still being followed correctly or to indicate a change of direction. There is an 'official' method of showing whether a left or right turn needs to be made but this has become

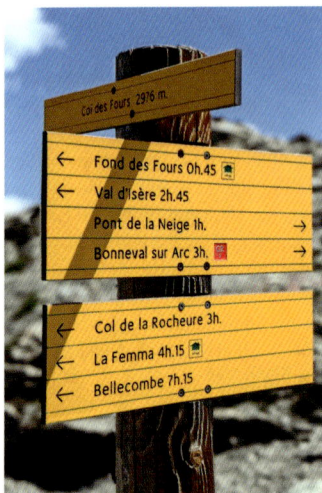

The highest signpost is found on a variant route on the GR5 that crosses Col des Fours (Stage 11a)

corrupted and is rarely used properly, so whenever you see the paint marks clearly bending left or right, assume that a turn needs to be made. If you inadvertently take a wrong turn at a junction, it is usually the case that you will quickly see a red stripe crossed at right angles by a white stripe. The red/white 'X' means that you are going the wrong way, and you should immediately turn round and retrace your steps.

In some areas, the course of the GR5 intersects with other GR routes or runs concurrent with them. Be sure to keep following the GR5, but also bear in mind that most variant and alternative routes are also marked with red/white flashes. Anticipate junctions with other trails and double-check that you are following the correct one each time. There are places where the GR5 has been rerouted, and it is usual for old red/white flashes to be painted over with grey paint or physically removed, but some faded markers may remain in place. In national parks, where the over-use of paint has been deemed an eyesore, some markers have been chiselled off rocks or repainted at a much smaller size and therefore aren't quite as obvious.

Waymarking and signposting varies from place to place, and the route description in this guidebook is intended to keep the reader alert when the GR5 switches from track to path, from riverside to forest, or from boulder-scree to grassy slopes. Always keep an eye open for markers and assume that something is wrong if none have been seen for a long time.

IGN maps show the GR routes as slightly bolder, magenta-coloured lines than are used for other walking trails and label them to confirm that they are GR routes. If the map is at odds with what is marked on the ground then common sense will have to be used. If the GR5 is found to be at variance with the description in this guidebook, the author would welcome news of any changes to the route, sent by email to updates@cicerone.co.uk or through the contact page at www.cicerone.co.uk.

GR5 GEOLOGY

The geology of the whole of the Alps is exceedingly complex, but as the French Alps form only part of the story, the geology of the GR5 is relatively simple to understand. For the most part, walkers tread on a variety of limestones, but in some places crystalline schists and gneisses are prominent. Other notable rock types include shale, sandstone, quartzite and chunky conglomerates.

The geological narrative starts with the break-up of an ancient landmass – a process known as continental drift. The massive 'plates' that carry Europe and Africa parted company, and the gap between them was filled by an ocean that came into being around 140 million years ago. The oldest Alpine rocks are therefore those that were exposed on the ancient seabed.

At different periods through geological time, the ocean was either deep or shallow, depending on the relative positions of the African and European plates. If the sea was shallow, corals colonised the seabed and built up into thick, lime-rich reefs. In deeper water, microscopic plankton thrived near the surface of the sea and their tiny skeletons fell to the seabed to create, over a very long period, thick, limey deposits.

All around the ocean, mountains were being eroded, and rivers carried rubble, sand and mud into the sea, forming alternating beds of sandstone, mudstone and cobbly conglomerates.

In some places, these became interbedded with the limey deposits. At certain times, the ocean was as deep as 5km, so there was plenty of space to be filled, resulting in a great thickness of rock.

After drifting apart for some considerable time, the African and European plates swung, as if on a pivot, setting them on a collision course, with devastating consequences. The ocean was squeezed out of existence some 60 million years ago, and the accumulated deposits were crushed together, suffering incredible heat and pressure, which often transformed the rock – a process known as metamorphism. With nowhere to go but upwards, the thick, crumpled and contorted beds of rock rose to form the Alps, and on the geological timescale, these are very 'young' mountains.

The practical outcome, as far as a walker on the GR5 is concerned, is that a number of rock types can be seen, representing a number of geological periods. The oldest rocks, which have undergone the most metamorphism, are wavy schists and hard, banded gneisses, mostly seen around Mont Blanc, the Vanoise and Mercantour. Triassic rocks include crumbling dolomitic limestones, often pitted with little holes like a sponge, and soft beds of gypsum. Jurassic limestones are hard and grey, and are the rocks that are encountered most often along the course of the GR5. Upper Jurassic rocks tend to be soft shale and

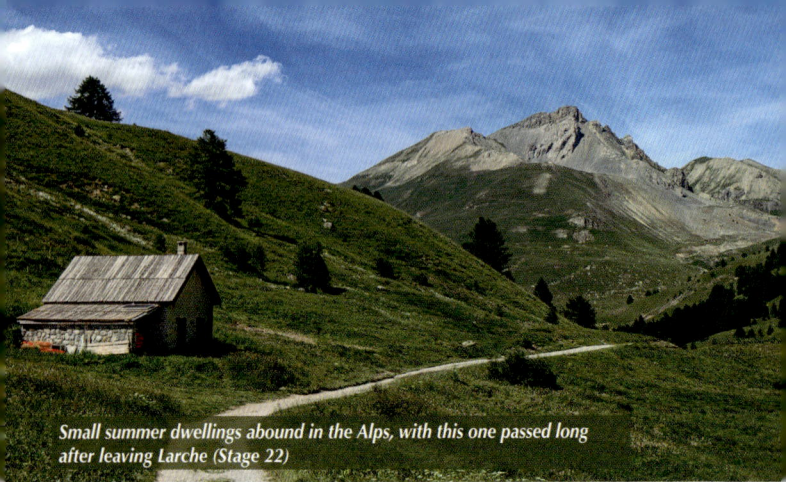
Small summer dwellings abound in the Alps, with this one passed long after leaving Larche (Stage 22)

sandstone, often inter-bedded, giving rise to slopes subject to landslip. On top of this series lies hard, dark, durable Cretaceous limestone.

In comparatively recent times – within the last couple of million years – the Alps were heavily glaciated. Monstrous glaciers carved their way through every rock type, tearing some apart with ease while slowly grinding away at harder bands. Classic U-shaped valleys and bowl-like mountain corries – or 'combes' – abound. Masses of ill-assorted bouldery moraine were dumped as the glaciers melted. Deep hollows ground out by the glaciers filled with water to become lakes. Geologists say that the Ice Age ended some 10,000 years ago, but of course, on the highest Alpine peaks, it is still in progress (although those who visit the Alps year after year are well aware that the glaciers are shrinking rapidly and may ultimately disappear altogether).

Anyone with a deep interest in geology can obtain geological maps of the Alps from the Bureau de Recherches Géologiques et Minières (BRGM); see www.brgm.fr. An easily understood 'crash course' in Alpine geology can be included in a walk along the GR5 by visiting the Espace Géologique at Château-Queyras on Stage 19 of the trek.

ALPINE FLOWERS

The Alps are famous for wildflowers and the colour and interest they lend to a walk is immense. It is simply not possible to do justice to the subject in a short space, but here are a few hints and tips to aid identification.

Flower species are divided into 'families', which often exhibit similar characteristics. If a flower looks like a daisy or buttercup then it is likely to be a member of the daisy or buttercup family. This 'rule' may apply even if colours and shapes are unexpected – such as the purple-petalled aster, which belongs to the daisy family, or the 'unopened' yellow petals of globeflowers, which belong to the buttercup family. If it looks like a tiny pansy, it will doubtless be the mountain pansy, and if it looks like clover, it will doubtless be clover, no matter how big or small or colourful it is.

Some flowers dominate the scene by virtue of their sheer size and colour, such as the tall, erect great yellow gentian. It grows in grassy places but is toxic and is therefore never eaten by grazing animals. Others are noticeable because of their colour and location, such as the blue gentian that grows across the higher cols and mountainsides, whose petals open in the full sun but twist tightly together on dull days. Some flowers have distinctive colours and shapes, such as the pink flowers with serrated edges to their petals, known simply as 'pinks'. Bell-shaped flowers, generally in shades of blue, are known as bellflowers. Seasonal variations occur, and the pale-mauve autumn crocus seems to sense when haymaking is over, since it flourishes in fields and pastures in the weeks after mowing.

Alpine rarities abound, of course, but even to shortlist them would be a pointless exercise. On the highest parts of the GR5, génepy – better known by its German name, edelweiss– can be found, but it suffers at the hands of collectors and is used to flavour a potent after-dinner digestif.

Similarly, there are plenty of humble plants that are common throughout Europe, such as rosebay willowherb, which nevertheless lend colour and interest to the scene. Many plants have short seasons, while others – such as alpenrose and blueberry (*myrtille*) – can always be spotted, since they are perennial and have woody stalks.

To assist identification when flowering plants are coming thick and fast, either carry a comprehensive guide, such as *Alpine Flowers* by Gillian Price (Cicerone, 2019), or look out for large posters showing a range of plants, often displayed along the GR5 by accommodation providers and tourist information centres.

ALPINE WILDLIFE

Anyone finding themselves in Chamonix or Les Houches, either before or during a trek along the GR5, could make a special visit to the Parc de Merlet (www.parcdemerlet.com) to see a range of Alpine animals. Walkers in the Alps may spot some species on a daily basis while obtaining only the briefest glimpses of other species. Look out for the following:

Marmot These chubby rodents live in colonies in high, grassy areas. Note their habits of standing upright, suddenly dropping into burrows, play fighting and mutual grooming. When disturbed, they give a piercing whistle. When you hear this, it may be because of your sudden appearance,

Clockwise from top left: Alpenrose, Blue gentian, Aster, a member of the daisy family

but also scan the skies, since it may indicate the presence of a large bird of prey. Marmots hibernate throughout winter, with their body temperature dropping as low as 5°C and their heart rate dropping to only three or four beats per minute.

Bouquetin These large, sure-footed, goat-like animals often travel in herds. The males have long, thick, curved horns. Young kids emit a heartbreaking bleat, while juveniles can often be seen head-butting each other. Although they are hunted in some areas, they cannot be hunted in the national parks and other reserves, where their numbers are increasing and where they seem to be more approachable than elsewhere.

Chamois These dainty, sure-footed, goat-like animals may travel in herds but are often spotted singly. Their horns are short, straight and slender, curving a little at their very tips. They were hunted almost to extinction but now enjoy protection in many places and their numbers are increasing. They are less likely to be spotted than bouquetin but may tolerate a close approach.

Deer Seldom seen because of their preference for forest cover, deer tend to graze around the margins of forests early and late in the day – and as most walkers aren't out at those times, they simply don't cross paths. Two types can be spotted – *cerf*, red deer, and *daim*, fallow deer.

Sanglier Bristly wild boar are hardly ever seen as they lie low in forests during the day. However, the damage they cause to Alpine pastures alongside forests is often clearly visible. They can literally plough up a pasture overnight while grubbing for food then vanish at dawn.

Wolf After centuries of persecution, wolves are making a comeback. Since 1992, small numbers have been present in the Parc National du Mercantour, having crossed the border from Italy. They are unlikely to be spotted. Those wishing to see wolves can visit Alpha at Le Boréon on the GR52 (GR52 Stages 1 and 2).

Squirrel Squirrels can be seen in woodlands but only by walkers who are alert to the sudden sound and sight of them scuttling for cover among the trees. They are dark brown, almost black, with small ears and bushy tails.

Ermine Stoat-like ermine wear their white coats only in the winter, to camouflage themselves against snow. During the summer, they wear brown coats, so are difficult to spot in woods or thick vegetation.

Golden eagle Although seldom seen, gliding silently over ridges then wheeling out of sight moments later, you can count on the piercing whistle of marmots to indicate when an eagle is present. Golden eagles are very large, so identification should not be a problem.

Vultures These large birds are sometimes confused with eagles. However, they are usually seen circling in the sky as a group, then they gather on the ground to squabble over the carcass of a dead animal.

Ptarmigan Ptarmigan are related to grouse and have a preference for high mountains. Their mottled plumage camouflages them on gravelly ground, and they might not be seen even if approached quite closely, unless they move.

Tétras lyre This black, grouse-like bird might not be seen often but is easily spotted when performing noisy, elaborate mating rituals. They spend most of their time on the ground, preferring forests with well-vegetated clearings.

Fish Many lakes and rivers attract fishermen – ask them what species are in the water. Generally, it will be trout. Lac Léman is the largest Alpine lake and has a long-established fishing fleet, with good stocks of fish which make their way onto restaurant menus. Trout, perch, char and carp are caught. There is a small fishing museum at the start of the GR5 at Thonon-les-Bains.

Insects Lovely butterflies, moths and honeybees flit around flowery pastures, while chirping crickets increase in size and number as you progress southwards. These are the 'benign' insects but there are also annoying ones. The livestock that grazes Alpine pastures is plagued by flies and some animals are driven to distraction by the painful jabs of horseflies. Given half a chance,

Marmots are large rodents and are widespread across the French Alps

buzzing and blood-sucking insects will pester walkers too. They tend to be worst on hot, still, sunny days and less troublesome on cold, windy or rainy days. If you are the sort of person who attracts their attention, invest in a strong repellant.

ALPINE FARMING

High Alpine farms are generally no more than *bergeries*, occupied only in the summer months by shepherds who tend flocks of sheep and herds of cattle on flower-rich pastures, or *alpages*. Generally, animals are grazed and fattened then driven down into the valleys before the onset of winter. Some small farms mow and bale hay for the winter months, even if their fields are tiny. Valley farms do this some weeks in advance of high Alpine farms.

Grazing flowery pastures may fatten beef cattle but dairy cattle are also grazed on those slopes to increase the richness of their milk, especially if that milk is to be made into cheese. In some places, rather than driving herds to and from dairy farms, mobile milking machines are parked high on the mountainsides and can be towed from one area to another as the cattle move from place to place. Sheep and goats are grazed, even to prodigious heights. The goats may be for milking but the sheep are generally there to be fattened. Free-range grazing animals can travel far in search of good food and they can disappear from sight on wooded or rocky ground, hence

the bongling bells that allow farmers and shepherds to locate their herds by sound.

Electric fences are often used to restrict grazing to certain areas. Such fences are not mentioned in the route description, since they are highly mobile and are often shifted across pastures from week to week. Usually, there is some means of passage, but if not, simply pull one of the slender fenceposts out of the ground and use it to hold the wire down while crossing, then replace the post.

PASTOUS

Huge flocks of sheep, or *troupeaux*, wander apparently untended over extensive pastures along the GR5, and signs often warn of their presence. On approaching a flock, walkers may find themselves face-to-face with large white dogs that bark menacingly. These are the famous *pastous*, related to sheepdogs from the Pyrenees. They work unsupervised by man, alone or in pairs, guarding flocks of sheep. *Pastous* are extremely loyal, living and travelling full-time with the sheep, and are fully accepted by the flock.

Pastous are not dangerous, provided they are treated properly. On approaching a flock, assume that the dogs are somewhere among the sheep – though their white coats make them difficult to spot. Do nothing to alarm the sheep, as the dogs will interpret this as a threat and will react accordingly. The best thing to do is to make

Sheep might be encountered, guarded by a pastou sheepdog hidden among the flock

a wide detour around them, if the terrain allows.

If approached by a *pastou*, do not threaten the dog by shouting or waving arms or sticks. Remain still, calm and quiet. The dog is simply trying to identify whether you are a 'threat', and while it may bark menacingly, it will not attack without provocation. Once the dog is satisfied that you pose no threat, it will return to the flock. Do not attempt to pet a *pastou* or feed it or distract it in any way. It is a working dog whose first responsibility is to the flock it guards.

LANGUAGE

French is spoken from start to finish along the GR5. Local variations in dialect should present no problem, although some people in Nice speak a dialect much closer to Italian. In

the Vallée Étroite, north of Briançon, Italian is far more likely to be heard than French, and in any case, Italian walkers are likely to be met whenever the route runs close to Italy. In such instances, if your Italian is better than your French, don't hesitate to use it.

Even if you know only a few words of French, be sure to use them and learn some more. The French appreciate being addressed in their native language and will render assistance if your command of the language is poor. Don't expect everyone you meet to speak English because some don't. However, when walkers from many nations land in the same place, English may well become the common tongue.

One of the most challenging times for those with limited fluency in French comes during a communal meal, when every topic under the

The village of Roure clings to a steep slope high above St-Sauveur sur Tinée (Stage 25)

sun is vigorously discussed, at speed, without a break. At such times, if you contribute nothing, you are quite likely to be ignored, but if you try your best, an effort will be made to include you. Remember that you are walking the GR5 and that it is quite likely that others are following the same route, so you do have something in common!

(A basic set of phrases for use on the GR5 is provided in Appendix B.)

TRAVEL TO THE ALPS

Walkers who live in London or another major European city will find Eurostar (www.eurostar.com) and TGV trains (www.sncf-connect.com) enable speedy access to the Alps. National Express coaches (www.nationalexpress.com) in Britain link with Flixbus coaches (www.flixbus.

com) serving Geneva, Chamonix and Nice. Geneva's tiny coach station has services to and from many parts of Europe, as does the coach station at Nice.

Those who prefer to fly will find that the most practical airports are Geneva, near the start of the GR5, and Nice, at the end of the route. Those who are breaking the trek into sections might also find an approach via the airport at Grenoble useful at some points, with ready access to the valleys around Modane and Briançon. Lyon is convenient for Grenoble, Chambery, etc, in the middle of the route. Easyjet (www.easyjet.com) and Jet2.com (www.jet2.com) fly direct from British airports to Geneva, Grenoble and Nice, as does the national carrier, Air France (www.airfrance.com), and connections are available with other European and international airports.

All three airports have good links with onward buses and trains, allowing many parts of the GR5 to be reached, even if the final link in the chain is little more than an irregular – and possible free – minibus (*navette*) service.

TRAVEL AROUND THE ALPS

Walkers who trek along the GR5 generally leave one village, climb over a high col, then descend to another village. Few have any idea whether public transport links one village with another, and in some cases it will but in others it won't. If a sudden storm or an unexpected dump of snow effectively closes a stretch of the route, and you want to keep moving, then you need to know what your options are. If you know that a bus is running to your next destination then you can use it. If you don't have a clue then you may be seriously inconvenienced. Useful bus and train services are noted throughout this guide, and timetables are often available online or information can sometimes be obtained from tourist information centres. Some popular towns and villages offer free bus services, or *navettes gratuites*.

SERVICES ON THE GR5

Useful services along the GR5 are noted throughout the route description. Most refuges double as restaurants during the day, and almost every restaurant doubles as a bar. Some places, known as *buvettes*, dispense

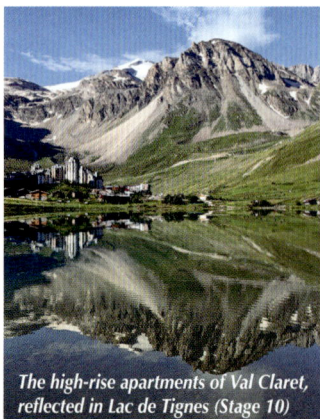

The high-rise apartments of Val Claret, reflected in Lac de Tignes (Stage 10)

only a very limited range of beverages and snacks.

Walkers requiring money will need to look out for banks and ATMs, or *distributeurs de billets*. Some places may have a range of shops while others may have only a small *épicerie* or *alimentation* selling basic groceries, or a more specialist *boulangerie* or *patisserie* selling bread or cakes respectively. Water is of course available at all lodgings along the way and at all towns and villages. Other isolated sources of drinking water are noted in the text: a notice stating '*eau potable*' means it is suitable for drinking while '*eau non potable*' isn't for drinking.

If the term 'all services' is used in the route description, this means that a town or village has a variety of accommodation options, a bank, ATM, post office, and a range of shops, bars and restaurants. Public transport is mentioned, and if there is a tourist information centre, the telephone number and website address is given.

ACCOMMODATION

Lodgings along the GR5 vary in every possible way. Some places boast a range of splendid hotels while others may have only a single basic refuge. Anyone wanting to walk the whole of the GR5 using a specific type of accommodation will find it impossible. In some places, there are no hotels, while in other places, there are no refuges, so overnights will be varied. Accommodation tariffs are often visible when checking into lodgings or are pinned behind the door of each room. Usually, you can pay for a bed or a room without taking meals. If you want to pay for dinner, bed and breakfast all together, ask for *demi-pension*. See Appendix A for an accommodation list.

Campsites

Carrying a tent along the GR5 allows trekkers to be completely independent. If hotels and refuges are full then maybe a nearby campsite will have space. Some campsites are very popular and get fully booked, which then leads trekkers to consider wild camping. In some places, a 'bivouac' is allowed as long as you pitch your tent after 7pm and pack it away before 7am. In other places, wild camping is strictly prohibited and subject to a fine if you are caught. Some refuges will allow a small number of tents to be pitched alongside while others won't allow any.

Refuges

These provide basic accommodation. In some areas, refuges are a few minutes apart, while in other areas, they are days apart. The Club Alpin Française runs many refuges while others are privately owned

The recently rebuilt Refuge de Longon fills a gap between accommodation at Roya and Roure (Stage 24)

and operated by families or municipal authorities. Sleeping is in mixed dormitories, and everyone is usually in bed by 10pm, with a view to rising early. Bunks have mattresses, with duvets or blankets, but you need your own sheets or a sleeping bag or silk liner. Some refuges are like small hotels, with hot showers and every comfort, while others are rough and ready, without showers or hot water. All refuges provide evening meals and breakfast and usually operate as restaurants during the day. A good site for checking the current details of refuges is www.refuges.info.

Gîtes d'étape

Gîtes d'étape fulfil a similar role to youth hostels in Britain. They generally offer more facilities than refuges, with smaller dormitories. Bunks or beds have mattresses, with duvets or blankets. Some provide sheets while others require you to provide your own. Some *gîtes* are almost as basic as a good refuge while others are like small hotels. Specific details of *gîtes* along the GR5 can be checked at www.gites-refuges.com.

Chambres d'hôte

These are often high-priced establishments providing individual rooms with all facilities. They are often translated as 'bed and breakfast' but may offer evening meals too. Some *chambres d'hôte* are quite luxurious while others are as basic as a good *gîte d'étape*.

Hotels

Hotels may be star-rated or unclassified, and standards vary enormously. More stars mean more services and facilities, and a higher price. Most hotels offer a full meals service but a few offer only a basic breakfast and no evening meal, so be sure to check. Some hotels operate under the Logis de France brand and can be checked at www.logishotels.com.

Advance booking

Some people like to book all their accommodation in advance and walk in the knowledge that there is a bed and a meal waiting for them at the end of each day. However, this may be inadvisable on the GR5, where a severe storm or heavy fall of snow could disrupt a carefully planned schedule. The loss of one day's walking could result in a nightmare round of phone calls, trying to cancel bookings and make new ones.

Most trekkers would have no problem booking a day or two in advance as they walk, and during peak-holiday-season weekends booking a couple of days ahead is advised. If language is a problem, refuge staff will book ahead on your behalf, though in many cases, you can make an online booking. Ask staff at *gîtes* or hotels if they will do the same (offering one or two euros for their trouble if they pull a face). In some towns and villages, staff at the tourist information office (*office de tourisme*, *maison de tourisme* or *syndicate d'initiative*) will assist. Sites such as www.airbnb.com and www.booking.com are useful for checking short-term availability and securing bookings. A basic accommodation list is provided in Appendix A.

FOOD AND DRINK

Walkers on the GR5 find plenty of food and drink at regular intervals, although there is the odd stage where nothing is available and supplies need to be carried. Shops and restaurants are noted throughout this guide. There may be supermarkets in some places but only a small *épicerie* stocking high-priced local specialities in other places.

Refuges operate as restaurants during the day then provide a set evening meal or menu for residents. In refuges and *gîtes*, it is usual for residents to dine communally, while hotels serve food at individual tables. Evening meals are substantial and rich in their variety and provide plenty of energy after the day's exertions. Those with special dietary requirements must give plenty of notice! Breakfast, on the other hand, is generally frugal and may consist of nothing more than bread and jam with coffee or tea. When asked what time you want breakfast, bear in mind that 7am is by no means considered early! You may have to declare, the evening beforehand, what type of hot drink you require for breakfast. A glossary of common terms for food and drink in French can be found in Appendix B.

Beaufort cheese in a 'cave' beneath the Chalet du Berger at Plan de la Lai (Stage 7)

TELEPHONES

Mobile phones do not always get a signal in the Alps. Sometimes, on cresting a col, half the mobiles carried by walkers spring to life, resulting in a string of messages to be answered. Those whose mobiles don't work generally ask the others which provider they are using. The strongest signal may not come from a French mast if you are near a border but rather a Swiss or Italian one. Talk to your provider before taking a mobile phone on this trek. Telephone kiosks, or *cabines téléphoniques*, are becoming scarce. They do not accept coins, so be prepared to pay for a call by credit/debit card. Some hotels provide telephones in rooms, but check the tariff as some charge exorbitant prices.

PATH CONDITIONS

Some of the mountain paths along the GR5 are steep and rocky while others were laid centuries ago for mule traffic, zigzagging uphill rather than climbing straight up. In some places, signs request that walkers do not shortcut zigzags, and as shortcutting makes things more difficult, it should be avoided anyway. On the other hand, the long and lazy zigzags taken by vehicular roads are frequently shortcut by paths.

Broad tracks have been made in recent years for occasional vehicle use, often in forests or to serve high farms and refuges. Tracks such as these allow walkers to stride out briskly, at least as far as the next steep slope and zigzag path. The GR5 seldom uses

A rugged path can be followed down to Maljasset in search of accommodation (Stage 20)

roads, but where it does, walk on the pavement if one is available, or on the left to face oncoming traffic, unless the nature of the road dictates otherwise. The most awkward roads are those leading into and out of towns, where there are numerous distractions and the red/white route markers and signposts are easily missed. To assist walkers, landmarks and street names are noted in this guide.

ALPINE WEATHER

The Alps, being high mountains, are quite capable of generating their own weather, which can be difficult to predict. However, it is well worth getting into a routine of checking weather forecasts, not only for the day but for the days ahead as well. If you have no access to radio or TV forecasts, simply look out for the forecasts, or *météos*, posted at tourist information offices and refuges. Most refuges will be aware of the weather forecast, and most *gîtes* will be happy to find one if they aren't already aware of it. In many places, the forecast is available only in French, but sometimes an English summary is also posted.

Even when you have the most up-to-date forecast, you should still keep a 'weather eye' open, watching especially for the build-up of heavy cloud that often precedes a storm. As far as possible, ensure that you are away from exposed cols and ridges, or better still, safely inside, before a storm breaks. Deep snow can, in theory, fall on any day in the summer, although it will be rare and should clear quickly.

A typical Alpine summer day will start cool – or even cold, clear and frosty at altitude – and will rapidly warm up as the sun rises. During the afternoon, clouds will form, and these may completely obscure the sun, possibly leading to rain or a storm. Often, the cloud simply disperses during the night and the next day starts clear again. Most walkers in the Alps start early and finish early, so they avoid being caught in rain later in the day. Sometimes, fine weather may last for weeks, while at other times, it can rain for weeks, with low cloud wiping out any chance of decent views. Keep a lookout for those forecasts, dress for the prevailing conditions, and be prepared to alter your plans in really nasty weather.

WHEN TO WALK THE GR5

The GR5 is primarily a summer trek. Starting too early or late in the season means you could have problems with deep snow. Most French people take their holidays between mid-July and mid-August, between Bastille Day and Assumption Day, and this particular period sees the best weather conditions on the GR5, although there can be stiff competition for beds along the way. Starting in the middle of June will almost certainly mean crossing deep snow on some high cols. Running late into September could spell running into early winter weather. Some refuges are open from mid-June to mid-September but some are only open in July and August. The more services that close, the more prospective trekkers must fend for themselves.

KIT CHECK

Some people trek the GR5 carrying full backpacking gear, aiming to camp almost every night along the way. Given the nature of the route, carrying a heavy pack is hard work. However, tents and sleeping bags can be lightweight and strong, so pack weight need not be excessive, and certainly no more than 10kg, with a tent, before adding food and water. It will seldom be necessary to pack more than a day's worth of food, and water is available at regular intervals. Only a few people camp all the way along the GR5, with most preferring to spend at least a few days indoors. Experienced backpackers will already be well aware of the kit they need for a successful trek.

Most walkers use refuges, *gîtes* and occasional hotels, so they aren't burdened with heavy packs. Apart from sheets or sleeping-bag liners (which are more lightweight) or a light sleeping bag, toiletries, and a complete change of clothes, nothing else is really essential on top of what you would normally carry on a day's hill walk. When the sun shines strongly at altitude, plenty of sunscreen, a sunhat

The dining room inside the wonderfully restored Refuge de Longon (Stage 24)

and sunglasses prove useful. Some people make the mistake of packing far too many clothes when regular rinsing and drying is adequate to keep a few clothes fresh. Others take things that may not even be used, carrying dead weight along the route.

Refuges and *gîtes* require you to wear 'house shoes' rather than your walking shoes or boots. You don't need to pack extra footwear as these places usually provide shoes in a variety of sizes. For the actual walking, use whatever shoes or boots you already feel comfortable with, but expect a trek along the whole of the GR5 to cause considerable wear!

To summarise, your normal hill-walking kit should be fine for a trek along the GR5, with the addition of a change of clothes and basic bedding if staying indoors. Those who intend to camp will manage fine with lightweight kit. The GR5 is just a long walk and so doesn't require specialist equipment.

MAPS

There are a few walkers, mainly French, who are happy to walk the whole of the GR5 without maps, relying entirely on the red/white route markers and signposts. Many French walkers rely on IGN map extracts in the FFRP Topoguide series (www. ffrandonnee.fr) that are printed at a scale of 1:50,000, but this means carrying four guidebooks to cover the whole route.

The best maps are the IGN 1:25,000 Serie Bleu, and 21 of these cover the route: numbers 3528 ET, 3428 ET, 3530 ET, 3531 ET, 3531 OT, 3532 OT, 3633 ET, 3534 OT, 3532 ET, 3634 OT, 3535 OT, 3536 OT, 3537 ET, 3637 OT, 3538 ET, 3639 OT, 3640 OT, 3641 ET, 3741 ET, 3742 OT, 3741 OT. These are available along the route, where they can be purchased one at a time, used as required, then posted home at intervals. Alternatively, they can be ordered in advance, either direct from the IGN in France (www.ign.fr) or from British suppliers such as Stanfords (tel 0207 836 1321 www.stanfords.co.uk), The Map Shop (tel 01684 593146 www. themapshop.co.uk) or Cordee (www. cordee.co.uk).

IGN mapping at various scales can be viewed online at www.geo-portail.gouv.fr. An incredibly useful, free app called 'Cartes IGN' works on mobile phones. It offers a wealth of useful tools, combined with seamless IGN mapping, allowing routes to be highlighted, distances to be checked and profiles to be generated. However, everything is in French and it needs to be translated in order to get the full benefit.

At the risk of worrying yourself sick, look out for the moulded plastic relief maps of various parts of the Alps, produced by the IGN. These are found on walls in refuges, *gîtes*, hotels, bars and tourist information offices. While tracing the course of the GR5 on these relief maps, bear in mind that the

The Col de la Vallée Étroite was formerly on the Franco-Italian border (Stage 16)

vertical gradient is hugely exaggerated and that the ascents and descents are nowhere near as steep as they appear!

There are three types of maps in this guidebook, as follows:

- An overview map on the inner cover sets the GR5 in its Alpine context, showing the whole route at a glance.
- Each of the six main sections along the route has its own introductory map, so that towns and potential transport links off route can be seen.
- The daily route maps are at a scale of 1:100,000, covering the entire GR5 and all the variant and alternative routes. Walking north to south, you read these maps

from the top of the page to the bottom. Certain placenames in the daily route descriptions have been highlighted in **bold**, meaning they are to be found on the maps. Facilities along the route are indicated so that it is easy to see at a glance what is available throughout each stage.

Route profiles are provided at the rate of one per stage, labelled with selected features, so that all the ascents and descents can also be observed at a glance.

CURRENCY AND COSTS

The euro is the currency of the GR5. (Banks and ATMs, or *distributeurs de billets*, along the route are noted in the route description.) Large denomination euro notes are difficult to spend, so avoid the €500 and €200 notes altogether, and avoid the €100 notes if you can. The rest are fine: €50, €20, €10 and €5. Coins come in €2 and €1. Small denomination coins, while officially termed cents throughout Europe, are referred to as *centimes* in France. They come in values of 50c, 20c, 10c, 5c, 2c and 1c. Prices are written as 5€20, for example, and spoken as *cinq euro vingt* (five euro twenty) or *cinq euro vingt centimes*. Even if you access the GR5 via Geneva in Switzerland, you will find that euros are often accepted instead of Swiss francs, and the two currencies differ only slightly in value.

Budgeting for a long trek and managing money supplies on the hoof involves a lot of unknown quantities, so you will have to resort to guesswork. The biggest expenses will be accommodation, food and drink, but sometimes, these will be available as a 'package' involving a single payment. Expect *demi-pension* (dinner, bed and breakfast) in a refuge to cost about €60 per person per night. The same deal in a *gîte d'étape* might cost about €75. A single person staying in a hotel might find themselves paying well over €100, depending on the quality of the establishment, and this will doubtless include a single supplement for the room. Two or more people sharing a room can expect to pay a little less.

At all lodgings the *demi-pension* rate will usually state, or at least imply, *'boissons non compris'*, drinks not included. If you enjoy a few beers after a day's walk, or a bottle of wine with your meal, then you need to budget separately for it. A simple cup of coffee after a meal might appear as another €3 or €4 on the bill.

During the day, many walkers will take a lunch break at a convenient refuge or restaurant if one appears at the right time. Expect small snacks to be quite pricey, with coffee and a cake maybe costing €7. A full meal might easily set you back €30 to €40. Remember that food and drink in the mountains has been driven up a rugged track, carried in by people or mules, or flown in by helicopter. The convenience of finding food high in the mountains must be balanced against the cost you pay for its transportation. You can, of course, carry your own food, but stores offering a wide range of goods are sometimes few and far between, and some small shops only offer rather expensive artisanal local produce. The longer the gaps between shops, the more you have to carry, otherwise you simply pay the price for someone else carrying it up there.

Surprisingly, some remote refuges are equipped to handle payment by credit/debit card, or *carte bancaire*, using electronic card readers. However, most remote places require payment in cash, and if you arrive without sufficient funds, it will cause embarrassment and annoyance. 'Pas de CB' means that payment by card is not available. Some French walkers still pay by cheque, but unless you have an account with a well-known French bank this option simply isn't available to you. So, you need to carry both cash and a credit/debit card to be covered for all eventualities. You can avoid many on-the-spot payments by booking and paying online.

Getting to and from the terminal points of the GR5 from the nearest airports – Geneva and Nice – involves using cheap and regular buses or trains. Bus travel is very cheap and trains cost only a little more. Depending on your start and finish points, travel between the terminal points and the nearest airports costs something in the region of €10–€20. Avoid using taxis since they are very expensive by comparison and not at all necessary. Similarly, if bus or train transport is needed to or from other parts of the GR5, expect a bus to be cheaper than a train, expect information to be readily available online, expect services to be reliable, and avoid taxis unless you have money to burn.

When cash reserves are running low, you need to be thinking ahead, and you need to know where to find an ATM to avoid having to leave the route for a nearby town. Locations of banks and ATMs are mentioned throughout this guidebook.

A café on Col du Granon, halfway between Vallée de la Clarée and Briançon (Stage 17)

Occasionally, an ATM might be inside a building, such as a *mairie*, supermarket or post office, rather than out on a street and available at all hours.

So, how much will it cost per day? If alternating between refuges and *gîtes*, with occasional hotels, taking *demi-pension*, with perhaps a couple of extra drinks, plus a few snack items in the pack from time to time, €150 per person per day should be ample. If you fancy using a few more hotels, you might expect the daily average to be closer to €200. A hardy backpacker, using a few campsites and several wild pitches, buying food from shops along the way, might get by on as little as €30 per day. The author has seen people settling hotel bills well in excess of €200, as well as others scrimping and saving every cent and spending less than €15 per day.

EMERGENCIES

Anyone walking for a month or so through the Alps can expect to suffer a cut, graze or bruise at some point, and will almost certainly get a jab from a horsefly! A simple first-aid kit will take care of most little problems. Other issues, such as an upset stomach, can often be resolved by visiting a pharmacy, where staff can advise on basic treatment.

Beyond that, if medical intervention is required, the Global Health Insurance Card (GHIC) is available free to UK residents, and the European Health Insurance Card (EHIC) is available free to EU residents. Both cards could prove useful for getting a partial reimbursement of costs.

To summon help, there are several ways to contact the emergency services, and if there is any doubt about which service is required, phone the general emergency number 112 (or text 114). If a specific emergency service is definitely required, there are separate numbers for each:

- police (*gendarmerie*) tel 17
- ambulance (*samu*) tel 15
- fire service (*pompiers*) tel 18

Mountain rescue teams, or Peloton de Gendarmerie de Haute Montagne (PGHM), can be alerted by phoning 112. However, bear in mind that each *département* in the Alps is covered by a separate team; each of their bases can be contacted directly as follows:

- Haute-Savoie – Chamonix tel 04 50 53 16 89
- Savoie (Tarentaise) – Bourg-St-Maurice tel 04 79 07 01 10
- Savoie (Maurienne) – Modane tel 04 79 05 18 04
- Hautes-Alpes – Briançon tel 04 92 22 22 22
- Alpes de Haute-Provence – Jausiers tel 04 92 81 07 60
- Alpes Maritimes – St-Sauveur sur Tinée tel 04 93 02 01 17

Anyone using a VHF radio can call for assistance on the emergency Canal E, on 161.300 Mhz.

Mountain rescue in France is usually provided free of charge but that cannot be guaranteed. If the rescue involves medical intervention, the doctor's fees must be paid, so **it is important to carry insurance** that includes medical, as well as rescue, cover. A very short stretch of the GR5 runs into Switzerland, where mountain rescue is an expensive, paid-for service.

KEY POINTS

Advice in a nutshell
- Don't walk too early or late in the year.
- Make sure you are fit and well prepared.
- Pack light and carry only what you need.
- Don't forget your sheets, sleeping bag or liner.
- Learn some basic French and use it.
- Look out for weather forecasts (*météos*).
- Take it slow and steady (as the French do).

- Be aware of your options every day.
- Protect yourself against the strong Alpine sun.
- Don't book accommodation too far ahead.

Points to bear in mind
- The GR5 is a walk not a mountaineering expedition.
- Waymarks are usually clear red/white stripes.
- Refuges usually operate as restaurants during the day.
- Meals in refuges and *gîtes* are usually communal.
- Sleeping arrangements in refuges and *gîtes* are mixed.
- Most people will be asleep in bed by 10pm.
- Mobile phones only rarely get a signal in the Alps.
- Refuge staff will help you book your accommodation ahead.
- *'VTT'* (*vélo tout terrain*) means cyclists may be using the path.
- It's fun – enjoy it!

SECTION 1:
LAC LÉMAN TO
LES HOUCHES

Aouille de Criou is glimpsed from a gap in the woodland on the way down to Samoëns (Stage 3)

This first, northern section of the GR5 is quite popular, fitting comfortably into a week. Many walkers use it as a way of reaching Chamonix, where they spend a few more days exploring. Most then go on to plan further trips, even to the extent of completing the whole of the GR5 over a period of years in sections of a few days apiece.

First and foremost, be realistic with your plans. There are two alternative starting points from which to reach La Chapelle-d'Abondance, and if you are full of energy, fit and ready for the mountains, then by all means start from St-Gingolph and walk to La Chapelle-d'Abondance on your first day. If you are not so fit, or less confident in your abilities, then consider the gentler alternative route from Thonon-les-Bains to La Chapelle-d'Abondance over a period of two days.

Be warned that Le Brévent, at the end of this section, is a huge mountain

Jet d'Eau, Geneva (Stage 1)

that can be an obstacle in bad weather. It holds snow well into the summer and is very exposed in storms. However, in clear weather, there is no finer stance for admiring Mont Blanc. Keep up to date with weather forecasts and ensure, as far as is possible, that

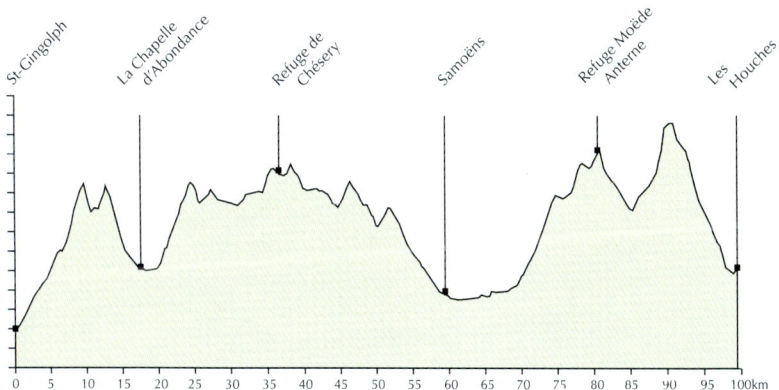

55

your summit bid coincides with opti-
mum conditions to cross in safety and
enjoy remarkable views.

The natural arrival and departure
airport for this section is Geneva,
which has regular transport links
to and from the terminal points of
Thonon-les-Bains, St-Gingolph and
Chamonix, as well as links with other
places along the way.

Travel to St-Gingolph

- **Ferry** This is the classic, scenic,
  but also the slowest and most
  expensive approach. Ferries
  operate from Swiss ports on Lac
  Léman, and while it is possible to
  sail from Geneva to St-Gingolph,
  it's best to allow a whole day for
  the journey. Check timetables
  with the Compagnie Générale

de Navigation sur le Lac Léman
(CGN): tel 0848 811 848 www.
cgn.ch.

- **Train** Access by train is possible
  only from Switzerland, since the
  line from France is closed between
  Évian-les-Bains and St-Gingolph,
  although there have been plans
  to restore it. Rail approaches are
  reasonably priced and run via
  St-Maurice and Monthey or can
  be combined with a ferry from
  Vevey. For timetables: tel 0848
  44 66 88 www.sbb.ch/en.

- **Bus** Bus travel is very cheap. On
  the Swiss side, CarPostal buses
  operate in conjunction with trains
  from Monthey. Details can be
  checked: tel 0848 818 818 www.
  postauto.ch/en. On the French
  side, buses operate from Geneva

Stage	Place	Altitude	Walking time	Distance
1	**St-Gingolph**	**374m**	**0hr 00min**	**0km**
1	Novel	950m	2hr 00min	4.5km
1	Chalets de Bise	1506m	3hr 45min	7.5km
1	**Chapelle-d'Abondance**	**1021m**	**3hr 00min**	**5.5km**
1a	**Thonon-les-Bains**	**374m**	**0hr 00min**	**0km**
1a	Armoy	645m	2hr 00min	7.5km
1a	Reyvroz	777m	1hr 45min	6km
1a	Bioge	534m	1hr 00min	3km
1a	**Vinzier**	**870m**	**1hr 30min**	**5.5km**
1b	*Refuge Dent d'Oche*	*1750m*	*5hr 15min/13km to turn off, +1hr 30min off main route*	
1b	Chalets de Bise	1506m	2hr 15min	5km

to Thonon-les-Bains or Évian-les-Bains, where a change of bus links with St-Gingolph. Buses are operated by SAT: tel 04 50 81 74 74 www.sat-leman.com.

Travel to Thonon-les-Bains

• **Ferry** This is the classic, scenic, but also the slowest and most expensive approach. Ferries do not run direct from Geneva to Thonon-les-Bains, so allow plenty of time if you choose this approach. Check timetables with the Compagnie Générale de Navigation sur le Lac Léman (CGN): tel 0848 811 848 www.cgn.ch.

• **Train** Rail approaches are reasonably priced, both from the French rail network and the Gare Eaux-Vives in Geneva in Switzerland, although using the latter may involve a change at Annemasse. Timetables can be checked with SNCF: tel 01 84 91 91 91 www.sncf-connect.com.

• **Bus** Bus travel is fairly cheap and regular between Geneva and Thonon-les-Bains. Check timetables with TPG: tel 00800 022 021 20, www.tpg.ch/en.

Key to symbols:
🏠 refuge/hut/gîte d'étape ⌂ hotel ⌂ home stay ⌂ unmanned hut/bothy ▲ camping ✱ bivouac 🍴 restaurant/refreshments ⊕ shop/groceries 💶 ATM ⓘ TIC ▣ train ◉ bus 🚡 lift/cable car

Facilities								
refuge/hut	hotel/homestay	camping	restaurant	shop	ATM	TIC	train	lift/cable car
	⌂		🍴	⊕	💶	ⓘ	▣	🚡
	⌂		🍴					
🏠			🍴					
🏠	⌂		🍴	⊕		ⓘ		🚡
	⌂	▲	🍴	⊕	💶	ⓘ	▣	🚡
	⌂		🍴	⊕				🚡
			🍴					
								🚡
🏠		▲	🍴	⊕	💶			🚡
🏠			🍴					
🏠			🍴					

Stage	Place	Altitude	Walking time	Distance
1b	**Chapelle-d'Abondance**	**1021m**	**3hr 00min**	**5.5km**
2	*Refuge Trébentaz*	*1524m*	*2hr 15min/5km to turn off, +1hr off main route*	
2	Col de Bassachaux	1780m	4hr 15min	9km
2	Alpage de Chaux Fleurie	1830m	0hr 30min	1.5km
2	**Refuge de Chésery**	**1985m**	**1hr 15min**	3.5m
3	Chaux Palin	1844m	0hr 45min	2.5km
3	Lapisa	1789m	0hr 45min	2.5km
3	Col de Coux	1920m	1hr 15min	4km
3	Col de Golèse	1600m	1hr 45min	5.5km
3	Les Allamands	1030m	1hr 00min	4.5km
3	Les Fontaines	762m	1hr 00min	2.5m
3	**Samoëns**	**703m**	**0hr 30min**	1.5km
4	*Pont des Nants (Sixt-Fer-á-Cheval)*	*768m*	*2hr 00min/6km to turn off*	
4	Cascade du Rouguet	960m	1hr 00min	3.5km
4	Le Lignon	1180m	0hr 30min	1.5km
4	Chalets d'Anterne	1808m	2hr 30min	5km
4	**Refuge Moëde Anterne**	**1996m**	**2hr 00min**	**5km**
5	Le Brévent	2525m	3hr 45min	9.5km
5	Refuge de Bellachat	2152m	0hr 45min	2.5km
5	*Merlet path junction*	*1648m*	*1hr 00min/2.5km to turn off*	
5	**Les Houches**	**1008m**	**1hr 30min**	4.5km

Facilities

STAGE 1
St-Gingolph to La Chapelle-d'Abondance

Start	St-Gingolph
Finish	La Chapelle-d'Abondance
Time	8hr 45min
Distance	17.5km
Total Ascent	1855m
Total Descent	1210m
Terrain	Rather steep and rugged ascents and descents for a first day, from a climb through a forested valley, crossing two rugged cols, then finishing with a descent through another forested valley.
Maps	3528 ET
Refreshments	Restaurants at St-Gingolph. Restaurants at Novel and Chalets de Bise. Plenty of choice at La Chapelle-d'Abondance.
Accommodation	Hotels at St-Gingolph. Hotel at Novel. Refuge at Chalets de Bise. Hotels and *gîtes d'étape* at La Chapelle-d'Abondance.

Only those who arrive fit and seasoned for a mountain walk are likely to cover the distance from St-Gingolph to La Chapelle-d'Abondance comfortably in a day; there are two steep-sided cols to be crossed. Those who arrive late in the morning could consider walking as far as Novel and spending the night there. Another approach is to split this long and arduous day at the Chalets de Bise. If in doubt, follow the gentler alternative two-day walk from Thonon-les-Bains to La Chapelle-d'Abondance (see Stages 1a and 1b).

ST-GINGOLPH

Founded in the year 755 by Gingulf, an officer in the service of Pépin le Bref, from 1204, the area was a property of the Abbaye d'Abondance. The village was divided in 1569 by a treaty between Savoie and Valais. On the Swiss side, the château dates from 1588 and contains a museum, while the church was built in 1677. The French half was burnt in 1944 as a reprisal against resistance activities, and most inhabitants lived as refugees in Switzerland.

There is a full range of services in St-Gingolph and these are mostly concentrated on the French side. The tourist information office is on the French side but it advises on facilities for the whole village: tel 04 80 16 10 64 www.st-gingolph.com.

St-Gingolph to Novel   2hr, 4.5km, +580m -5m

There are three ways to reach the start of the GR5. If arriving by ferry in the Swiss half of St-Gingolph, at the lake level of 374m, stay close to the shore to find a metal footbridge spanning a river, **La Morge**. This leads to the French half of the village, where the start of the GR5 is marked on the ground as 'Nice/Menton 620km'. Walk up Rue du Lac as marked. If arriving by train, walk down Rue du Lac in the Swiss half of the village, cross the metal footbridge, then walk up Rue du Lac in the French half of the village. If arriving by bus from Évian-les-Bains, walk down Rue du Lac in the French half of the village, admire the view across Lac Léman, then turn around and walk back up the street.

Cross the main road in the village and walk straight up the narrow Rue de la Morge, under an old railway bridge, past Place Charles de Gaulle and straight ahead up Rue des Gaules, as signposted for Novel and the GR5. Continue climbing Chemin du Cret and Rue des Granges, leaving the village, to reach the entrance to Léman Forest, an arboreal adventure park.

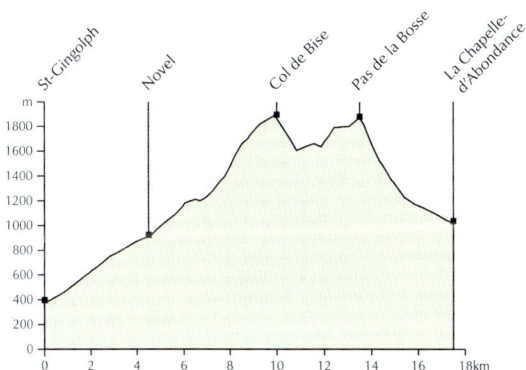

61

Follow a winding track up through the valley of La Morge, enjoying fine cascades. The woods are predominantly beech, lush with ferns and mosses. **Le**

Freney is to the left, across the river in Switzerland, while the GR5 stays on French soil. Cross a road at a higher level and continue along a track past houses. A tiny cemetery is reached (water), and a narrow, winding road climbs further uphill to **Novel**, at 950m, where the only hotel and restaurant lie just to the right.

Novel to Col de Bise   3hr, 5.5km, +960m -0m

A flight of steps leads up to the *mairie* (town hall), and a short tarmac path continues up to a church. Turn left along a road, but watch for GR5 markers, which later show a shortcut up a track on the right. Pass a road bend and keep right again, up a track, passing the wayside **Chapelle des Bergers**. Walk further up the road from a bend to find another track climbing to the right. At the next road bend, walk up a narrow road and pass between chalets to continue up a track. At a path junction, turn left for the GR5, passing a sign indicating 'Nice 21 jours – Novel 21 minutes'. The path descends slightly to reach a car park at 1210m at **La Planche**.

Leave the car park by turning left down an undulating forest track, which becomes a path. Walk across a meadow and turn right along a track, heading back into the forest. Turn left to follow a path up through a clearing at Les Nezs, later emerging close to a stream, which is La Morge again, still marking the Franco-Swiss border. Turn right to climb higher through the forest, reaching a steep, open slope with cliffs above. The GR5 exploits a rugged breach in the cliffs. Turn right beyond it to follow a level path, then climb a little to reach the **Chalets de Neuteu**, at 1690m (water).

Climb a steep and rugged path up flowery slopes as marked, passing two signposted junctions at 1820m and 1834m. (The second junction is where the

The little village of Novel is passed during a long and steep climb to Col de Bise

GR5 from Thonon-les-Bains joins.) Keep left at both junctions and climb further to reach **Col de Bise** at 1915m, from where views stretch beyond the Chalets de Bise to Pas de la Bosse, Mont de Grange and higher mountains beyond.

Col de Bise to Pas de la Bosse   1hr 45min, 3.5km, +310m -405m

Continue over the col. Take care on the initial steep descent, as the path is worn and gritty and has had extensive work done to prevent further erosion. It later levels out and becomes a delightful grassy path, crossing a stream and leading directly to some large, tin-roofed buildings at the **Chalets de Bise**, at 1506m (refuge, restaurants and small museum). The nearby Marais de Bise is a swampy area that was formerly a lake.

Leave the chalets as signposted and follow a narrow path that winds uphill. Look for marmots, goats and bouquetin on the steep ascent, while admiring the soaring cliffs of the Cornettes de Bise above. Reach **Pas de la Bosse** at 1816m, where views ahead take in the Vallée d'Abondance, Châtel, Mont de Grange, Dents du Midi and Dents Blanches.

Pas de la Bosse to La Chapelle-d'Abondance   2hr, 4km, +5m -800m

Three paths leave the col; take the middle one, which descends past the ruined Chalets Cote. Further downhill, the restored Chalet de la Cheneau is passed at 1590m. Follow the path down a steep, cow-grazed pasture, entering a forest, to zigzag down to a junction of tracks near the **Chalets de Chevenne**, at 1290m.

Walk down a forest track to reach a road. A left turn along the road leads straight to La Chapelle-d'Abondance. The GR5, however, turns right along the road then almost immediately turns left to cross a footbridge. Turn left again to follow a riverside path, which is part nature trail and part health trail (*parcours santé*). The path broadens to a track and re-joins the road. All that remains is to walk straight down into the village of **La Chapelle-d'Abondance**, at 1021m, where you pass an 18th-century farmhouse on the right before reaching the centre (accommodation, post office, shops, bars and restaurants).

LA CHAPELLE-D'ABONDANCE

This village has transformed itself from a quiet farming settlement into a busy ski resort and year-round tourist destination. Old barns made of thick, dark, timber beams and planks recall the days gone by. Modern architecture tries to mirror the old style, but largely fails, and new developments continue to spread. Locally grazed cows produce milk for a fine range of cheeses.

A good range of services are available. Buses operate to and from Chevenoz, Vinzier and Thonon-les-Bains.

STAGE 1A

Thonon-les-Bains to Vinzier

Start	Thonon-les-Bains
Finish	Vinzier
Time	6hr 15min
Distance	22km
Total Ascent	910m
Total Descent	370m
Terrain	One of the gentlest days on the entire route, rising and falling through forest and farmland, passing occasional villages.
Maps	3428 ET and 3528 ET
Refreshments	Plenty of choice at Thonon-les-Bains. Shop, bakery and hotel restaurant at Armoy. Café at Reyvroz. Supermarket, café/bar and pizza kiosk off route at Vinzier.
Accommodation	Plenty of choice at Thonon-les-Bains. Hotels at Armoy. Basic GR5 lodging and campsite off route at Vinzier.

The GR5 from Thonon-les-Bains takes two longer but easier days to reach La Chapelle-d'Abondance, compared with the direct, one-day approach from St-Gingolph (see Stage 1). The first day's walk is fairly easy, passing through gentle countryside and woods, with occasional views of the towering peak of Dent d'Oche and possibly distant Mont Blanc. There are steep slopes on either side of the Dranse valley. Small villages offer very few services and it is best to detour into Vinzier for basic accommodation.

THONON-LES-BAINS

This Stone Age and Bronze Age lakeside port had its thermal springs developed by the Romans. A fishing museum stands by the Port des Pêcheurs. The 14th-century church, dedicated to St-Hippolyte, stands on the site of an older, Roman church. There are several prominent châteaux, including: Montjoux, by the port, with Ripaille along the shore, Sonnaz above the port, and Bellegard in town. Fine belvederes offer good lake views, and a short funicular railway, built in 1888, links the port with the town centre.

A full range of services are available. Tourist information office tel 04 50 71 55 55 www.thononlesbains.com.

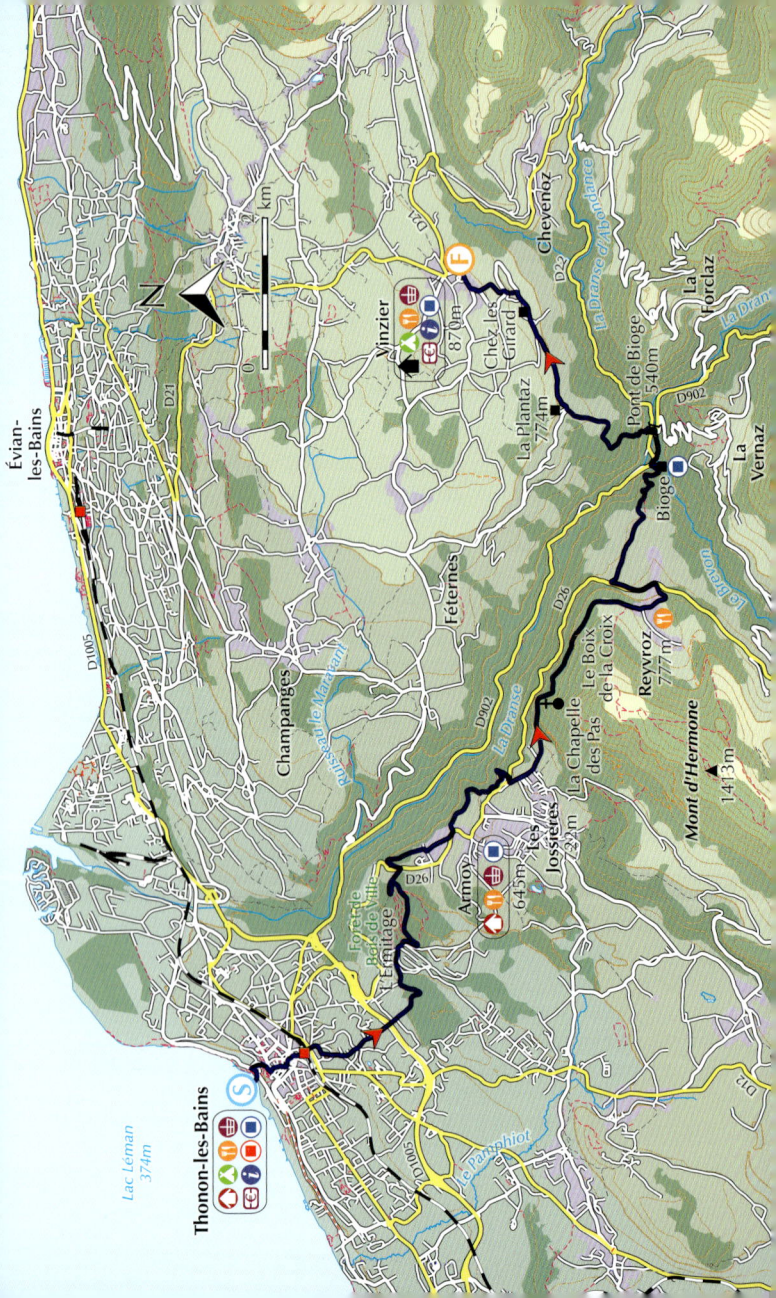

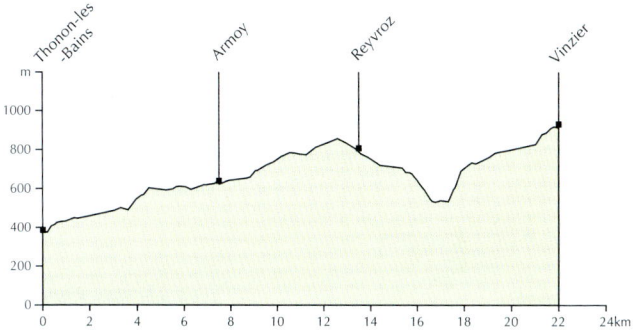

Thonon-les-Bains to Armoy   2hr, 7.5km, +280m -10m

There are three ways to reach the start of the GR5. If arriving by ferry, at the lake level of 374m, there is no specific marked route into town, so follow a steep path climbing roughly parallel to a funicular railway to reach the tourist information centre and *mairie* (town hall), where the first GR5 signpost stands at 426m. Follow the short Rue de l'Hôtel de Ville to a church and turn right to follow the pedestrianised Grande Rue past a square. Turn left along Rue des Arts then head diagonally right through Place des Arts as marked. This leads to a small bus station, the second starting point, and the **railway station**, the third starting point, is only a short walk away, where another GR5 signpost stands at 435m.

Leave the railway station by crossing a broad, pedestrian footbridge over the line, then follow a broad path with steps leading up to Place de Crête (hotel and café/bakery). Turn right to pass a car park then turn left to walk down and up Chemin de Trossy. Turn left up Chemin des Harpes, which leads to a five-way road junction; walk straight through and continue up Chemin de la Vionnaz to reach the edge of town, where a bridge spans a bypass.

Cross the bypass and walk straight ahead to follow a track into a forest. The forest is predominantly oak, with some chestnut and beech. There are many tracks and paths, so watch for GR5 markers and signposts. A gentle ascent is followed by a pronounced left turn, then a gentle descent. Later, turn right at a wire-fenced enclosure to walk up to a road. Cross the road and climb to a car park on the outskirts of **L'Ermitage**. Walk through the car park to find a GR5 signpost indicating a path into the Forêt de Thonon, then climb steeply to a viewpoint at Repos de l'Aigle, at 600m. If growing trees allow, enjoy a view back to Thonon-les-Bains and Lac Léman, and to the Jura and Switzerland.

Turn left along a track called Chemin du Dessus, which includes a fitness trail (*parcours sportif*) through the forest. Turn right along Chemin de Lonnaz, which runs gently downhill through a track intersection to reach a junction at Carrefour du Comte Rouge. Keep straight ahead to curve up around a wooded hollow. Turn right later to walk down a gentle track to reach a road near Le Cornabut. Cross the road and turn left down a path, then keep right to follow a track to some houses. Turn right along a tarmac road then quickly turn left to follow Chemin des Chartreux, which climbs to the village of **Armoy**, at 645m, where there is a church, and just off route, hotels, a shop, a bakery and buses to Thonon-les-Bains and Reyvroz.

Armoy to Reyvroz   1hr 45min, 6km, +240m -105m

Walk down a road and a track below the church, then turn right up a path. Roughly contour along the top edge of a beech wood, keeping a watch for markers. Pass a metal mast then turn left after passing a barn. Watch for markers while crossing an awkward ravine, then climb steeply, cross a track and follow a path up to a road. Turn right along the road, but quickly step up to the left to reach another road and turn left again. This is Route des Champs de Beule, leading to the hamlet of **Les Jossières**, at 722m.

Turn left along Route de la Capité then walk up a track called Chemin des Pas, which passes a couple of houses and runs through forest. Pass the wayside shrine of **La Chapelle des Pas** and follow the track onwards. It undulates but generally climbs, keeping right, to reach 880m before descending. Enjoy a fine view across the Dranse valley to the peak of Dent d'Oche, then head down to a church in the village of **Reyvroz**. Walk down a road, keeping right at a junction and curving downhill below a cemetery, to reach a crossroads and a simple café at 777m.

Reyvroz to Vinzier   2hr 30min, 8.5km, +390m -255m

Walk down the main road to leave the village then turn right down Route du Perrozet. Turn right again down Route de la Ferme. Before the tarmac ends, a track continues through fields, with views ahead to Dent d'Oche. Later, parts of the track have landslipped, so turn left as marked down a woodland path, rejoining the track later as it winds down through mixed woods, deep into the valley of the Dranse. Land on a road near a tunnel mouth at **Bioge** (buses to Thonon-les-Bains), turn right to cross a bridge then turn right again at a roundabout as signposted for Morzine, passing an adventure centre.

Walk up the road until a boulder is reached on the left, where a path runs downhill. Cross the restored **Pont de Bioge** at 540m, which is dated 1736 and spans the milky Dranse river, below the dam of a hydroelectric station. Cross

Vinzier, where basic accommodation is available beside the church

another main road, walk up an access road and quickly turn right up a steep, rough and winding track through mixed woodland. The gradient eases, and a right turn is marked at Les Chênes. The track leaves the woods for fields and becomes a tarmac road. Branch right to follow another short track up to a road junction at **La Plantaz**, at 774m.

Turn right to follow the road through the little settlements of Chaux and **Chez les Girard**. Since accommodation is so sparse in this area, this is probably far enough for one day, and most walkers will be happy to detour off route for lodgings. Pass the Gîtes de Vinzier and spot a signpost on the left. Walk up the path, turn right up a track and pass straight through a crossroads. Follow a quiet road signposted 'Accueil GR5', which turns right and then left as it climbs, then turn right and right again to enter the village of **Vinzier**, at 870m (basic GR5 lodging, supermarket with ATM, café/bar, pizza kiosk, post office, nearby campsite, and buses to Thonon-les-Bains, Chevenoz and La Chapelle-d'Abondance).

STAGE 1B
Vinzier to La Chapelle-d'Abondance

Start	Vinzier
Finish	La Chapelle-d'Abondance
Time	10hr 30min
Distance	23.5km
Total Ascent	1920m
Total Descent	1810m
Terrain	A forested valley gives way to hills, which in turn give way to rugged cols in the mountains, finishing with a descent through another forested valley.
Maps	3528 ET
Refreshments	Restaurants at the Chalets de Bise. Plenty of choice at La Chapelle-d'Abondance.
Accommodation	Refuge de la Dent d'Oche lies off route. Refuge at Chalets de Bise. Hotels and *gîtes d'étape* at La Chapelle-d'Abondance.

After an easy first day, the GR5 climbs high across forested slopes and wanders along grassy, flowery crests. The trail skips from one rugged col to another, passing close to the towering peak of Dent d'Oche. Just before Col de Bise, it joins the route that climbs more steeply from St-Gingolph (see Stage 1), from where a single route proceeds onwards to the Chalets de Bise. Another col, Pas de la Bosse, is crossed before the descent to La Chapelle-d'Abondance.

Vinzier to Le Grand Chesnay   2hr 45min, 6.5km, +635m -135m

Double back from Vinzier, down roads, a track and a path as marked, to rejoin the GR5 on the outskirts of Chez les Girard. Turn left to follow the road to nearby Mérou, then turn right down Chemin du Moulin and later, turn right again, down a track. This winds down through woods to reach a metal footbridge over L'Ugine at 780m. Climb a steep and rugged path through mixed woods, crossing a road, to follow a short, steep path up to another road.

Turn right to walk to a little settlement at **Le Crêt** at 917m and turn left as signposted for the GR5 to follow a road uphill. (Turning right leads to Chevenoz, for buses to Thonon-les-Bains, Vinzier and La Chapelle-d'Abondance.) On reaching

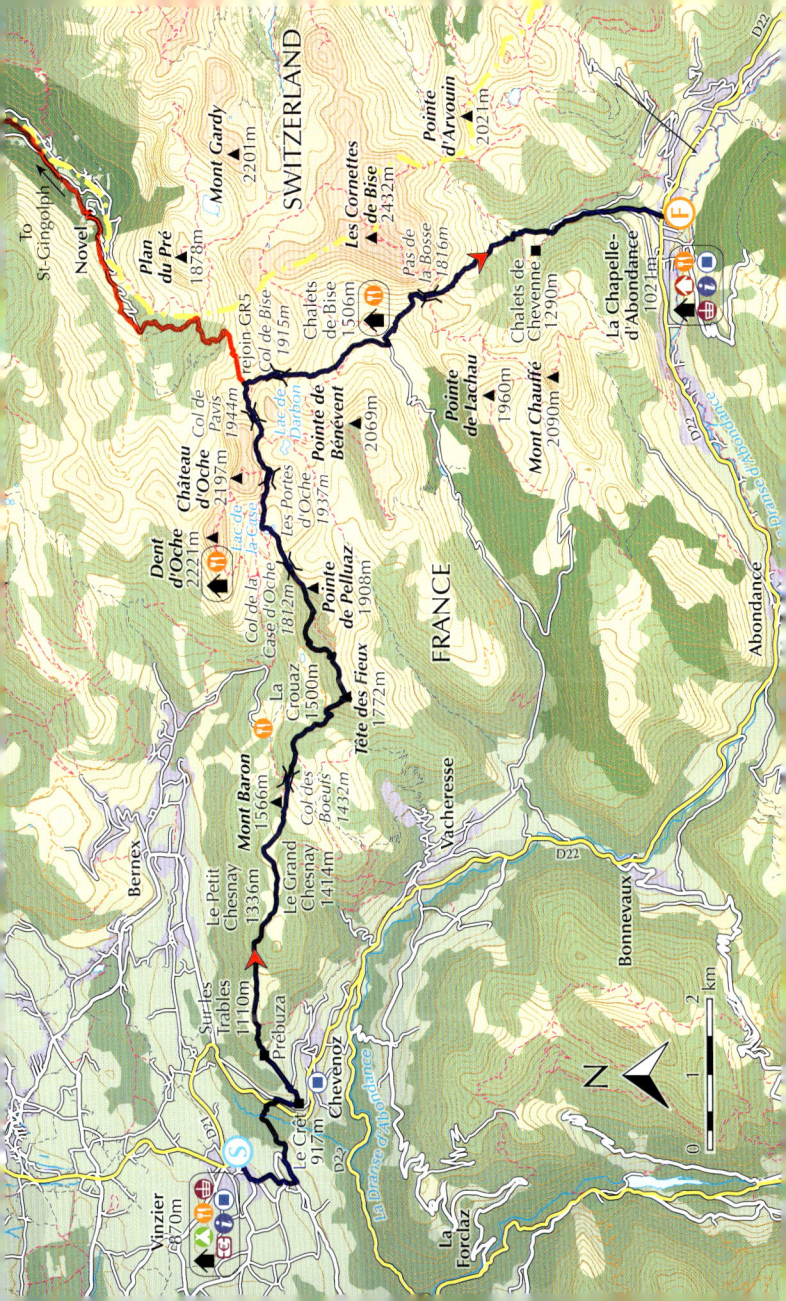

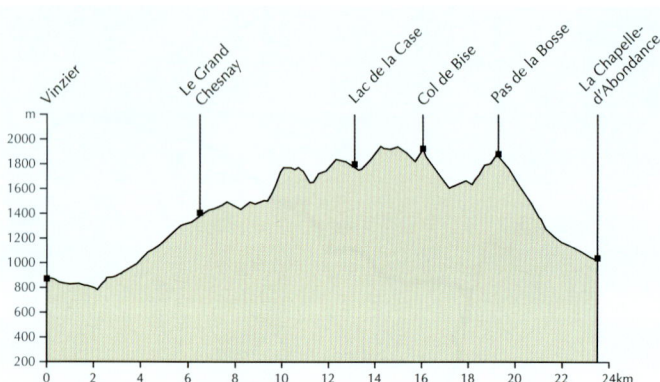

the highest houses, turn left up a road, which climbs even higher, passing a few more houses at **Prébuza**.

Turn left up a steep and possibly muddy forest track, watching for markers at junctions, to emerge into a meadow, where the gradient eases. Follow the track past a couple of buildings at **Sur les Trables**, at 1110m. The track continues uphill, surfaced with tree trunks, with views of Lac Léman, then enters forest again. Climb very steeply, then the gradient eases as the track approaches a couple of chalets at **Le Petit Chesnay**, at 1336m. A path rises through a large, flowery pasture, with views of Lac Léman and the peak of Dent d'Oche, to reach a higher building at **Le Grand Chesnay**, at 1414m (water).

Le Grand Chesnay to Lac de la Case   2hr 30min, 6.5km, +660m -320m

The path climbs around a grassy hump and crosses a slight, grassy gap, climbing towards pine forest. In clear conditions, views from a higher gap may feature Mont Blanc. There is an option to turn left and climb to the 1566m summit of **Mont Baron**; otherwise, follow the path across the forested slopes and down to **Col des Boeufs**, at 1432m. (Restaurants off route at Pré Richard, but following the path down to them is currently discouraged.)

Climb into forest and walk through a large clearing, then back into forest, more or less following a crest. Pass a pylon at the top of a chairlift (*télésiège*) then drop down to a gap at **La Crouaz**, at 1500m. Climb a forested slope and zigzag up to a slight gap at 1600m. Pass the top of another chairlift and climb again, steeply at times, up a well-wooded crest. The path later reaches the open crest of **Tête des Fieux** at 1772m. There is a splendid panorama: follow the undulating crest to a

Looking from Col des Boeufs to the striking peaks of Dent d'Oche

view indicator for details. Views stretch from the Jura and Lac Léman, past nearby Dent d'Oche, to Dents du Midi and Mont Blanc.

Drop down to the next gap, at 1750m, which is dominated by the hump of **Pointe de Pelluaz**. Follow a narrow path across a steep and grassy slope, passing under a chairlift before entering a combe and dropping down to the ruined Chalet Vert. Climb uphill, passing alder scrub, then walk along a flowery crest to the **Col de la Case d'Oche**, at 1812m. Drop down to the left to reach the small **Lac de la Case**, at 1750m. (The Refuge de la Dent d'Oche lies 1hr 30min off route, reached by way of a rocky scramble assisted by a chain and cable.)

Lac de la Case to Col de Bise   1hr 30min, 3km, +310m -145m

Keep to the left of the lake to pass between it and a grassed-over lake, then head left to skirt a heap of huge boulders. Keep right while climbing, to follow the path marked with red/white flashes. Climb across grassy and scree slopes to the rugged gap of **Les Portes d'Oche** at 1937m, where there is a view back to Thonon-les-Bains and Lac Léman. Roughly contour across scree slopes in a boulder-strewn combe, high above Lac de Darbon. There is a brief glimpse of Mont Blanc on the way to **Col de Pavis**, at 1944m, where bouquetin often congregate.

Turn left to cross the col and follow the path downhill, eventually reaching a point where paths head either side of a large boulder. Turn right and keep right again at another junction soon afterwards, where the direct route climbing from St-Gingolph joins. Turn right and climb further to reach **Col de Bise** at 1915m, from where views stretch beyond the Chalets de Bise to Pas de la Bosse, Mont de Grange and higher mountains beyond.

Col de Bise to Pas de la Bosse   1hr 45min, 3.5km, +315m -415m

Continue over the col. Take care on the initial steep descent, as the path is worn and gritty and has had extensive work done to prevent further erosion. It later levels out and becomes a delightful grassy path, crossing a stream and leading directly to some large, tin-roofed buildings at the **Chalets de Bise**, at 1506m (refuge, restaurants and small museum). The nearby Marais de Bise is a swampy area that was formerly a lake.

Leave the chalets as signposted and follow a narrow path that winds uphill. Look for marmots, goats and bouquetin on the steep ascent, while admiring the soaring cliffs of the Cornettes de Bise above. Reach **Pas de la Bosse** at 1816m, where views ahead take in the Vallée d'Abondance, Châtel, Mont de Grange, Dents du Midi and Dents Blanches.

Pas de la Bosse to La Chapelle-d'Abondance   2hr, 4km, +0m -795m

Three paths leave the col; take the middle one, which descends past the ruined Chalets Cote. Further downhill, the restored Chalet de la Cheneau is passed at 1590m. Follow the path down a steep, cow-grazed pasture, entering a forest, to zigzag down to a junction of tracks near the **Chalets de Chevenne**, at 1290m.

Walk down a forest track to reach a road. A left turn along the road leads straight to La Chapelle-d'Abondance. The GR5, however, turns right along the road then almost immediately turns left to cross a footbridge. Turn left again to follow a riverside path, which is part nature trail and part health trail (*parcours santé*). The path broadens to a track and re-joins the road. All that remains is to walk straight down into the village of **La Chapelle-d'Abondance**, at 1021m, where you pass an 18th-century farmhouse on the right before reaching the centre (accommodation, post office, shops, bars and restaurants).

Start	La Chapelle-d'Abondance
Finish	Refuge de Chésery
Time	8hr 15min
Distance	19km
Total Ascent	1435m
Total Descent	470m
Terrain	Riverside path, followed by steep forest paths, giving way to more open slopes. Easier tracks and paths are used later in the day.
Maps	3528 ET
Refreshments	Restaurant off route at Trébentaz. Restaurants at Col de Bassachaux, Alpage de Chaux Fleurie and Refuge de Chésery.
Accommodation	Refuge de Trébentaz is off route. Refuge de Chésery.

Mont de Grange is a large mountain and it takes half a day to trek round its sprawling slopes. Most of the ascent is forested, so views are limited. The higher slopes are open and are grazed by cattle, and a high shoulder above Lenlevay offers an optional ridge route to the summit, suitable for those with time and energy to spare. The latter half of the route is mostly along good tracks and paths, climbing gradually out of France and into Switzerland.

La Chapelle-d'Abondance to Les Crottes   2hr 15min, 5km, +515m -15m
Leave La Chapelle-d'Abondance by following the main road in the direction of Châtel, turning right at a metal cow sculpture (hotel, restaurant and specialist food shop) to walk down a track. Turn left to follow a path upstream beside **La Dranse d'Abondance**. When a road is reached, turn right to cross **Pont du Moulin**, at 1018m. Follow a track uphill, passing the waterfall of **La Cascade**. The track climbs steeply, then a path heads up to the right on a wooded slope, later emerging onto an open slope at **Sur Bayard**, at 1230m, from where there is a view back across the Vallée d'Abondance to Pas de la Bosse. There is the option to climb off route to the Refuge de Trébentaz.

The broad path runs slightly downhill then enters a forest and climbs quite steeply at times, sometimes zigzagging, sometimes level and occasionally

Mont Chauffé ▲
2090m

La Jorette
▲
1643m

La Chapelle-
d'Abondance
1021m (S)

Pont du Moulin
1018m

La Cascade

Sur Bayard
1230m

Refuge de Trébentaz
1866m

Les Crottes
1524m

Châtel

Mont de Grange
▲
2432m

Les Mattes
1925m

L'Etrye
1694m

Le Pron
1751m

Cheneau de Grange

Lenlevay
1733m

Les Covagnes

FRANCE

La Dranse d'Abondance

N

Les Grands Plans
1660m

Col de Bassachaux
1780m

0   1   2
km

Alpage de
Chaux Fleurie

La Dranse de Montriond

*Pointe de
Chésery*
▲
2251m

SWITZERLAND

(F)

Avoriaz

Col de Chésery
1992m

Lac Vert

Refuge de
Chésery
1985m

*Pointe de
Chavanette*
▲ 2219m

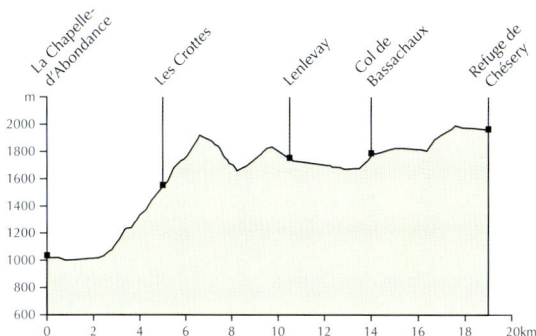

descending a little. Keep an eye on the path and markers, eventually reaching a clearing at **Les Crottes**, where there is a chalet at 1524m. (This is the start of a variant route, via the Refuge de Trébentaz, to Les Mattes.)

Les Crottes to Lenlevay   2hr 45min, 5.5km, +590m -375m

Take the path as marked, back into the forest, though it later begins to follow a broad swathe between the trees, which allows for views. The path is steep and rugged in places, then there is a further clearing at the Chalet de la Torrens, at 1733m. Pass to the left-hand side of the chalet and watch carefully for markers, as cattle have trodden the ground hereabouts. The GR5 climbs through alder scrub and aims for a prominent stump of rock before crossing a high, grassy shoulder of Mont de Grange to reach another chalet at **Les Mattes**, at 1925m. There are views of Dents du Midi and Dents Blanches, flanked by Mont Blanc and Dent Blanche.

Pass to the right-hand side of the chalet to pick up a trodden path, bending right then later bending left, making a dramatic loop to negotiate a steep and flowery slope. I lead towards a few pines then zigzag down a steep slope trodden by cattle to reach buildings at **Le Pron**, at 1751m (water). Turn right then left, keeping an eye open for markers. The GR5 winds down to the foot of a waterfall. Cross the stream and turn left, down to a junction of tracks at 1660m.

Turn right and follow the track up to **L'Étrye**, at 1694m. Pass a building and keep climbing, enjoying wonderful views along the Vallée d'Abondance. Zigzag up a wooded slope to reach a shoulder at 1840m. There is a view of distant Dent Blanche on the way up, then a view of Mont Blanc on the way down through forest. The track leads to a huddle of chalets at **Lenlevay**, at 1733m (water).

Lenlevay to Col de Bassachaux   1hr 30min, 3.5km, +120m -70m

Continue straight ahead through a couple of track junctions on a well-vege-tated crest at **Les Covagnes**. Roughly contour across shale slopes then drop while traversing a partly forested slope, with views across the head of the Vallée d'Abondance to peaks on the Franco-Swiss frontier. When a junction of tracks is reached at **Les Grands Plans**, at 1660m, follow none of them. Instead, walk up a narrow path and cross duck-boards and little footbridges through a marshy area rich in orchids, butterworts and alder scrub. Eventually, the path climbs across a road to reach a car park on **Col de Bassachaux**, at 1780m (restaurant).

Col de Bassachaux to Refuge de Chésery   1hr 45min, 5km, +210m -10m

A level track runs beyond the restaurant, crossing a partly forested slope. The track serves as a nature trail, with information boards about birds and views down to Lac de Motriond, near Morzine. Keep right at a junction then right again at the **Alpage de Chaux Fleurie** (restaurant) to pass beneath a chairlift. Reach a junc-tion of paths and tracks (beware speeding cyclists). Two paths run ahead across a slope; keep right for the GR5 walking route and avoid the parallel cycling route. The paths join later.

Continue across a grassy, flowery slope, noting a prominent ski station on top of Pointe des Mossettes. Cross the **Col de Chésery** at 1992m, where the GR5 passes from France into Switzerland. Continue along the path as signposted, aim-ing for a building with a tall pole flying a Swiss flag alongside. This is the **Refuge de Chésery**, at 1985m (refuge and restaurant).

Looking back to Mont de Grange, which takes half a day to pass on the GR5

The little Refuge de Chésery is the first building encountered in Switzerland

Variant route via Refuge de Trébentaz

If you spend a night at the Chalets de Bise, before La Chapelle-d'Abondance, you could pass through the village and later detour off route to stay at the Refuge de Trébentaz. The following description leaves the GR5 at Les Crottes and rejoins the route at Les Mattes. It takes an hour longer than the main route to cover an extra 2km, with a further 150m of ascent and descent.

Leave **Les Crottes**, at 1524m, and follow a track signposted for the Refuge de Trébentaz. This curves round a forested slope, drops downhill then climbs to a signpost at 1550m. Turn left to follow a path uphill, passing a few trees then rising across steep slopes of grass and limestone scree. The path winds more steeply uphill, keeping well to the left of a ruin, and soon reaches the **Refuge de Trébentaz**, at 1866m (refuge, bivouac and restaurant). Turn left to leave the refuge, contouring along a narrow path. Later, climb a steep, narrow, winding path up a crumbling shale slope to reach a col. Cross a fence and turn left to follow an easy path down to a chalet at **Les Mattes**, at 1925m.

STAGE 3
Refuge de Chésery to Samoëns

Start	Refuge de Chésery
Finish	Samoëns
Time	7hr
Distance	23km
Total Ascent	725m
Total Descent	2005m
Terrain	Pastures, high passes and forest. Mostly along dirt roads, with road walking at the end. Some linking paths are rugged.
Maps	3528 ET and 3530 ET
Refreshments	Restaurants at Chaux Palin, Lapisa and Col de Coux. Restaurant off route at the Refuge de Chardonnière. Restaurant at Col de la Golèse. Plenty of choice at Samoëns.
Accommodation	*Gîtes* at Chaux Palin and Lapisa, with a refuge at Col de Coux. Refuge de Chardonnière off route. Refuge de la Golèse. *Chambre d'hôtes* at Les Fontaines. Plenty of choice at Samoëns.
Notes	Signposting and waymarking is different in Switzerland. Most signposts mention the GR5 and some mention Col de Cou (or Col de Coux). Euros are accepted in this part of Switzerland.

The GR5 through Switzerland is mostly along clear and obvious tracks, passing from one col to another before crossing back into France. Most of the route to Samoëns is along tracks, but some of these are very steep and some linking paths are rugged. However, despite the distance, the route can be covered fairly quickly and easily. At the end of the day, the bustling village of Samoëns offers every comfort for walkers.

Refuge de Chésery to Col de Coux   2hr 45min, 9km, +395m -460m

Leave the Refuge de Chésery and follow a path along the rugged right-hand side of **Lac Vert**, climbing to the gap of **Portes de l'Hiver** at 2096m. Note that a track covers the same distance more easily on the other side of Lac Vert. Cross the gap and turn left down a track, enjoying magnificent views of the glaciated Dents

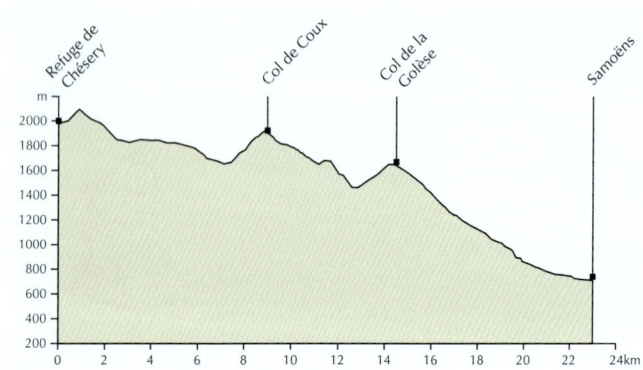

Blanches. Turn right at a junction of tracks to continue downhill; the way becomes more rugged towards the bottom, reaching a dirt road at **Chaux Palin**, at 1844m (gîte d'étape and restaurant, under reconstruction in 2024).

Turn right to follow the dirt road, keeping left at one junction to head downhill a little then keeping right at another junction to climb a little. (Turning left and left again leads down to Les Crosets, for hotels, bars and restaurants.) The dirt road basically contours from one farmstead to another, passing **Les Pas** to reach **Lapisa** (gîte d'alpage and café). Keep to the left of the farm buildings to find a path short-cutting down to the dirt road at **La Pierre**. Turn right to follow the dirt road uphill a little then downhill to a hairpin bend at **La Poyat**, at 1645m.

Turn right up a track, which winds considerably on a slope of shale covered in alpenrose. A former customs post (refuge and restaurant) is reached on **Col de Coux** at 1920m on the Franco-Swiss border. A view indicator is split between Switzerland and France, looking back to Dents du Midi and Dents Blanches, and ahead to Col de la Golèse, past the curved, boilerplate flanks of Les Terres Maudites.

Col de Coux to Col de la Golèse   1hr 45min, 5.5km, +240m -560m

Cross from Switzerland into France and follow a track across an open slope then past alder scrub. The track descends steeply through forest and is quite bendy. Avoid turnings to either side until you come close to the **Torrente de Chardonnière**, at 1500m. Turn left to leave the track and step across the stream to follow a pleasant path out of the forest and down through a pasture. Keep to the left as marked at **Plan des Heures**, at 1435m (right leads down to the nearby Refuge de Chardonnière and its restaurant).

Col de la Golèse is crossed by an easy track, and a refuge stands only a short walk off route

A narrow, rugged path runs across a steep slope grazed by cows then back into forest. Cross another open slope and again head back into forest, keeping left at a junction where another path leads down to the Refuge de Chardonnière. Follow the path uphill to join a track at **Sous Bonnevalette**, at 1525m. Turn left to follow the track up past alder scrub to cross the grassy **Col de la Golèse**, at 1600m, which is overlooked by rocky towers of limestone. Refuge de la Golèse and its restaurant are immediately off route to the left.

Col de la Golèse to Samoëns   2hr 30min, 8.5km, +90m -985m

Simply walk down the rugged dirt road, catching a brief glimpse of Samoëns deep in the valley. Grassy slopes give way to patchy forest, and a few chalets are passed. Continue to follow the track below a few houses at **Les Chavonnes**, at 1245m. The dirt road later becomes a tarmac road, passing a forest car park at **Plan aux Arches**, at 1096m (bus service to Samoëns), and runs down to the small village of **Les Allamands** (water), where there is a little church. The village was established by German-speaking Swiss foresters, hence the name.

Walk down the road to a car park at **Le Crêt**, at 997m, then turn right, as signposted for Samoëns. The path is partly based on the original old highway serving the village, descending a well-wooded slope and crossing a substantial bridge. Cross the tarmac road as marked and signposted at **Pied du Crêt**, at 900m. Follow a woodland path, which never strays far from the road, before joining the road again at **Les Fontaines** (chambre d'hôte). Continue onwards to reach a road junction at Le Chevreret.

Watch for signposts and markers at a series of road junctions and pass a former mill and mill race at **Les Moulins**. Keep turning left at these junctions to cross a bridge over a river, **Le Clévieux**. Follow a road downstream alongside the river, passing through the suburbs but avoiding the centre of **Samoëns**, until you reach the end of the stage at a crossroads at 703m.

Little buildings are spotted on grassy pastures on the way down to Les Chavonnes

SAMOËNS

In 1438, Comte Amédée VIII of Savoie gave people the right to use seven *alpages* (Alpine pastures) to the north, hence the name *septimontains*, from which Samoëns is derived. These days, the old part of the town, clustered around a 500-year-old lime tree, is surrounded by new developments. The area attracts outdoor enthusiasts throughout the year, with walking and skiing being popular.

Samoëns has a full range of services. Buses serve nearby Les Allamands, Sixt-Fer-à-Cheval and Le Lignon, as well as running down the valley to Annemasse. Timetables can be checked with SAT: tel 04 50 37 22 13 www. sat-annemasse.com. Tourist information office: tel 04 50 34 40 28 www. samoens.com.

Start	Samoëns
Finish	Refuge Moëde Anterne
Time	8hr
Distance	21km
Total Ascent	1820m
Total Descent	530m
Terrain	Easy riverside walking, then metal ladders in the Gorges des Tines, followed by a climb through forest on good paths to pastures and high passes.
Maps	3530 ET
Refreshments	Restaurants off route at Sixt-Fer-à-Cheval and Salvagny. Also at Cascade du Rouget, Le Lignon, Refuge d'Anterne and Refuge Moëde Anterne.
Accommodation	Plenty off route at Sixt-Fer-à-Cheval. *Gîte* at Salvagny. Refuge d'Anterne and Refuge Moëde Anterne.

Easy riverside walking leads to a ladder-assisted climb through the Gorges des Tines. More riverside walking leads to the spectacular Cascade du Rouget and the twin falls of Cascade de la Sauffaz and Cascade de la Pleureuse. Climbing further, a pleasant pasture is passed on the way to the Refuge d'Anterne, with glimpses of Mont Blanc ahead. Some walkers will be happy to stop while others will press on across Col d'Anterne to finish at the Refuge Moëde Anterne.

Samoëns to Pont des Nants   2hr, 6km, +210m -145m

Start on the main road on the outskirts of Samoëns and walk downstream beside **Le Clévieux** to pass through another crossroads. Follow a dirt road to a footbridge, the **Passerelle de Clévieux**, but don't cross it. Instead, turn left to follow a track away from it then turn right to reach the banks of **Le Giffre**. Simply follow a well-wooded riverside path upstream until you are diverted onto a track leading to the main road at Pont du Perret, at 731m (water and buses to Samoëns and Sixt-Fer-à-Cheval).

Cross the bridge and follow a road up past a few houses. Continue down a woodland track and maybe detour left to see the Chapelle de Notre Dame des Grâces. Walk down through a riverside meadow to reach **Pelly Renadé** at 748m.

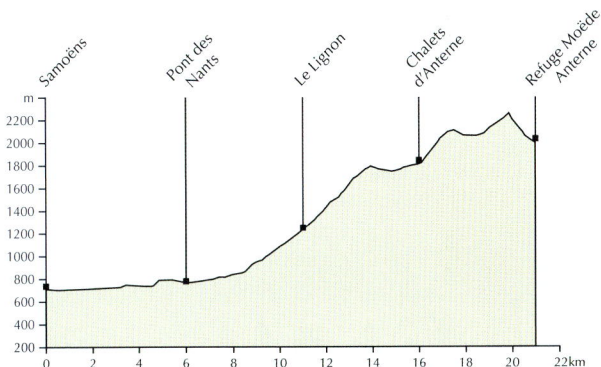

Go onto a bridge to see the river in a narrow gorge, but don't cross the bridge (unless you wish to reach the main road, for buses and a snack bar).

Follow the path up through a beech wood to reach the dramatic **Gorges des Tines**. Climb through the gorge using metal ladders: first 24 steps, followed by 12 steps. Follow a winding, bouldery path straight past a path junction beside a cliff at **Dessus les Tines**. Climb 33 steps then hold onto cables to climb further into the woods. A zigzag descent on a devastated, formerly forested slope to **Le Béné** gives way to an easy path leading through meadows to **Pont des Nants**, at 768m. (You can access Sixt-Fer-à-Cheval from here, for all services and buses to Samoëns and Le Lignon. Tourist information office: tel 04 50 34 49 36 www.haut-giffre.fr.)

Pont des Nants to Le Lignon   1hr 30min, 5km, +415m -5m
Cross the bridge and turn right along a riverside track. Don't cross the next bridge (bar, closed in 2024), unless you wish to inspect the nearby **Cascade du Déchargeux**, but continue upstream through mixed woodlands. Cross a bouldery streambed and turn right along another track, then turn right again. The track reaches a road, which leads straight ahead across **Pont de Sales**. Walk up the road then turn left up a track, cutting a bend from the road, rejoining it near a higher bridge. A path on the slope just above the road leads to the impressive **Cascade de Rouget**, at 960m (restaurant). The waterfall is in two parts and the spray is often like rain!

Continue up the road but watch out for about a dozen short paths that short-cut bends. Pass the hamlet of **Les Fardelays** (water) and a patchwork of woods and pastures. The road ends at a car park at **Le Lignon**, at 1180m (restaurant and buses to Sixt-Fer-à-Cheval).

Le Lignon to Chalets d'Anterne   2hr 30min, 5km, +690m -60m

Follow a stony track straight up through the forest, enjoying fine valley views wherever there are gaps between the trees. The path becomes steep and boulder-strewn but is very popular with school groups and coach parties. The spectacular twin waterfalls of **Cascade de la Sauffaz** (left) and **Cascade de la Pleureuse** (right) are reached at 1450m.

Turn left and continue climbing, as signposted. The path follows a rugged, partly wooded, inclined terrace, with the cliffs of Pointe de Sales above. The path

The twin falls of Cascade de la Sauffaz (left) and Cascade de la Pleureuse (right)

passes close to a pylon as it crosses a gentle grassy gap at **Collet d'Anterne**, at 1796m. There is a view back towards the Gorges des Tines and ahead to Mont Blanc beyond Col d'Anterne. Descend easily through a boulder-strewn area to cross a footbridge over **Ruisseau d'Anterne**. The path, which is vague at times, runs through a pleasant pasture, with magnificent views of sheer cliffs, to reach the **Chalets d'Anterne** at 1808m (refuge and restaurant, named after Alfred Wills, founder of the Alpine Club). This may be far enough for some while others may wish to press on to the next refuge.

Chalets d'Anterne to Refuge Moëde Anterne   2hr, 5km, +505m -320m

Leave the refuge and cross the Ruisseau d'Anterne, then follow a clear path, zigzagging across crumbling, banded shale and limestone. The path wanders past limestone outcrops at around 2090m then drops down past a signpost at Croisement du Lac. Cross a broad and gentle grassy dip, keeping to the left-hand side of the fine **Lac d'Anterne**, at 2064m, and crossing many inflowing streams.

The path zigzags uphill, across more banded shale and limestone, crossing either snow patches early in summer or slopes of rubble later in the summer. Look ahead to spot a prominent cross beside a high col and climb up to it to enjoy magnificent mountain scenery. On a clear day, the view from the **Col d'Anterne**, at 2257m, is one of the finest in the Alps, looking ahead to the Aiguilles Rouges and Le Brévent, with Mont Blanc beyond.

Pick a way down a steep and winding path below crumbling, banded cliffs to reach a path junction. Turn left to walk down to a track then head straight for a prominent, large building that has been in view throughout the descent. This is the **Refuge Moëde Anterne**, at 1996m (refuge, bivouac and restaurant).

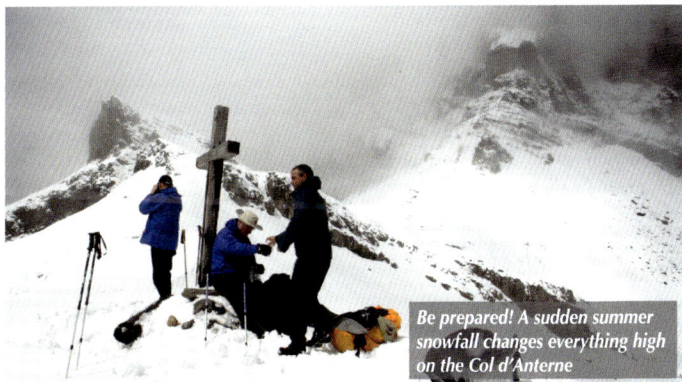

Be prepared! A sudden summer snowfall changes everything high on the Col d'Anterne

STAGE 5
Refuge Moëde Anterne to Les Houches

Start	Refuge Moëde Anterne
Finish	Les Houches
Time	7hr
Distance	19km
Total Ascent	975m
Total Descent	1965m
Terrain	After crossing a wooded valley, an increasingly steep and rugged climb ends on metal ladders high on Le Brévent. A long, steep, rugged descent becomes densely forested.
Maps	3530 ET
Refreshments	Restaurants on Le Brévent, at Refuge de Bellachat and off route at Parc de Merlet. Plenty of choice at Les Houches.
Accommodation	Refuge de Bellachat. Plenty of choice at Les Houches.

Today's objective is to climb Le Brévent, but this should be avoided if a storm is imminent or if there is snow or ice on the steep, rocky slopes. In foul weather, head down the valley to Servoz, where buses and trains run to Les Houches. Once trekkers pass the Col du Brévent, the only options are to continue over Le Brévent or turn back and descend. In clear weather, views of Mont Blanc are without equal, but the summit must be shared with numerous tourists who arrive by cable car (*téléphérique*).

Refuge Möede Anterne to Col du Brévent
3hr, 8km, +785m -410m

Leave the Refuge Moëde Anterne and follow a clear track down towards the huddled **Chalets de Moëde Anterne**. Before reaching them, turn right, down a narrow path, crossing squelchy slopes, to drop through scrubby woodland. With Le Brévent looming large ahead, the path drops deep into a wild valley, becoming firmer underfoot.

Cross a footbridge, **Pont d'Arlevé**, at 1597m, and turn right, climbing gradually and fairly easily across a rugged slope covered in alder scrub. For the most part, the path has been built in stone, and it passes the ruined **Chalets d'Arlevé**. Small streams are crossed on slopes of alpenrose and blueberry then the path starts zigzagging uphill. There are flights of rough stone steps, as well as airy terrace paths. Tufts of parsley fern grow among hard gneiss blocks. Massive rocky

Aiguille
de Bérard
2663m

Lac d'Anterne
2064m

Tête de Moëde
2459m

Pointe
d'Anterne
2733m

Aiguille de
la Glière Sud
2836m

Refuge Moëde
Anterne
1996m

S

Chalets de Moëde Anterne

Torrent de la Floria

Pont d'Arlevé
1597m

Torrent de Moëde

Pointe Noire
de Pormenaz
2323m

Chalets
d'Arlevé

Aiguille de
la Charlanon
2549m

Le Souay

La Diosaz

Col du Brévent
2368m

Tête de la
Fontaine
1206m

D13

Lac du Brévent
2125m

Le Brévent
2525m

Servoz

N205

Pointe
de Lapaz
2313m

Refuge de
Bellachat
2152m

Chamonix-
Mont-Blanc

D243

Merlet

L'Arve

N205

Christ Roi

Torrent de Tacconnaz

Les
Houches
1008m

F

Le Petit
Béchard
2150m

N

Mont Lachat
2115m

Torrent de la Griaz

0   1   2
km

buttresses are circumvented before the path finally climbs past huge boulders to reach a tall cairn on **Col du Brévent** at 2368m. If the weather is bad, or if the higher slopes are icy, a descent to Planpraz and Chamonix should be considered.

Looking into the heart of the Aiguilles Rouges from the summit of Le Brévent

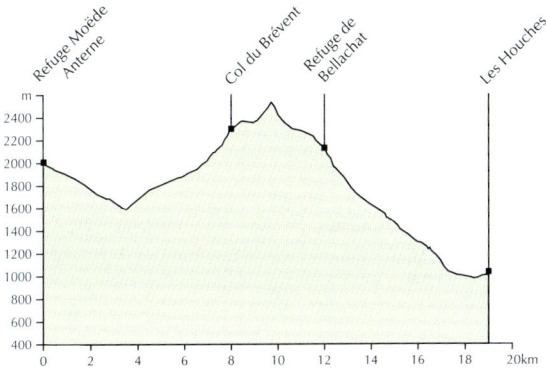

Col du Brévent to Refuge de Bellachat

1hr 30min, 4km, +150m -375m

The GR5 turns right on reaching the cairn, but look carefully for the yellow markers, which lead up and down on rugged, bouldery slopes. Several rocky peaks rise ahead, but the route goes down through a small, bouldery valley. Climbing again, a rocky part of the route features two fixed ladders, each with 11 rungs, as well as handrails and metal footplates.

Walkers suddenly find themselves on a broad dirt road and this leads effortlessly onwards. Simply climb to what is actually the artificial summit of **Le Brévent**, at 2525m (restaurant, view indicator, panoramic terrace, display about the Réserve Naturelle des Aiguilles Rouges and cable car down to Chamonix.)

Mont Blanc dominates the view, which also stretches back to Col d'Anterne and Dents Blanches and ahead to Col de Voza and Col de Tricot. Regular visitors over the past few decades are aware of how rapidly the glaciers on Mont Blanc are retreating.

Backtrack down to the dirt road, where a path is signposted for Bel-Lachat. The path has been built with stone but it often crosses hard, bare, banded gneiss. Follow it as it zigzags down a rough and rocky slope overlooking Lac du Brévent, but don't be tempted off route to the lake. A length of rail protects against overshooting a sudden left turn where the path has been cut into a cliff. A fine promenade leads along the top of a steep brow, from where there are bird's-eye views of Chamonix. As the path drops from this brow, the roof of the **Refuge de Bellachat** appears, and the building is reached at 2152m (refuge, restaurant, views of Mont Blanc and Col de Tricot). Note that the name is written as 'Bel-Lachat' on signposts but as 'Bellachat' on the building.

CHAMONIX

A good reason to visit Chamonix is that it is the 'capital of mountaineering', although it is also just a town, like many others, and it's the location that makes it special. Chamonix has a full range of services and offers the chance to access many scenic, high-level walks using ski lifts. Chamonix tourist information office: tel 04 50 53 00 24 www.chamonix.com.

Refuge de Bellachat to Les Houches   2hr 30min, 7km, +40m -1180m

Watch carefully for a signpost for Les Houches and red/white markers, as there is a confusing tangle of paths near the refuge. Start at a tall cairn just above the refuge and zigzag down a steep slope to cross a ravine before entering a forest. Keep to the path which, despite being badly worn in places, has been engineered to provide the best passage, with wooden steps in various states of repair. Use metal handrails to cross another ravine and enter another stand of forest. Later, watch for a path junction, where there is an option to visit a wildlife park at **Merlet** (restaurant). Alpine wildlife can be observed at close quarters: tel 07 67 22 82 69 www. parcdemerlet.com.

If you are not visiting the park, keep right, as marked for the GR5 and signposted for Les Houches, and the path later zigzags down beside the enclosure fence before landing on a road. Turn right, down the road, then left as signposted. Keep to the waymarked paths on a forested slope or follow signposts for **Christ Roi** – an imposing statue of Christ built over a small chapel. Watch carefully for more markers, avoiding a very steep track. Later, gentle tracks and roads cross a railway and a dam. Climb a little by road and turn right into the bustling little town of **Les Houches** at 1008m.

LES HOUCHES

Although forever in the shadow of big, brash Chamonix, Les Houches attracts its fair share of visitors and is a thriving skiing and outdoor centre. An arch offers a photo opportunity for those starting and finishing the famous Tour du Mont Blanc.

Anyone wanting to visit Chamonix can use the Chamonix Mobilité bus, which links Les Houches with Chamonix and Argentière, stopping at numerous points, including all the main lifts up the mountainsides. Timetables can be checked: tel 04 50 53 05 55 www.chamonix-mobilite.com. The bus links with Le Mulet, a bus service around the centre of Chamonix. SAT buses run between Chamonix, Les Houches and Geneva: tel 04 50 78 05 33 www. sat-montblanc.com.

Tourist information office: tel 04 50 55 50 62 www.chamonix.com.

SECTION 2:
LES HOUCHES
TO LANDRY

*Snow lies late into the summer across the GR5 as it climbs
towards the Col du Bonhomme (Stage 7)*

There are two choices of route for Stage 6: the main route is described first and the higher-level route is described second.

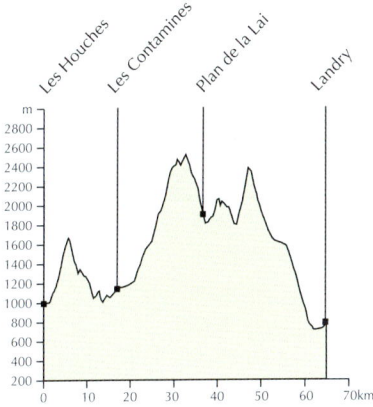

The main route starts by following the course of the Route du Sel, or Salt Route, over Col de Voza, through Les Contamines. The traverse of Col de Voza is steep but otherwise quite easy, and it would suit walkers who are only just starting this section from Les Houches. Those who already have a taste for the mountains should consider the variant route from Col de Voza, over the higher Col de Tricot, to Les Contamines.

Bear in mind that Col du Bonhomme (Stage 7) can carry snow late into the summer, and also note that facilities along the first couple of days of this section come under a

The view down to Plan de la Lai from the ridge path on Crête des Gittes (Stage 7)

lot of pressure, because the popular Tour du Mont Blanc follows the same course as the GR5.

After crossing Col du Bonhomme, the departmental boundary is crossed between Haute-Savoie and Savoie. The crowds following the Tour du Mont Blanc are left behind and instead cheese-tasting enthusiasts are encountered on the Tour du Beaufortain (towards the end of Stage 7). If you haven't sampled Beaufort cheese, then you are now in the heartland of its production. As a consequence, expect many paths across pastures to be heavily trodden by dairy cows.

This is only a short section, and it can be covered in as little as three or four days. Landry is a sensible place

Stage	Place	Altitude	Walking time	Distance
6	**Les Houches**	**1008m**	**0hr 00min**	0km
6	Col de Voza	1653m	2hr 15min	6km
6	Refuge du Fioux	1505m	0hr 15min	1km
6	Bionnassay	1320m	0hr 30min	1km
6	Tresse d'en bas	1000m	1hr 45min	5.5km
6	**Les Contamines-Montjoie**	**1164m**	**1hr 00min**	3.5km
6a	Col de Voza	1653m	2hr 15min	6km
6a	Chalets de Miage	1550m	3hr 45min	8km
6a	Chalets du Truc	1720m	0hr 30min	1.5km
6a	**Les Contamines-Montjoie**	**1164m**	**1hr 15min**	**3.5km**
7	Le Pontet	1175m	0hr 45min	2.5km
7	Chalet de Nant Borrant	1459m	1hr 00min	3km
7	Refuge de la Balme	1706m	1hr 15min	2.5km
7	Refuge du Col de la Croix du Bonhomme	2443m	3hr 00min	5.5km
7	**Plan de la Lai**	**1815m**	**2hr 15min**	**6.5km**
8	*Refuge de Presset*	*2469m*	*4hr 30min/10.5km to turn off at Col du Bresson, +20min off main route*	
8	Refuge de la Balme	2009m	1hr 00min	2.5km
8	Valezan	1240m	2hr 30min	8.5km
8	Bellentre	719m	0hr 45min	3.5km
8	**Landry**	**777m**	**0hr 45min**	**3km**

to call a halt because it has a railway station offering easy departure and/or arrival for those covering the GR5 in easier sections. Those who continue beyond Landry, intending to finish this section at Tignes le Lac, could take advantage of a bus link between Tignes le Lac and the railway station at Bourg-St-Maurice.

Legend:
- ⬆ refuge/hut/gîte d'étape
- ◐ hotel
- ◯ home stay
- ⬆ unmanned hut/bothy
- ◐ camping
- ✶ bivouac
- 🍴 restaurant/refreshments
- ⊕ shop/groceries
- 💶 ATM
- ⓘ TIC
- ◉ train
- ◉ bus
- 🚡 lift/cable car

Facilities								
Refuge/hut	Hotel	Camping/Bivouac	Restaurant	Shop	ATM	TIC	Train	Bus
	hotel	camping	restaurant	shop	ATM	TIC	train	bus
	hotel		restaurant				train	
refuge		bivouac	restaurant					
refuge			restaurant					
								bus
refuge	hotel	camping	restaurant	shop	ATM	TIC		bus
	hotel		restaurant				train	
refuge		bivouac	restaurant					
refuge			restaurant					
refuge	hotel	camping	restaurant	shop	ATM	TIC		bus
refuge		camping	restaurant					bus
refuge			restaurant					
refuge		bivouac	restaurant					
refuge			restaurant					
refuge			restaurant					
refuge			restaurant					
refuge		bivouac	restaurant					
refuge			restaurant	shop				
			restaurant	shop				
refuge	hotel	camping	restaurant	shop			train	bus

STAGE 6
Les Houches to Les Contamines

Start	Les Houches
Finish	Les Contamines
Time	5hr 45min
Distance	17km
Total Ascent	975m
Total Descent	820m
Terrain	Fairly easy walking, mostly along tracks and minor roads.
Maps	3531 ET
Refreshments	Restaurants at intervals across Col de Voza, at Refuge du Fioux and at Bionnassay. Plenty of choice at Les Contamines.
Accommodation	Hotel at Col de Voza. *Gîtes* at Le Fioux and Bionnassay. Plenty of choice at Les Contamines.

After the increasingly difficult walking of the previous week, this day's walk is relatively easy and mostly along good tracks and paths, although gradients are steep in places. The high point of the stage is Col de Voza, which is also traversed by the Tour du Mont Blanc and the Tramway du Mont Blanc. Expect to see plenty of people throughout the day. Anyone pining for the higher mountains could consider the alternative route from Col de Voza over the higher Col de Tricot (Stage 6a).

Les Houches to Col de Voza   2hr 15min, 6km, +675m -30m

Follow the road through the village and pass the Téléphérique de Bellevue. Go through a tunnel and continue along the road to reach the Grand Balcon apartment building. Turn left as signposted, and a broad and obvious path climbs steeply up wooden steps. Turn right, along a track, then turn left up a short path, then left again up a road to reach a signposted junction. Turn right to walk up a very bendy road past more chalets, watching for two opportunities to shortcut bends. Turn right at **Maison Neuve** to walk up a track.

Continue up the dirt road called Chemin de la Carbotte, winding up through woods and steep meadows, passing a chalet restaurant, followed later by another restaurant. The track finally levels out before descending a little to **Col de Voza**, at 1653m (hotel, restaurant, view of the flanks of Mont Blanc; reached by the

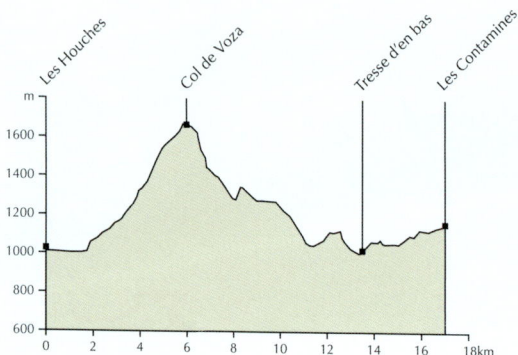

Tramway du Mont Blanc, constructed from 1904 with the original intention of reaching the summit). Note that Stage 6a, offering a high-level route over Col du Tricot, splits from the main GR5 route here.

Col de Voza to Tresse d'en bas   2hr 30min, 7.5km, +145m -780m

Cross the tramway line at a level crossing and follow a track heading straight downhill. A steep and winding descent, through forest and meadows, passes

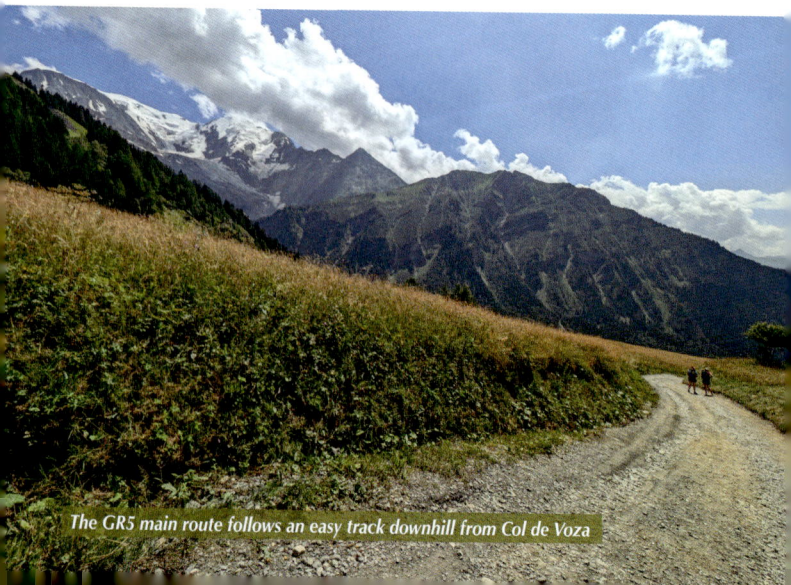

The GR5 main route follows an easy track downhill from Col de Voza

the **Refuge du Fioux**, at 1505m (gîte d'étape, bivouac and restaurant), to reach a car park at Le Crozat at 1420m. Walk down the road, eventually reaching the quaint village of **Bionnassay**, at 1320m (gîte d'étape and restaurant).

BIONNASSAY

In 1784 and 1785, this was the basecamp for expeditions intent on climbing Mont Blanc. A series of information panels titled 'Sur les Pas des Premiers Guides' outlines the history and development of mountain guiding in the area. On 12 July 1892, the Glacier de Tête Rousse, which contained an enormous volume of water, ruptured, with disastrous results. Some 200,000,000 litres of water surged down the valley, tearing up mud and rubble, causing devastation all the way to St-Gervais and leaving 200 people dead.

Turn left just before the Auberge de Bionnassay, down a track called Chemin des Tétras, to pass a chapel. Continue down into mixed woodland in a valley and cross a footbridge over the milky, glacial **Ruisseau de Bionnassay**, then zigzag up to a forest track at L'Ormey, at 1340m. There is another option to turn left for the high-level route over Col de Tricot, but the main GR5 turns right to follow an undulating track until it leaves the forest and drops down to the village of **Le Champel**, at 1225m (water).

Follow the tarmac Route du Champel, with views down the valley to St-Gervais, and turn left after a chapel for views up the valley to Col du Bonhomme. Go straight down a steep woodland track, the Chemin des Chevreuils, to land on a tarmac road in **La Villette**, at 1050m. Turn left at a large, stone water trough to follow the Chemin de la Fontaine uphill. Shortcut higher bends by walking straight up a narrow track, as signposted for **La Gruvaz** (water).

Continue up and down the road into a forested valley and cross a river at a car park at 1085m. Turn right to walk down a woodland path, which drops steeply over awkward pine roots to reach the village of Tresse d'en haut, then walk down to a crossroads at **Tresse d'en bas**, at 1225m (buses to Les Contamines and St-Gervais).

Tresse d'en bas to Les Contamines   1hr, 3.5km, +155m -10m
Walk straight along the Chemin du Quy to cross a river, **Le Bon Nant**. The road loops uphill then continues as a track, becoming a woodland path. Emerge into a meadow, with a view of Col de Voza and Col de Tricot. Turn left, down a track, at Les Meuniers, cross a stream then walk down a road through **Les Hoches**. Les Hoches was the birthplace of Alexis Bouvard, who discovered the planet Neptune. Walk along a road to reach a junction at **Le Molliex**. Turn left to cross a river via

Looking across the valley from the Refuge du Fioux to Mont Joly

Pont du Plan du Moulin then turn right to follow a well-wooded path between the river and the main road, climbing steeply at times. A path is later signposted left, uphill, for the busy town centre of **Les Contamines**, at 1164m; otherwise, continue walking along the riverside path to reach a small hydro-electric dam at Pont des Loyers then turn sharp left for the town centre.

LES CONTAMINES-MONTJOIE

Les Contamines is on the Tour du Mont Blanc and can be very busy, with lots of people coming and going. Although small, the town offers a full range of services. Visit the Maison de la Reserve Naturelle to appreciate the natural history of the area. SAT buses run to St-Gervais and Sallanches for onward bus and rail travel: tel 04 50 78 05 33 www.sat-montblanc.com. Tourist information office: tel 04 50 47 01 58 www.lescontamines.com.

Les Houches to Les Contamines (via Col de Tricot)

Start	Les Houches
Finish	Les Contamines
Time	7hr 45min
Distance	19km
Total Ascent	1455m
Total Descent	1300m
Terrain	Easy walking at first, mostly along tracks and minor roads. Steep and rugged paths and tracks are used later.
Maps	3531 ET
Refreshments	Restaurants at intervals across Col de Voza, off route at La Chalette, and at the Chalets de Miage and Chalets du Truc. Plenty of choice at Les Contamines.
Accommodation	Hotel at Col de Voza. Refuges at Chalets de Miage and Chalets du Truc. Plenty of choice at Les Contamines.

This variant climbs from the Col de Voza high over the Col de Tricot, offering a longer, tougher alternative to the main route (it is also an alternative on the Tour du Mont Blanc). There is an option to visit the snout of the Glacier de Bionnassay, and no other part of the GR5 runs as close to a glacier. Stunning views take in the flanks of Mont Blanc. There are options to stay or eat at the Chalets de Miage and Chalets du Truc before reaching Les Contamines.

Les Houches to Col de Voza
2hr 15min, 6km, +675m -30m

Follow the road through the village and pass the Téléphérique de Bellevue. Go through a tunnel and continue along the road to reach the Grand Balcon apartment building. Turn left as signposted, and a broad and obvious path climbs steeply up wooden steps. Turn right, along a track, then turn left up a short path, then left again up a road to reach a signposted junction. Turn right to walk up a very bendy road past more chalets, watching for two opportunities to shortcut bends. Turn right at **Maison Neuve** to walk up a track.

Continue up the dirt road called Chemin de la Carbotte, winding up through woods and steep meadows, passing a chalet restaurant, followed later by another restaurant. The track finally levels out before descending a little to **Col de Voza**, at 1653m (hotel, restaurant, view of the flanks of Mont Blanc; reached by the

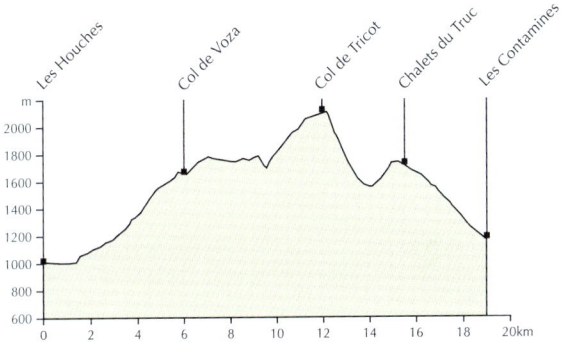

Enjoying a picnic, with a view of the Glacier de Bionnassay, on the way to the Col de Tricot

Tramway du Mont Blanc, constructed from 1904 with the original intention of reaching the summit).

Col de Voza to Col de Tricot

2hr 30min, 6km, +590m -125m

Cross the tramway line at a level crossing and turn left, up a track, the Chemin de Bellevue, running parallel to the line. Climb steeply at times and cross a hump near the rebuilt but subsequently abandoned Hotel Bellevue. There are views back to Col d'Anterne and Le Brévent, as well as to the flanks of Mont Blanc. Don't cross the tramway again, unless you wish to visit La Chalette (restaurant), but follow a grassy track towards a forest. Follow a path across a steep slope, with occasional views down the Bionnassay

107

valley and up towards the Glacier de Bionnassay. The marked route leads down a steep and bouldery path to the **Passerelle du Glacier**, at 1600m. There is an option to leave the route and visit the snout of the Glacier de Bionnassay.

Cross the wobbly suspension footbridge over the milky torrent spouting from the glacier. Climb to a path junction and keep left (right runs down to Bionnassay). Climb past trees and alder scrub onto a pleasant, flowery pasture, then the path is smoother and gentler as it climbs, with fine views on the way to **Col de Tricot**, at 2120m.

Col de Tricot to Chalets du Truc   1hr 45min, 3.5km, +190m -595m

Descend along a steep, worn, stony, zigzag path. The bottom of the slope is in view all the time but progress is slow. Eventually, reach the **Chalets de Miage**, at 1550m (refuge, bivouac and restaurant). Leave the chalets, either along a track or a path – both of which meet at a stone bridge. Turn left, up a zigzag path, to climb through woods, then cross a pasture. Keep left at a junction of paths and walk down past the **Chalets du Truc**, at 1720m (refuge and restaurant).

Chalets du Truc to Les Contamines   1hr 15min, 3.5km, +0m -550m

Walk down a track into a forest. After taking a sharp right bend, turn left along a rugged forest path, taking care over boulders and tree roots. Watch for a left turn then later turn right to reach a track. Turn left, down a steep and bendy track, sign-posted for Les Contamines, to reach a junction at **Les Granges de la Frasse**. Turn right, steeply downhill, to reach a road at La Frasse d'en Haut (water, navette shuttle bus into Les Contamines). Head left, down a road, then turn left to go straight down the Chemin du P'tou, watching for its continuation across road bends, to land beside a church in the busy town centre of **Les Contamines**, at 1164m (all services).

LES CONTAMINES-MONTJOIE

Les Contamines is on the Tour du Mont Blanc and can be very busy, with lots of people coming and going. Although small, the town offers a full range of services. Visit the Maison de la Reserve Naturelle to appreciate the natural history of the area. SAT buses run to St-Gervais and Sallanches for onward bus and rail travel: tel 04 50 78 05 33 www.sat-montblanc.com. Tourist information office: tel 04 50 47 01 58 www.lescontamines.com.

STAGE 7
Les Contamines to Plan de la Lai

Start	Les Contamines
Finish	Plan de la Lai
Time	8hr 15min
Distance	20km
Total Ascent	1470m
Total Descent	815m
Terrain	The valley walk becomes increasingly wild as roads and tracks give way to rugged paths and perhaps snow. After taking a rocky path from col to col, a fine ridge gives way to a long, grassy descent.
Maps	3531 ET, 3531 OT and 3532 OT
Refreshments	Restaurants on the ascent at Le Pontet, Notre Dame de la Gorge, Chalet de Nant Borrant, Refuge de la Balme and Refuge du Col de la Croix du Bonhomme. Restaurants at Plan de la Lai.
Accommodation	Campsite and *gîte* at Le Pontet. Refuges at Nant Borrant, La Balme, Col de la Croix du Bonhomme and Plan de la Lai.

The route from Les Contamines through the Bon Nant valley and over Col du Bonhomme was for centuries part of the Route du Sel, or Salt Route. It takes the best part of the day to reach the Col du Bonhomme, which holds snow well into the summer. Beyond the Refuge du Col de la Croix du Bonhomme, a fine ridge walk traces the Crête des Gittes before you descend into Beaufortain, which is famous for the golden-brown Tarentaise cows that produce rich milk for fine Beaufort cheeses.

Les Contamines to La Balme
3hr, 8km, +555m -15m

Leave Les Contamines by picking up the wooded riverside path beside Le Bon Nant at Pont des Loyers. Don't cross the road bridge but instead cross a footbridge just upstream. Head upstream to another road bridge but only cross the road, not the bridge. Cross a footbridge over an inflowing river then walk up to the next road bridge, Pont du Lay, and cross that too. Continue upstream to join a road

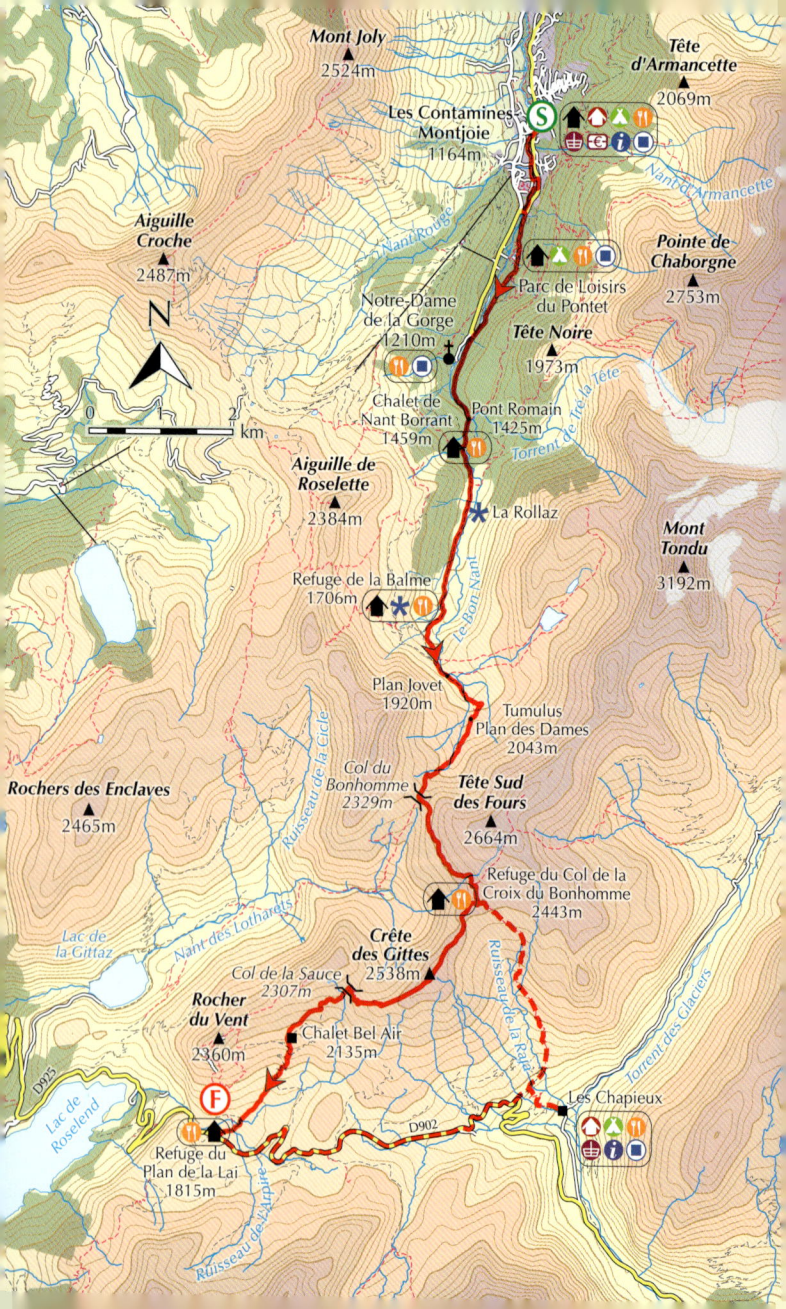

Mont Joly
2524m

Tête d'Armancette
2069m

Les Contamines Montjoie
1164m

Nant d'Armancette

Aiguille Croche
2487m

Nant Rouge

N

Parc de Loisirs du Pontet

Pointe de Chaborgne
2753m

Notre-Dame de la Gorge
1210m

Tête Noire
1973m

0   1   2
├────────┼────────┤ km

Chalet de Nant Borrant
1459m

Pont Romain
1425m

Torrent de Tre la Tête

Aiguille de Roselette
2384m

✴ **La Rollaz**

Mont Tondu
3192m

Refuge de la Balme
1706m ✴

Le Bon Nant

Plan Jovet
1920m

Tumulus Plan des Dames
2043m

Rochers des Enclaves
2465m

Ruisseau de la Gircle

Col du Bonhomme
2329m

Tête Sud des Fours
2664m

Refuge du Col de la Croix du Bonhomme
2443m

Crête des Gittes
2538m

Ruisseau de la Raja

Nant des Lotharets

Lac de la Gittaz

Col de la Sauce
2307m

Rocher du Vent
2360m

Chalet Bel Air
2135m

Les Chapieux

D925

Ⓕ

Lac de Roselend

Refuge du Plan de la Lai
1815m

D902

Torrent des Glaciers

Ruisseau de la Neuve

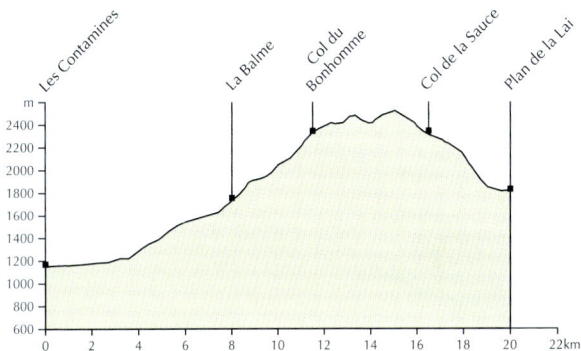

then keep to the left of a car park and restaurant, as signposted for the Parc de Loisirs.

A good track continues, often flanked by trees, passing a sports area and restaurant, followed by **Le Pontet** (campsite and gîte). When a wayside oratory is reached, keep straight ahead as signposted, along the wooded riverside track. A bridge on the right allows the pilgrim church of **Notre Dame de la Gorge** to be visited, at 1210m; otherwise, keep straight ahead along the track.

The track climbs steeply, at times boulder-paved, at times running across bare gneiss bedrock. Keep right to cross **Pont Romain**, at 1425m, where there is a waterfall viewpoint. Climb past a bar/restaurant to reach the **Chalet de Nant Borrant** at 1459m (refuge and restaurant). Keep climbing along the track, passing **La Rollaz** at 1535m (basic bivouac site). Views open up as a fine meadow is entered. There are some chalets on the left, but stay on the track as it climbs gently onwards (water). Walk up through a little more forest then cross a bridge over the river, beside some enormous limestone boulders. Reach the **Refuge de la Balme** at 1706m (refuge, restaurant and nearby basic bivouac site).

La Balme to Col du Bonhomme   2hr, 3.5km, +625m -0m

Just above the refuge, turn left, up a path, and climb to a prominent pylon to rejoin the track. Turn left and walk down the track a short way to reach a small concrete dam at **Plan Jovet**, at 1920m. Turn right as signposted and follow a path to cross a footbridge over a stream. Climb further, later following a path worn into the schist bedrock.

Pass a prominent cairn, the **Tumulus Plan des Dames**, at 2043m. A little further uphill, note how a small stream is swallowed by a band of limestone.

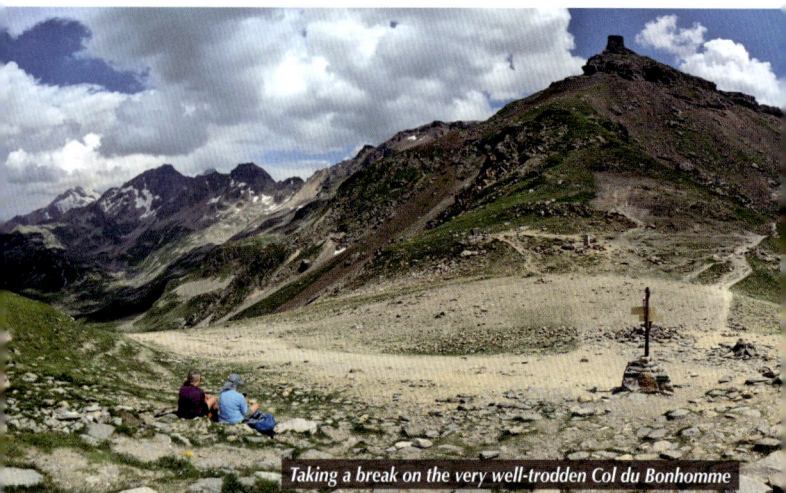
Taking a break on the very well-trodden Col du Bonhomme

Depending on the season, the path may cross the valley on snow or on stony ground. Either way, climb more steeply, noting how the badly eroded path traces a junction between flaky slate and crumbling dolomitic limestone. The path finally reaches the **Col du Bonhomme** at 2329m, where there is a wooden shelter and views ahead of the Crête des Gittes.

Col du Bonhomme to Col de la Sauce   2hr, 5km, +280m -300m

Turn left and climb gradually across a rocky slope, with some short descents, as marked. Cross a variety of rock types and note other types in rockfall debris. After crossing a stream, climb a little around a corner to pass a monument. Cross the departmental boundary, Haute-Savoie to Savoie, and descend to the **Refuge du Col de la Croix du Bonhomme**, at 2443m (refuge and restaurant). A view indicator is available: take note of the direction to Crête des Gittes.

> **Note:** The walk along Crête des Gittes is inadvisable in very strong wind or if snow and ice cover the path. In such conditions, follow the Tour du Mont Blanc down to Les Chapieux then follow the winding road to Plan de la Lai (see map).

The ridge path along Crête des Gittes is delightful in clear, calm weather

Don't get mixed up with the Tour du Mont Blanc, which heads down to Les Chapieux, but cross a nearby col at 2408m and climb uphill. A zigzag path crosses crumbling slates, later passing through a notch hammered out of the ridge. A fine path leads along the **Crête des Gittes**, but before reaching a pyramidal peak, head down to the right, across the flank of the mountain. Walk along the ridge then head down to the right, across the flank again. Cross the ridge then later, cross back again, and finally, zigzag down to **Col de la Sauce**, at 2307m. There are views back to Col du Bonhomme and Mont Blanc, and ahead to La Terrasse and Aiguille de Grand Fond.

Col de la Sauce to Plan de la Lai   1hr 15min, 3.5km, +10m -500m

The lowest part of the col is on a junction between flaky slate and more durable limestone. Turn left to descend, overlooking steep, grassy, flowery slopes grazed by cattle. The track crosses wet patches and can be muddy. Switch to a path heading to the right and continue down to a lower part of the track at the stone-built **Chalet Bel Air**, at 2135m.

The track makes sweeping zigzags down a steep, grassy slope, while a signposted and waymarked path shortcuts through as many bends as possible. The path levels out in pastures dotted with huge boulders. Aim for a footbridge crossing a river then follow a track onwards. Pass the Chalet du Berger (gîte and restaurant) to reach a road then turn right for **Plan de la Lai**, at 1815m (refuge, yurt and restaurant).

STAGE 8
Plan de la Lai to Landry

Start	Plan de la Lai
Finish	Landry
Time	9hr 30min
Distance	28km
Total Ascent	1040m
Total Descent	2080m
Terrain	Some muddy paths, followed by steep, bouldery slopes. Good tracks and paths towards the end of the stage lead deep into a valley.
Maps	3532 OT
Refreshments	Restaurants at Refuge de la Balme, Valezan, Bellentre and Landry.
Accommodation	Refuge de Presset is off route, along a rugged path. Refuge de la Balme. *Auberge* and *gîte* at Valezan. Hotel, *gîte*, and campsite at Landry.

This long day's walk probably ranks as the muddiest on the GR5. The flaky slate bedrock crumbles to slimy mud and is often trampled by cattle. When limestone appears on either side of the Col du Bresson, it is often in the form of monstrous boulders. However, things speed up beyond the Refuge de la Balme, with good tracks and paths on the way down to the Isère valley. There is no need to walk all the way to Landry if a night at Valezan appeals.

Plan de la Lai to Lavachay   2hr, 6.5km, +300m -280m

Cross the road from the refuge and follow a track up past the **Gîte d'Alpage de Plan Mya** (refuge and restaurant). Slabs of limestone slope down, and a line of sink-holes is visible where another rock type is encountered. The limestone becomes flaky before the **Chalet de Mora** is reached. Afterwards, the predominant rock is a very flaky slate. The track climbs in a sweeping zigzag, so shortcut straight uphill along a winding path. The bedrock is soft and the path runs through a deeply worn groove. Rejoin the track and turn right to follow it to the solitary building of **La Petite Berge**, at 2060m, from where there is a view back to Mont Blanc beyond Col de la Sauce.

Refugé du
Plan de la Lai
1815m

Plan Mya

Chalet de
Mora

La Petite Berge
2060m

La Grande Berge
2053m

Aiguille du
Grand Fond
2920m

N

0   1
km

Lavachay
1821m

Refuge de Presset
2514m

Le Roignais
2995m

Presset
2021m

Col du Bresson
2469m

La Pierra Menta
2714m

Refuge de la Balme
2009m

Bourg-St-Maurice

Chalet des Plans
1620m

Chapelle-St-Guérin

Les Fours
1553m

Les
Chapelles

Valezan
1240m

Le Rocheray
910m

Landry
777m

Bellentre

La-Côte-
d'Aime

73m

Pont de
Bellentre
719m

Aime

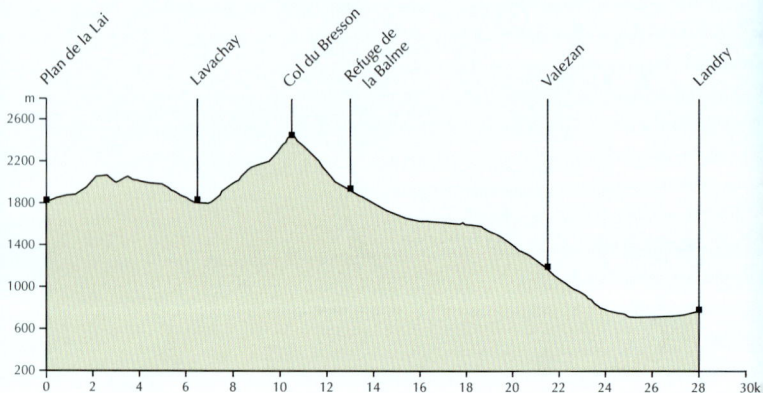

A track gives way to a muddy path, which continues across grassy, flowery slopes, with one stretch on duckboards. There are views down to Lac de Roselend, a reservoir created for hydro-electric power. Look ahead to spot a gentle col but don't head directly to it. The waymarked path drifts down to the right to avoid a wet and muddy stretch then climbs to the grassy col. Pass the ruins of **La Grande Berge** at 2053m then descend past another ruin, cross duckboards and go down some steps.

Cross a steep slope covered in alder scrub, where the path is muddy, then cross a grassy slope above a chalet. There is a view of a valley full of dairy farms, with the prominent rock tower of La Pierra Menta ahead. Walk down to a track and turn left, then shortcut through a bend, as marked. There is one other opportunity to shortcut; otherwise, walk around all the bends until the track leads down to a solitary building at **Lavachay**, at 1821m.

Lavachay to Col du Bresson   2hr 30min, 4km, +675m -40m

Before reaching the building, turn left along a narrow path to cross cattle-grazed slopes studded with boulders. Cross a winding track and climb up a path on a slope of alder scrub, passing bouldery rock-fall. Rejoin the track at a waterfall, crossing the flow. Continue walking up the track until a signpost points to the left at **Presset**, at 2021m.

A path climbs up a grassy slope studded with big boulders (including coarse limestone conglomerate and quartz-rich metamorphic rock). The boulders become bigger further uphill, fallen from two prominent peaks. The peak rising to the left of the path is metamorphic rock, while the one to the right is conglomerate. Also

La Pierra Menta from Col du Bresson

note the parsley fern growing in crevices. After passing around a buttress of rock and climbing further, witness how the junction of the two rock types appears to create a weak area forming the **Col du Bresson**, at 2469m. Refuge de Presset is 20min off route. There are views beyond the valley of the glaciated heart of the Vanoise and of La Pierra Menta, first climbed in 1922, on the descent.

Col du Bresson to Refuge de la Balme   1hr, 2.5km, +0m -465m

Zigzag down a path on a bouldery slope, passing some immense blocks of rock. Walk roughly parallel to a stream then cross it where it is flanked by huge boulders to reach a tumbled ruin. Continue downstream, eventually walking through masses of tall, blue Alpine sow-thistle to reach the **Refuge de la Balme** at 2009m (refuge, bivouac and restaurant), formerly a cheese-producing farm.

Refuge de la Balme to Valezan   2hr 30min, 8.5km, +0m -785m

A stony track drops from the refuge into a valley flanked by steep, grassy slopes. Pass huge limestone boulders fallen from slabby slopes, then cross a stream. After a bendy stretch, which can be shortcut, the track runs more directly and at a gentler gradient. Walk down through the valley until the first house is seen on the left-hand side of the valley. Well before the house, but not obvious, an indistinct path heads left across a grassy slope, following a horizontal line which was once a water channel.

Pass in front of the house, **Chalet des Plans**, at 1620m, then watch for the continuation of the path to the left of its access track. (Alternatively, follow the access track to the **Chapelle-St-Guérin**, rejoining the main GR5 at Les Fours.) The course of the old channel is clearer as it enters a forest, but some stretches are wet and muddy. Emerge from the forest and cross a grassy slope. Pass a few houses while following a track downhill to a signposted junction at **Les Fours**, at 1553m. Views ahead reach almost to Col du Palet in the Vanoise.

Walk down the stony track but later watch for a grassy track signposted down to the right, beside a little stream. The track later passes beneath a pylon line to reach a road bend. Walk down the road, and after passing beneath another pylon line, watch for a track down to the right. This leads to a road at the top end of the village of **Valezan**. Walk down to a church at 1240m (nearby auberge, gîte d'étape, shop and restaurant).

Valezan to Landry   1hr 30min, 6.5km, +65m -510m

Watch for signs reading *'passage pieton'* for a traffic-free descent from the church. Walk down steep, narrow roads and later follow a track beside a field to leave the village at Pied de Ville, at 1120m. Cross a road to pick up an old track that was formerly the highway out of the village. When the road is reached again, walk down it a little to spot a track heading down from a slope of apple trees. Later, simply cross over the road. One stretch of path offers a fine view of the valley, with Bellentre and Landry in view.

Avoid old buildings at **Le Rocheray**, at 910m, and follow the signposted path downhill. Cross an access road, follow the path onwards then later go down steps to follow a road through the hamlet of Le Crey. Step off the road at a little shelter and go down through woods. Continue straight down a road to reach the village of **Bellentre** at 773m and turn left to walk into it (bar/shop and post office).

Follow the road to the right of the church and continue on, later passing through a tunnel under a busy road. Follow a path beside a field, dropping down to a bridge, **Pont de Bellentre**, at 719m. Cross the bridge and turn left to follow a tarmac cycleway parallel to the **L'Isère river**, passing woodland and fields. A road bridge is reached near a watersports business. Turn right and follow the road up into the village of **Landry**, reaching a crossroads at 777m (hotel, chambres d'hôte, campsite, restaurants, bars, shop; trains to Bourg-St-Maurice for Belle Savoie Express buses to Tignes le Lac and Val d'Isère: tel 04 80 00 70 00 www.altibus. com; free bus, or *navette gratuite*, to Peisey-Nancroix and Rosuel).

SECTION 3:
LANDRY TO MODANE/FOURNEAUX

View from a steep, forested descent from La Norma to Modane/Fourneaux (GR5E Stage 2)

Bourg-St-Maurice

(S) Landry

9

Peisey-Nancroix

FRANCE

Lac du Chevril

Refuge d'Entre le Lac

GR55 1   10   Tignes le Lac

Col du Palet

Col de la Leisse

Col de la Vanoise

Pralognan

GR55 2   Refuge d'Entre Deux Eaux

13   Refuge du Plan du Lac

Refuge du Roc de la Pêche   GR55 3

Refuge de Vallonbrun

Col de Chavière

Le Montana

GR5E 2   Termignon

14

Aussois   Bramans

Fourneaux (F) (F)   La Norma

Modane

ITALY

Val d'Isère

11

11a

Col de l'Iseran

Pont de la Neige

Col des Fours

Bonneval-sur-Arc

GR5E 1

12   Bessans

Lanslebourg-Mont-Cenis

Lac du Mont Cenis

Susa

N

0   5   10
km

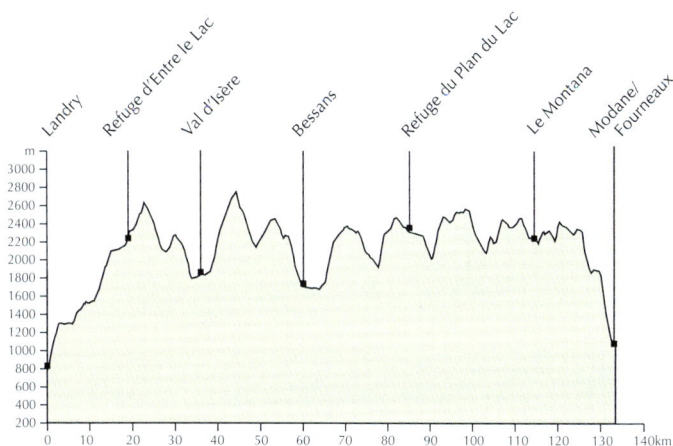

This is the most complex section along the whole trail, as there are three widely differing routes to choose between, which need careful consideration – see the Section 3 map.

The **GR5 main route** climbs from Landry to Tignes le Lac (Stage 9), then heads for Val d'Isère and crosses Col de l'Iseran, which is the highest point reached on the main route, at 2770m. However, there is a variant route crossing the higher Col des Fours, at 2976m. Descending from either col, the trail heads for Bessans.

The variant route over Col des Fours rejoins the main GR5 at Pont de la Neige (Stage 11a)

From Bessans, the GR5 very roughly contours around the high southern flanks of the Vanoise, often enjoying wonderful views, before descending to Modane/Fourneaux (Stage 14).

The **GR55 high-level route** offers a more exciting, remote and scenic experience. It parts company with the GR5 at Tignes le Lac (Stage 10), climbing high through the wild heart of the Vanoise to reach Pralognan. From there, the route crosses Col de Chavière, at 2796m. Afterwards, a long descent rejoins the GR5 on its way down through forests to Modane/Fourneaux. This is quicker than the main route and saves two days; pick up the onward route description at Section 4, Stage 15.

The **GR5E low-level route** can be joined at Bonneval-sur-Arc (Stage 11) and followed down through the Arc valley. This route, also known as the Chemin du Petit Bonheur, leads from village to village, following clear tracks. Walkers who have over-exerted

Stage	Place	Altitude	Walking time	Distance
9	**Landry**	**777m**	**0hr 00min**	**0km**
9	Peisey-Nancroix	1300m	1hr 45min	5.5km
9	Pont Romano (Nancroix)	1450m	1hr 00min	2.5km
9	Les Lanches	1520m	0hr 30min	1.5km
9	Chalet-Refuge de Rosuel	1556m	0hr 30min	1.5km
9	**Refuge d'Entre le Lac**	**2155m**	**3hr 00min**	**8km**
10	Refuge du Col du Palet	2600m	1hr 30min	4km
10	Tignes le Lac	2100m	2hr 00min	5km
10	**Val d'Isère**	**1809m**	**2hr 30min**	**9.5km**
11	*Restaurant d'Altitude Le Signal*	*2310m*	*1hr 45min/3.5km to turn off at D902 junction, +10min off main route*	
11	Col de l'Iseran	2770m	1hr 30min	3.5km
11	**Bessans**	**1710m**	**4hr 45min**	**15.5km**
11a	La Ferme de l'Arsellaz	2130m	1hr 15min	5.5km
11a	Refuge du Fond des Fours	2537m	1hr 15min	2.5km
11a	**Bessans**	**1710m**	**6hr 45min**	**18.5km**
12	Refuge de Vallonbrun	2270m	3hr 15min	7.5km
12	Refuge du Cuchet	2160m	1hr 45min	5.5km

themselves on the early sections of the GR5 might prefer this route, and it could prove useful if really bad weather rules out following either the GR5 or GR55. When the route reaches Modane, it rejoins the main GR5.

There are further options. Walkers can switch easily between the GR5 and GR5E at Bessans on Stage 12, where the two routes run concurrent. There is also a simple half-hour linking path between the GR55 (GR55 Stage 1 or 2) and the GR5 (Stage 13) via the Refuge d'Entre Deux Eaux.

Legend

- ⬆ refuge/hut/gîte d'étape
- ◯ hotel
- ◯ home stay
- ⬆ unmanned hut/bothy
- ◯ camping
- ✳ bivouac
- ◯ restaurant/refreshments
- ⬤ shop/groceries
- ⊟ ATM
- ⓘ TIC
- ⬤ train
- ⬤ bus
- ⬤ lift/cable car

Facilities								
refuge/hut	hotel	camping/bivouac	restaurant	shop	ATM	TIC	train	bus
⬆	◯	◯ camping	◯	⬤			⬤ train	⬤
	◯		◯	⬤		ⓘ		⬤
⬆		◯ camping	◯					
⬆			◯					
⬆			◯					⬤
⬆		✳ bivouac	◯					
⬆		✳ bivouac	◯					
	◯		◯	⬤	⊟	ⓘ		⬤
	◯	◯ camping	◯	⬤	⊟	ⓘ		⬤
			◯					
			◯					
⬆	◯	◯ camping	◯	⬤	⊟	ⓘ		⬤
			◯					
⬆		✳ bivouac	◯					
⬆	◯	◯ camping	◯	⬤	⊟	ⓘ		⬤
⬆		✳ bivouac	◯					
⬆ unmanned hut								

Stage	Place	Altitude	Walking time	Distance
12	Bellecombe	2307m	4hr 30min	10.5km
12	**Plan du Lac**	**2365m**	**0hr 30min**	**2km**
13	Pont de la Renaudière	2045m	0hr 45min	2.5km
13	Refuge de l'Arpont	2309m	3hr 45min	11km
13	**Le Montana**	**2190m**	**5hr 45min**	**15.5km**
14	Refuge de Plan Sec	2330m	0hr 20min	1.5km
14	Refuge de la Fournache	2340m	0hr 15min	1km
14	*Refuge de l'Orgère*	*1945m*	*4hr 55min, 11km to turn off/ +5min off route*	
14	**Modane**	**1070m**	**1hr 55min**	**4.5km**
14	*Fourneaux*	*1050m*	*2hr 15min, 5.5km from Refuge de l'Orgère turn off*	

GR55

Stage	Place	Altitude	Walking time	Distance
1	**Refuge d'Entre-le-Lac**	**2155m**	**0hr 00min**	**0km**
1	Refuge du Col du Palet	2600m	1hr 30min	4km
1	Tignes le Lac	2100m	2hr 00min	5km
1	Val Claret	2140m	0hr 30min	1.5km
1	Refuge de la Leisse	2487m	3hr 30min	10km
1	**Refuge d'Entre Deux Eaux**	**2120m**	**1hr 45min**	**6.5km**
2	Refuge du Col de la Vanoise	2518m	2hr 30min	6km
2	Refuge des Barmettes	2010m	1hr 15min	4.5km
2	Les Fontanettes	1650m	0hr 45min	2km
2	Pralognan	1418m	0hr 30min	1km
2	Les Prioux	1715m	1hr 15min	4.5km
2	**Refuge du Roc de la Pêche**	**1911m**	**1hr 00min**	**3km**
3	Alpage de Ritord	1971m	0hr 30min	1.5km
3	Refuge de Péclet-Polset	2474m	1hr 30min	4km

| | | | Facilities | | | | | |

| | | | Facilities | | | | | |

Stage	Place	Altitude	Walking time	Distance	
3	**Modane**	**1070m**	**5hr 10min**	**13.5km**	
3	*Fourneaux*	*1050m*	*5hr 30min, 14.5km from Refuge de Péclet-Polset*		

GR5E					

Stage	Place	Altitude	Walking time	Distance	
1	**Bonneval-sur-Arc**	**1800m**	**0hr 00min**	**0km**	
1	Le Villaron	1740m	1hr 15min	6km	
1	Bessans	1710m	0hr 45min	2.5km	
1	Les Chardonnettes	1680m	0hr 45min	3km	
1	Lanslevillard	1480m	1hr 45min	6.5km	
1	Lanslebourg-Mont-Cenis	1400m	0hr 45min	2.5km	
1	**Termignon**	**1290m**	**1hr 30min**	**6.5km**	
2	Sollières L'Envers	1275m	0hr 45min	3km	
2	Le Verney	1224m	1hr 00min	4km	
2	Bramans	1250m	0hr 15min	1.5km	
2	Fort Marie-Thèrése	1258m	1hr 15min	4km	
2	La Norma	1370m	1hr 00min	4km	
2	Modane	1070m	1hr 00min	3.5km	
2	**Fourneaux**	**1050m**	**0hr 30min**	**1.5km**	

GR5 MAIN ROUTE
STAGE 9
Landry to Refuge d'Entre le Lac

Start	Landry
Finish	Refuge d'Entre le Lac
Time	6hr 45min
Distance	19km
Total Ascent	1590m
Total Descent	210m
Terrain	Good paths, tracks and roads run from village to village. Paths through a high valley are steep and rugged in some places but easy and almost level in other places.
Maps	3532 ET
Refreshments	Restaurants at Peisey-Nancroix, Pont Baudin, Les Lanches (*buvette*), Chalet-Refuge de Rosuel and Refuge d'Entre le Lac.
Accommodation	Hotels and *chambres d'hôte* at Peisey-Nancroix. *Gîte* and campsite near Pont Baudin. Lodging and campsite near Les Lanches. Chalet-Refuge de Rosuel and Refuge d'Entre le Lac.

The course of an old highway, now merely a path, is used to climb from Landry to Peisey-Nancroix. Some walkers might spend time exploring these and other nearby villages then break early at the Chalet-Refuge de Rosuel. Strong walkers might climb all the way to the Refuge du Col du Palet. In between both refuges, a short detour leads to the Refuge d'Entre le Lac.

Landry to Peisey-Nancroix   1hr 45min, 5.5km, +545m -5m

Leave the crossroads in the centre of Landry by following the road signposted for Hauteville-Gondon, crossing a bridge over a river, **Le Ponturin**. Turn left at Hôtel l'Alpin, as signposted and marked, along a narrow road, passing between houses. Find and follow Chemin de l'Église uphill. The road ends abruptly and a path continues climbing up a wooded slope.

The path joins a road and a left turn reveals the village church, Église St-Michel, at **La Vignerie**, at 849m. Keep well to the right of it and adjacent

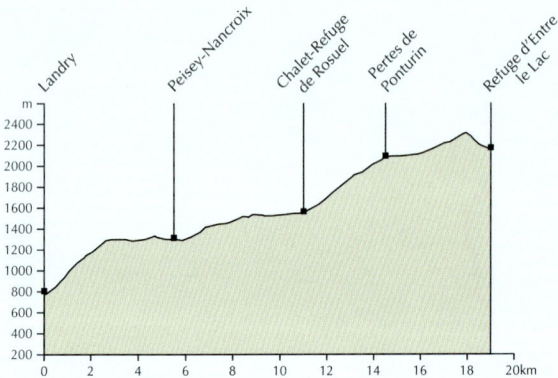

buildings to follow a path signposted further up the wooded slope, keeping left at a junction. When another stretch of road is reached, turn left then right and climb further up the wooded slope. When the next stretch of road is reached, turn right then quickly left to continue up another path. There are clearings in the wood, and the next time the road is crossed, simply continue straight ahead, climbing past a building, to reach a vehicle track, where the hamlet of **Le Martorey** lies to the left, at 1132m.

Cross over the track, turn right at a signposted junction and continue along paths that rise across the wooded slope.The path rejoins the track at a bend and continues undulating through woods to reach buildings at Les Côtes. Follow the track through woods and small meadows, rising gently, to join a road at **Le Villaret**, at 1295m.

Walk along Route des Côtes, which is narrow as it squeezes past buildings. Reach a junction and turn left to pass the wayside chapel of St-Pierre, continuing along the Route de la Lonzagne. Look up to see the cables of the Vanoise Express high above. At the top of the road, turn left, as signposted, up a grassy path and keep straight ahead along a road to pass below a church. Turn right, down a short, narrow road, then left along Rue des Monts d'Argent. Follow this through **Peisey-Nancroix**, along with Rue de la Chenalette, down to a junction with the main **D87** road, at 1300m (hotel, chambres d'hôte, restaurants, bars, shop; free bus, or *navette gratuite*, to Landry and Rosuel; tourist information office: tel 04 79 07 94 28 www.peisey-vallandry.com).

Peisey-Nancroix to Chalet-Refuge de Rosuel   2hr, 5.5km, +275m -35m

Turn left to follow the main road, which soon has a fenced-off path alongside it. Turn right at a junction and follow a winding road downhill, passing the chapel of Ste-Agathe. Keep to the left of the Place des Quatre Zoé and follow the Route du Vieux Moulin down to Pont de Vieux Moulin at 1290m. Cross the bridge, turn left and follow a track upstream, climbing steeply at times.

Join another track and walk down to **Pont Romano**, at 1440m (access to Nancroix for restaurant and free bus, or *navette gratuite*, to Landry, Peisey-Nancroix and Rosuel). Walk further up the track to pass a campsite (snacks) and a sporting area at Les Lanchettes, continuing along a tarmac road. Walk straight ahead, up the road, then the GR5 steps up to the right to continue along a track. This crosses a stream and runs through a forest to reach a large building, **Palais de la Mine**, at 1440m (restaurant and bus stop nearby at Pont Baudin).

PALAIS DE LA MINE

L'École Française des Mines was created in Paris in 1783 to regulate the mining industry and train workers in all aspects of mining. The Corps des Mines was instituted in 1784, consisting of uniformed mining engineers. The Palais de la Mine, now derelict, was the centre of an 18th to 19th-century lead and silver-mining site. The ore veins ran through schist and quartzite beds in the mountains. The metal was largely destined for military use, and English and German miners were employed when specialist knowledge was needed.

Pass below the building then turn right up another track, crossing two rivers using bridges which are close together. Walk down to a road and turn quickly right and left, then right again at **Les Lanches**, at 1520m (buvette). Follow a track past lovely little houses then turn left to cross a bridge (lodging) and right to continue upstream. (A diversion along the road was in place in 2024, due to a missing footbridge.)

Follow the track towards farm buildings, enjoying a fine view of the higher valley. Either ford the river as signposted, where a footbridge is missing, then turn left upstream, or continue walking upstream to find the next footbridge then double back. Either way, reach a large car park beside the **Chalet-Refuge de Rosuel**, at 1556m (refuge, restaurant, Parc de la Vanoise information centre, viewing area for nearby nesting bearded vultures; free bus, or *navette gratuite*, to Peisey-Nancroix and Landry).

Chalet-Refuge de Rosuel to Pertes du Ponturin

1hr 45min, 3.5km, +520m -0m

Walk past the refuge, turn right along a track then turn right again along a path. Pass larches then climb gently across a flowery slope and continue through low woodland. Cross a streambed and traverse another open slope, then follow the path up through more extensive woodland. Pass beneath a frowning cliff of schist, then the gradient eases among larches, and views stretch back along the valley and up to nearby peaks, while slender cascades pour down the mountainsides.

A splendid waterfall is seen on the climb from Rosuel to Pertes du Ponturin

Pass a viewpoint and climb steeply, and the gradient eases again near a little chalet. Climb again past ice-smoothed gneiss bedrock, on which masses of limestone boulders lie. Cross a stream and head for a signpost at **Pertes du Ponturin**, at 2068m. (Choose now between following the GR5 or a variant route to the Refuge d'Entre le Lac.)

Pertes du Ponturin to Refuge d'Entre le Lac   1hr 15min, 4.5km, +250m -170m

Turn left to stay on the GR5, climbing at a gentle gradient on a rugged, boulder-strewn slope. Cross a footbridge over a stream and keep climbing, levelling out on even more boulders, where the Parc National de la Vanoise is entered. Enjoy all-round mountain views, noting the glaciated dome of La Grande Motte far ahead, which will be seen over successive days. Boulder-hopping gives way to a cattle-grazed pasture, with the **Chalets de la Plagne** beyond, at 2100m.

Keep to the right of the chalets to climb around a rocky rib then climb more gently past the Chalet des Gardes, at 2220m, on the **Rocher des Mindières**. There are splendid views down to Lac de la Plagne beneath the cliffs of Mont

Blanc de Peisey. The path climbs gently and briefly levels out at a junction around 2300m.

Turn right to leave the GR5 and follow a clear path down across a grassy, bouldery slope. There are fine views of Lac de la Plagne on the way down to the **Refuge d'Entre le Lac**, at 2155m (refuge, yurts, bivouac and restaurant).

Variant: to Refuge d'Entre le Lac   **45min, 3km, +255m -110m**

Turn right to leave the GR5 as indicated for the Refuge d'Entre-le-Lac, following a bouldery path gently uphill. The route runs upstream beside a river, which winds through lush grasslands, with occasional waterfalls. Eventually, the path climbs to **Lac de la Plagne**, popular with walkers and fishermen. Although easy at first, the path becomes more difficult as it weaves through massive boulder scree. Cross a footbridge and stony ground to reach the **Refuge d'Entre le Lac**.

The lovely Lac de la Plagne, where the Refuge d'Entre-le-Lac is located

STAGE 10
Refuge d'Entre le Lac to Val d'Isère

Start	Refuge d'Entre le Lac
Finish	Val d'Isère
Time	6hr
Distance	18.5km
Total Ascent	725m
Total Descent	1060m
Terrain	Mostly gently graded ascents and descents, with some short, steep ascents and descents. Good mountain paths, with forest and riverside paths towards the end.
Maps	3532 ET and 3633 ET
Refreshments	Refuge du Col du Palet. Plenty of choice at Tignes le Lac and Val d'Isère.
Accommodation	Refuge du Col du Palet. Plenty of choice at Tignes le Lac and Val d'Isère. Campsite just beyond Val d'Isère.

On today's walk, enjoy crossing the Col du Palet then make haste through the bizarre, high-rise ski development of Tignes le Lac. Although every service is available, most walkers prefer to put the town behind them as quickly as possible. The GR5 crosses an easy shoulder, offering one last chance to look back at receding Mont Blanc, then drops down through forest to Val d'Isère. This is another ski town that continues to expand apace but it avoids the worst excesses of Tignes.

Refuge d'Entre le Lac to Refuge du Col du Palet   1hr 30min, 4km, +430m -0m
Leave the refuge and follow the signposted path back uphill, across a slope of grass and boulders, to get straight back to a junction with the GR5, then turn right and look ahead to spot the white dome of La Grande Motte. Keep to the right of grassy **Plan de la Grassaz**, away from a little stone chalet. Look out for marmots. Cross a stream-bed and climb more steeply, crossing the outflow and inflow of **Lac du Grattaleu**. Head left at a path junction to reach the **Refuge du Col du Palet** at 2600m (refuge, bivouac and restaurant).

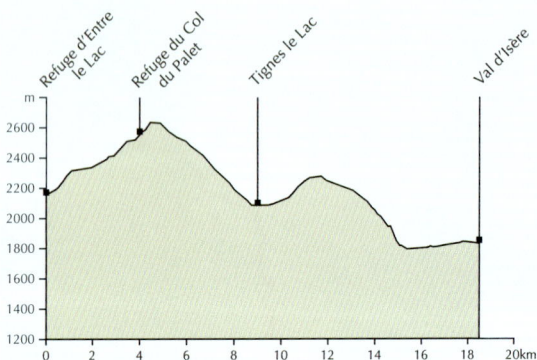

Refuge du Col du Palet to Tignes le Lac   2hr, 5km, +70m -570m

Leave the refuge and either climb straight up a path or take a slightly longer, easier track uphill. Both routes meet to cross the **Col du Palet**, at 2652m, which might be flanked by snow patches late into summer. Enjoy the views of nearby glaciated peaks as you exit the Parc National de la Vanoise.

The geology around the Col du Palet is quite mixed. On the ascent, the underlying rock is a mixture of limestone and schist. On the col itself, both can be found, while nearby, grey, crumbling humps are rich in gypsum. On the way downhill, the limestone is dolomitic and full of tiny holes. Pass a couple of dolines, or solution hollows, one of which contains a small pool. When a track is reached, climb a short way up it and pass under a chairlift, then follow a path further downhill to the Tichot *télésiège* station, at 2469m.

Keep to the left of the chairlift and follow a path across a track. The Tignes and Val Claret conurbations are evident below, and the high-rise buildings seem quite incongruous so close to a national park. After passing tall poles stuck into the mountainside, the route reaches a viewpoint at **Croix de Lognan**, at 2300m.

Walk down into a little valley at Combe des Militaires to reach a junction of paths. Keep left to follow the GR5 down to Tignes le Lac. (Turn right for a shortcut down to Val Claret to link with the GR55. See GR55 Stage 1 for details.) Follow the path across two tracks and zigzag down to a busy road. Cross the road to reach the shore of **Lac de Tignes** and turn left to follow the GR5 along a lakeshore path towards **Tignes le Lac**, at 2100m (all services). (The GR55 turns right along the lakeshore path for nearby Val Claret.)

TIGNES LE LAC

This high-altitude resort thrives on the fact that it can offer all-year-round skiing, courtesy of the Glacier de la Grande Motte. In the summer months, it sells itself as a sporting and family resort. Surprisingly, much of the land nearby is designated as the Réserve Naturelle de la Tignes-Champagny, and presumably, this limits further development.

A full range of services is available in the town, and at nearby Val Claret, with free buses, or *navettes gratuites*, linking both sites. Belle Savoie Express buses run to and from Tignes le Lac and Bourg-St-Maurice: tel 04 80 00 70 00 www.altibus.com. Tourist information office: tel 04 79 40 04 40 www. tignes.net.

Tignes le Lac to Val d'Isère
2hr 30min, 9.5km, +225m -490m

Cross the outflow of the lake and aim for a combined cycleway and footpath rising from the resort. Follow this to **Le Rosset** and keep right, as signposted for the GR5 to Val d'Isère. Continue as marked up a path that crosses a long ridge of rubbly moraine. Watch carefully for markers as the path climbs in a huge zigzag then proceed over a rough and bouldery slope to cross the gentle **Pas de la Tovière**, at 2252m. Look back for a last view of Mont Blanc.

Walk downhill and keep to the left of a hut. The land nearby is used as a landing strip by a local aero club, so stay on the marked path in **Vallon de la Tovière**. A track continues down smooth, grassy slopes, with a view of Val d'Isère and the

View from a clearing while descending through forest to La Daille

mountains flanking Col de l'Iseran. Zigzag down into larch forest, taking great care to spot signposts and markers, as the route is very convoluted and intersects with equally convoluted cycle trails.

Eventually, cross a footbridge and continue down the last part of the forested slope to emerge into an open space overlooked by apartment blocks at **La Daille**. Head for the Télécabine de la Daille and turn right to pick up and follow a riverside track. This later becomes a riverside path, passing through an area where springs burst from limestone on the forest floor. Pass a hydro-electric station, go through a car park and turn right to follow a road straight into the suburbs of Val d'Isère.

Leaving Val d'Isère, at the start of the long climb towards Col de l'Iseran

Keep straight ahead at a junction, signposted for Le Joseray. Follow the road uphill, through a tunnel, then soon afterwards, turn left across a bridge, signposted for La Legettaz. Don't go through a road tunnel but go under a wooden bridge to follow the Chemin du Charvet. A dirt road and a tarmac road lead to a church with a prominent stone steeple in **Val d'Isère**, at 1809m (all services). Note that on the following stage, there are two routes leaving town: the main GR5 crossing Col de l'Iseran and a variant route crossing Col des Fours.

VAL D'ISÈRE

This is a high-rise ski development, although there are a few old stone buildings near the church. Most GR5 walkers don't visit the roundabout in the middle of the main road in the town centre; those who do will find an announcement that this is the middle of the Grande Traversée des Alpes from Thonon-les-Bains to Menton!

Free buses, or *navettes gratuites*, serve different parts of Val d'Isère. Each bus, known as a *train*, is colour-coded as follows: Train Rouge serves Le Fornet and La Daille, Train Bleu serves La Légettaz, and Train Vert serves Parc des Sports du Manchet. Belle Savoie Express buses run to and from Val d'Isère and Bourg-St-Maurice: tel 04 80 00 70 00 www.altibus.com. From Bourg-St-Maurice, trains run to Paris and Lyon via Chambery. Tourist information office: tel 04 79 06 06 60 www.valdisere.com.

Start	Val d'Isère
Finish	Bessans
Time	8hr
Distance	22.5km
Total Ascent	1365m
Total Descent	1485m
Terrain	Steep climbing gives way to gentler gradients on Col de l'Iseran. A steep and rugged descent is followed by a climb to a balcony path before a track and a rugged path lead down into a valley.
Maps	3633 ET
Refreshments	Restaurants on the way to and at Col de l'Iseran. Plenty of choice off route at Bonneval-sur-Arc and at Bessans.
Accommodation	Hotels, *chambres d'hôte* and refuge off route at Bonneval-sur-Arc. *Gîte d'étape* off route at Le Villaron. Hotels, *gîte d'étape* and campsite at Bessans.

The road over the Col de l'Iseran was built in 1937 and is one of the highest in France. The old highway survives as a path and the GR5 follows it. The road has to be crossed several times but very little of it is followed. The top of the Col de l'Iseran is the highest point on the main GR5 route and it is often very busy. The descent can optionally include Bonneval-sur-Arc (linking with the GR5E low-level variant) while the main route enjoys a fine balcony path before descending to Bessans.

Val d'Isère to Col de l'Iseran   3hr 15min, 7km, +945m -0m

The old church in Val d'Isère is a fine landmark and there is a GR5 marker on its wall, indicating a quiet road, Rue Nicolas Bazile, leading away from the town centre. Walk up the road and branch right along a stone-paved path called Voie Romane. Continue up another road, which gives way to a gravel path which runs through fields, passing above a campsite.

Pass between buildings and a tiny chapel at **Le Laisinant** then head straight up a track to pass a building called Les Mélezes. Watch for markers while passing under a chairlift and crossing a footbridge over a stream, making sure to follow

La Daille

L'Isère

Rocher de
Bellevarde ▲
2826m

Val d'Isère
1809m

Le
Laisinant

L'Isère

Forêt du Fornet

Rocher du Charvet
▲
2856m

Pointe
du Monte
▲
3428m

D902

Ruisseau de l'Isseran

Col de l'Iseran
2770m

Pointe Nord
des Lores
▲
2903m

N

Pont de la Neige
2530m

Pont de l'Ouliette
Pied Montet
2274m

Col des Fours
2976m

VALLON DE LA LENTA

Ruisseau de la Lenta

D902

0   1   2
km

Tralenta

L'Arc

Pointe de
Méan-Martin
▲
3330m

Chalets
des Roches
2453m

Bonneval-
sur-Arc
1800m

Pont
du Vallon
2242m

Ruisseau du Vallon

Le Mollard

Rocher du Château

Ouille Allégra
▲
3130m

Ruisseau de Pis

Le Villaron
1740m

Bessans
1710m

Le Reclus

L'Arc

D902

Torrent d'Averole

Pointe
de Tierce

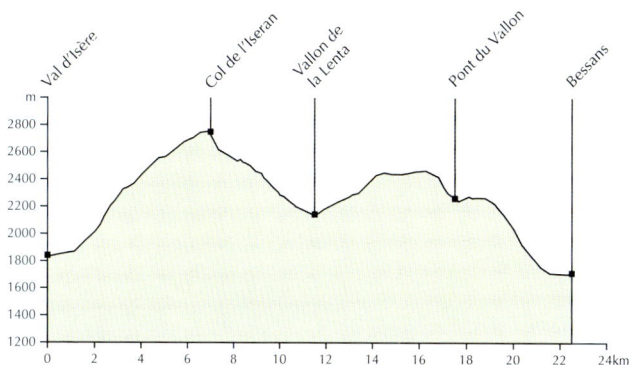

a path zigzagging up into the **Forêt du Fornet** and not some other path. Turn right only when signposted for the GR5, climbing through the forest to cross a ski piste, then the trees thin out on flowery slopes and there is a view back to Val d'Isère and La Grande Motte.

Reach a main road at 2310m and turn left to find the continuation of the path a few paces down the road (restaurant off route). Climb again to cross the **Ruisseau de l'Iseran**, which may contain snow into the summer. Keep climbing and join a track, crossing the stream at a higher level. Leave the track to follow a path up to the main road. Turn left to walk up the road to a bend then find the path, climbing again. Every time the road is encountered, the path will be found on the other side, until you eventually reach a stone hut. Just beyond is the top of the **Col de l'Iseran**, at 2770m (restaurant, gift shop, former chalet-hotel and the little church of Notre Dame de Toute Prudence). This is the highest point on the main GR5, with views of glaciated peaks on the Franco-Italian border.

Col de l'Iseran to Vallon de la Lenta   1hr 15min, 4.5km, +0m -630m

Start the long descent from a tall, square-built cairn. The path is initially steep, narrow and worn. It cuts across a grassy slope, and there is no need to touch the main road. Enter the Parc National de la Vanoise. The path leads close to a bridge, **Pont de la Neige**, at 2530m, where snow patches linger well into the summer. Turn right, away from the road, then left to ford a stream, heading down a path to cross a footbridge over the main flow. However, if the first stream is in spate, cross the road bridge and pick up the path, without using the footbridge.

The way down is initially rocky, narrow and crumbling, with a chain for assistance. Enjoy fine waterfalls, but keep an eye on the rough and rocky ground.

Looking down through Vallon de la Lenta after passing Pont de la Neige

Turn left to pass a building and a bridge to reach a road bend at **Pied Montet**, at 2274m. Step onto the road but look for and take the path dropping down again, passing bigger waterfalls. One area of smooth outcrops has a boulder-paved path, then a track leads past small farms in the **Vallon de la Lenta**. Either cross a foot-bridge on the right, at 2134m, or leave the main GR5 to follow a link route down to Bonneval-sur-Arc for the low-level GR5E.

Vallon de la Lenta to Pont du Vallon   2hr, 6km, +385m -275m

After crossing the footbridge over **Ruisseau de la Lenta**, follow a track uphill. Look out for views of hanging glaciers on the Franco–Italian frontier. Keep right at a track junction near Les Druges, at 2260m, then turn left shortly afterwards, up a narrow path. This climbs steeply at times up a grassy, flowery slope, offering splendid views of the Arc valley. A few streams have to be crossed, and the more vigorous ones may feature wobbly plank footbridges. Climb to a path junction at the **Chalets des Roches**, at 2453m. There is another option to follow a path off route down to Bonneval-sur-Arc; otherwise, climb a little further to pass stone cabins.

After the small stone cabins pass a couple of small pools – if they haven't dried up in a hot spell. Reach another cabin and follow the path as it winds down into Le Vallon, where a valley is watered by cascades and has patches of snow lingering through the summer. Cross a footbridge, the **Pont du Vallon**, at 2242m, near which cattle and sheep graze around small cabins.

Pont du Vallon to Bessans   1hr 30min, 5km, +35m -580m

Follow an undulating track onwards and later look left to catch a glimpse of the Chalet des Gardes before passing the ruins of **Le Mollard**. Bessans is in view, but don't follow the track all the way downhill, as it actually runs off route to Villaron (gîte d'étape). Go down a track on the left, but leave it to follow a path, which is actually the old way to Bessans. Watch carefully for the old path shortcutting loops on the modern track, as there are few markers. Be sure to spot the last stretch of the old path, leaving a bend and making a beeline for Bessans, exiting the Parc National de la Vanoise.

Pass below a cliff to land on a track at the foot of the **Ruisseau de Pis**, at the junction of the GR5 and GR5E. Turn right and follow the track alongside a river, **L'Arc**, until you reach a bridge. The GR5E crosses the bridge but the GR5 doesn't. However, most walkers will cross the bridge to visit the village of **Bessans**, at 1710m (all services; Cars Région Savoie buses to Bonneval-sur-Arc and Modane/Fourneaux: www.cars-region-savoie.fr; tourist information office: tel 04 79 05 96 52 www.haute-maurienne-vanoise.com).

Variant: Link from GR5 at Vallon de la Lenta to GR5E at Bonneval-sur-Arc   1hr, 2.5km, +10m, -345m

Leave the GR5 at the **Ruisseau de la Lenta** and head for a nearby road bridge. Cross the bridge and follow the road, watching for a path dropping down to the left, which passes a concrete hut. A steep and rugged zigzag path continues downhill, with fine views over the Arc valley. Gates towards the bottom give way to a track and a road, which winds down past houses to reach the main road just above the tourist information office at **Tralenta**, adjacent to **Bonneval-sur-Arc**, at 1800m (hotels, chambres d'hôte, refuge, restaurants, bars, shop; morning minibus up to Vallon de la Lenta; Cars Région Savoie buses to Modane/Fourneaux: www.cars-region-savoie.fr; tourist information office: tel 04 79 05 95 95 www.bonneval-sur-arc.com). To continue to Bessans, follow the GR5E as described in GR5E Stage 1.

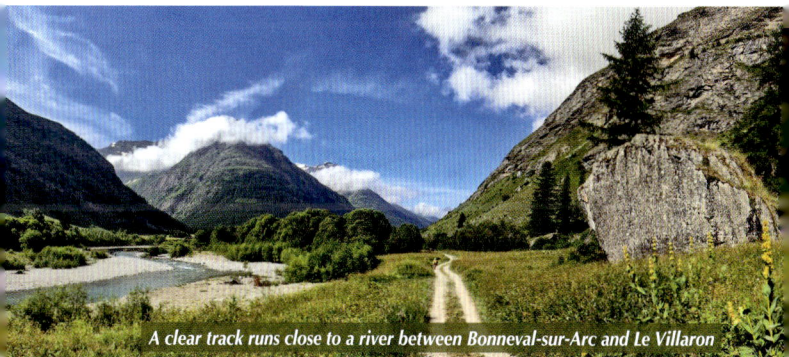
A clear track runs close to a river between Bonneval-sur-Arc and Le Villaron

STAGE 11A
Val d'Isère to Bessans (via Col des Fours)

Start	Val d'Isère
Finish	Bessans
Time	9hr 15min
Distance	26.5km
Total Ascent	1600m
Total Descent	1720m
Terrain	Steep climbing to Col des Fours. A steep and rocky descent is followed by a climb to a balcony path before a track and a rugged path lead down into a valley.
Maps	3633 ET
Refreshments	La Ferme de l'Arsellaz. Refuge du Fond des Fours. Plenty of choice off route at Bonneval-sur-Arc and at Bessans.
Accommodation	Refuge du Fond des Fours. Hotels, *chambres d'hôte* and refuge off route at Bonneval-sur-Arc. *Gîte d'étape* off route at Le Villaron. Hotels, *gîte* and campsite at Bessans.

The route over Col des Fours is one of the latest variant routes on the GR5. Using it takes trekkers higher than any other part of the trail, to 2976m. It is well worth the effort in good weather, although snow cover is likely well into the summer. The descent can optionally include Bonneval-sur-Arc (linking with the GR5E low-level variant) while the main route enjoys a fine balcony path before descending to Bessans.

Val d'Isère to Le Manchet   1hr, 4km, +165m -30m
The old church in Val d'Isère is a fine landmark and there is a GR5 marker on its wall, indicating a quiet road, Rue de l'Église, leading away from the town centre. After leaving town, turn left to pass the tiny Chapelle St-Jean. Follow a dusty dirt road uphill, continuing along a tarmac road as signposted. When the road drops a little, a signpost for the Refuge du Fond de Fours points between chalets at **Le Legattaz**, where a track continues through a valley. Watch out to spot a grassy path on the left, which climbs a little then turns right. It contours across the lower slopes of a mountain, passing abundant yellow gentians and a few bushes. Pass beneath a chairlift and later turn right down a track, not far from ruined buildings at **Le Manchet**, at 1957m. Turn left along a road and cross a bridge over a river, entering the Parc National de la Vanoise, to reach some noticeboards.

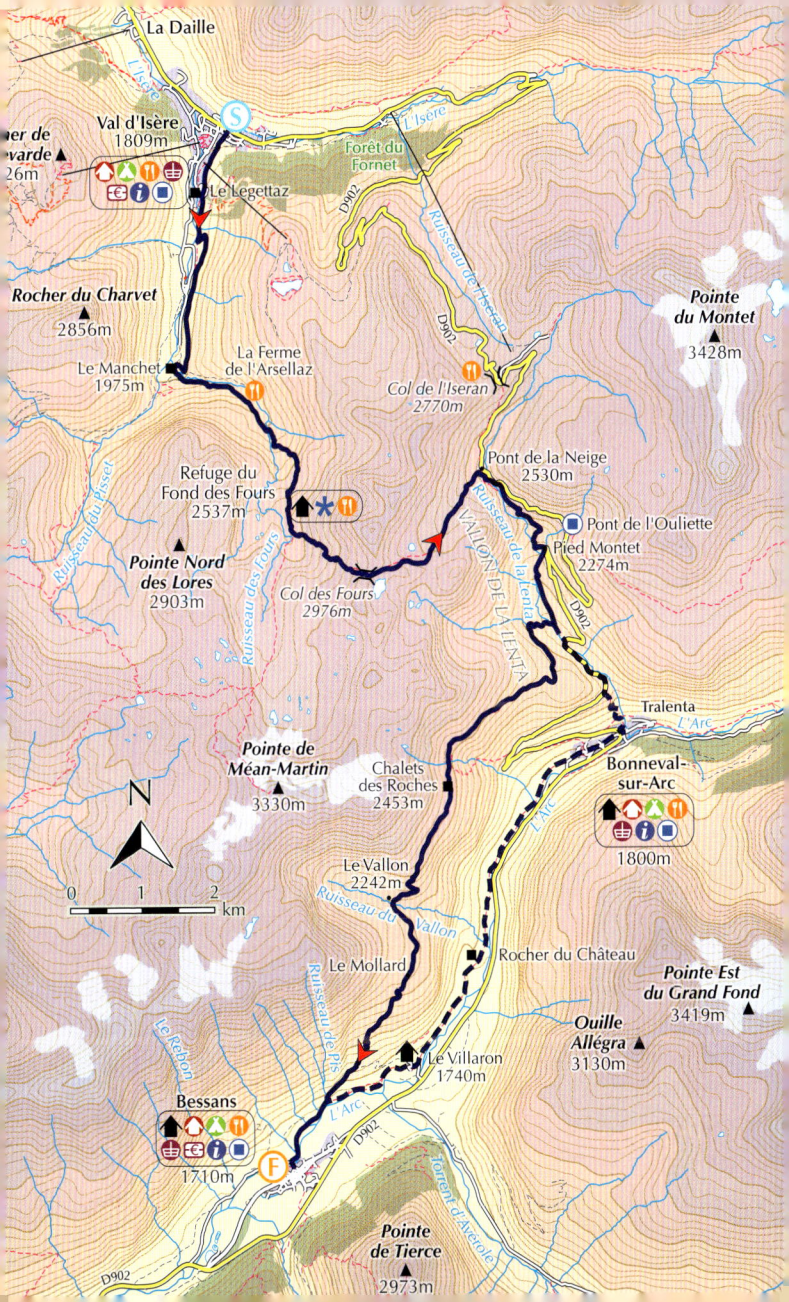

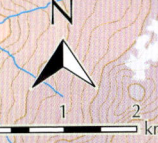

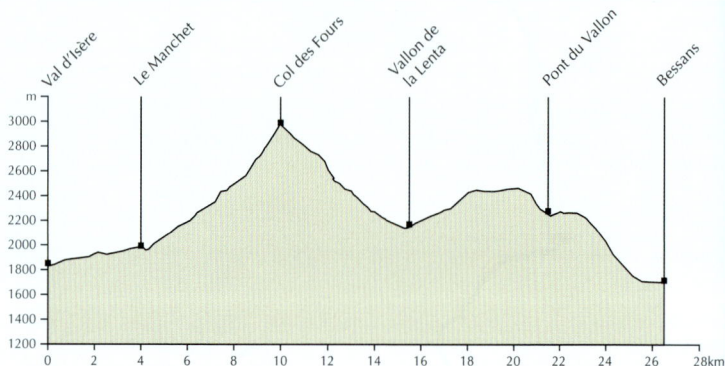

Le Manchet to Col des Fours

3hr, 6km, +1020m -5m

Turn left, as signposted, and follow a path uphill to join a track. Turn left to follow the track gently uphill then turn right to leave it, climbing a rugged path. Later, pass well to the right of **La Ferme de l'Arsellaz** or detour left to visit it (restaurant) and rejoin the route afterwards. After an easy stretch of path, cross a footbridge below a fine waterfall and climb further. Ford a stream and continue climbing, later crossing a footbridge below another fine waterfall.

Climb steeply up through a boulder-strewn valley, climbing some chunky stone steps. Spot a pole on the skyline, marking the location of the **Refuge du**

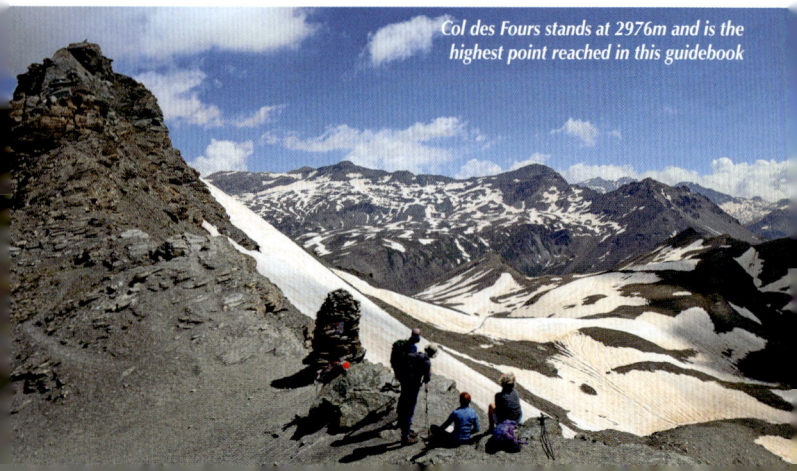

Col des Fours stands at 2976m and is the highest point reached in this guidebook

Fond des Fours, the highest refuge in this guidebook, at 2537m (refuge, bivouac and restaurant). Continue onwards to reach a signposted junction and turn left. The path climbs a grassy slope, which gives way to broken, crumbling rock, leading to a signpost and cairn on **Col des Fours** at 2976m, where there is a splendid view from what is the highest point reached on any of the paths in this guidebook. Snow tends to linger well into the summer at this altitude.

Col des Fours to Vallon de la Lenta   1hr 45min, 5.5km, +0m -835m

Carefully, pick a way down from the col, walking on flaky rock trodden to dust, overlooking a small lake, to reach a lower col which looks towards Col de l'Iseran. Carefully, walk further downhill, keeping well to the right of another small lake. The path aligns itself with a crumbling crest of dolomitic limestone, then a clear path winds further downhill. Don't ford the stream to reach the road near **Pont de la Neige**, at 2530m, but instead keep right and cross a footbridge.

The way down is initially rocky, narrow and crumbling, with a chain for assistance. Enjoy fine waterfalls, but keep an eye on the rough and rocky ground. Turn left to pass a building and a bridge to reach a road bend at **Pied Montet**, at 2274m. Step onto the road but look for and take the path dropping down again, passing bigger waterfalls. One area of smooth outcrops has a boulder-paved path, then a track leads past small farms in the **Vallon de la Lenta**. Either cross a footbridge on the right, at 2134m, or leave the main GR5 to follow a link route down to Bonneval-sur-Arc for the low-level GR5E (see Stage 11 for details).

Vallon de la Lenta to Pont du Vallon   2hr, 6km, +385m -280m

After crossing the footbridge over **Ruisseau de la Lenta**, follow a track uphill. Look out for views of hanging glaciers on the Franco–Italian frontier. Keep right at a track junction near Les Druges, at 2260m, then turn left shortly afterwards, up a narrow path. This climbs steeply at times up a grassy, flowery slope, offering splendid views of the Arc valley. A few streams have to be crossed, and the more vigorous ones may feature wobbly plank footbridges. Climb to a path junction at the **Chalets des Roches**, at 2453m. There is another option to follow a path off route down to Bonneval-sur-Arc; otherwise, climb a little further to pass stone cabins.

Climb a little to pass a couple of small stone cabins and pass a couple of small pools – if they haven't dried up in a hot spell. Reach another cabin and follow the path as it winds down into Le Vallon, where a valley is watered by cascades and has patches of snow lingering through the summer. Cross a footbridge, the **Pont du Vallon**, at 2242m, near which cattle and sheep graze around small cabins.

Approaching the village of Bessans, where the GR5 and GR5E follow the same track

Pont du Vallon to Bessans   1hr 30min, 5km, +30m -570m

Follow an undulating track onwards and later look left to catch a glimpse of the Chalet des Gardes before passing the ruins of **Le Mollard**. Bessans is in view, but don't follow the track all the way downhill, as it actually runs off route to Villaron (gîte d'étape). Go down a track on the left, but leave it to follow a path, which is actually the old way to Bessans. Watch carefully for the old path shortcutting loops on the modern track, as there are few markers. Be sure to spot the last stretch of the old path, leaving a bend and making a beeline for Bessans, exiting the Parc National de la Vanoise.

Pass below a cliff to land on a track at the foot of the **Ruisseau de Pis**, at the junction of the GR5 and GR5E. Turn right and follow the track alongside a river, **L'Arc**, until you reach a bridge. The GR5E crosses the bridge but the GR5 doesn't. However, most walkers will cross the bridge to visit the village of **Bessans**, at 1710m (all services; Cars Région Savoie buses to Bonneval-sur-Arc and Modane/Fourneaux: www.cars-region-savoie.fr; tourist information office: tel 04 79 05 96 52 www.haute-maurienne-vanoise.com).

STAGE 12
Bessans to Refuge du Plan du Lac

Start	Bessans
Finish	Refuge du Plan du Lac
Time	10hr
Distance	25.5km
Total Ascent	1415m
Total Descent	755m
Terrain	Some steep climbs but mostly gentle gradients along a balcony path overlooking the valley.
Maps	3633 ET
Refreshments	Refuge de Vallonbrun, Auberge de Bellecombe and Refuge du Plan du Lac.
Accommodation	Refuge de Vallonbrun, Refuge du Cuchet (unstaffed), Auberge de Bellecombe and Refuge du Plan du Lac.

After an easy riverside stroll, the GR5 climbs back into the mountains. A splendid balcony path runs just inside the Parc National de la Vanoise, from the Refuge de Vallonbrun to the Refuge du Cuchet. Fine views take in the peaks along the Franco-Italian frontier, with a peep through the Col du Mont-Cenis. The route makes a long traverse around the deep and rocky gorge of the Doron, penetrating into the heart of the Vanoise.

Bessans to Refuge de Vallonbrun   3hr 15min, 7.5km, +635m -65m

Leave Bessans by crossing the bridge over the river, turning left to follow a track downstream. Turn right at a junction, rising slightly and pulling away from the river to walk between fields (campsite). Pass Chapelle St-Maurice at La Chalp and continue to the **D902** road, around 1700m. Turn right to follow the main road, but as it swings left, watch for a signpost on the right.

A narrow path rises through woods and continues along an overgrown ridge of rubble, rising through fields to houses and an old chapel at **Col de la Madeleine**, at 1752m (water). A path climbs uphill, hacked from bare rock and equipped with steps on an early steep stretch. Gentler zigzags climb a grassy, flowery slope, passing ruined buildings at **Le Mollard**. Enjoy widening prospects, and turn left, up to the **Chapelle St-Antoine**, perched on top of a grassy slope.

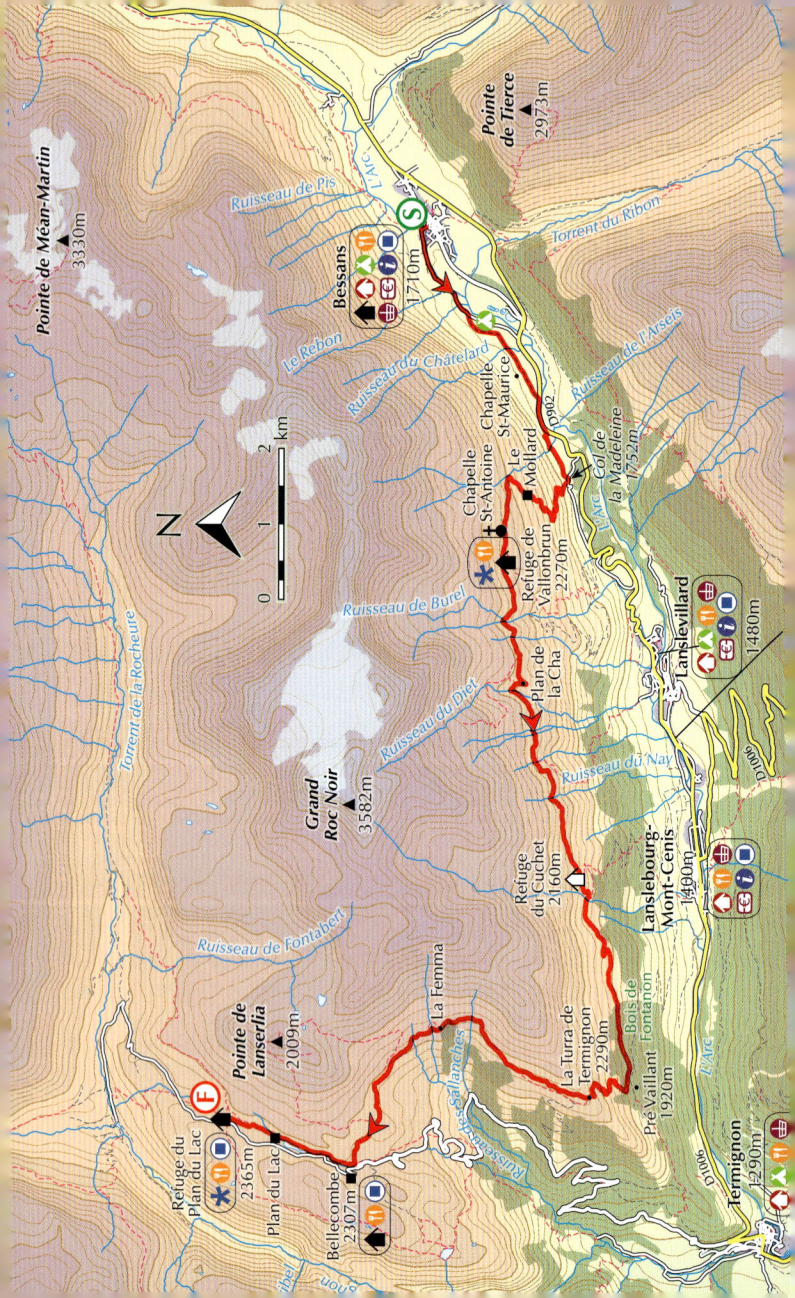

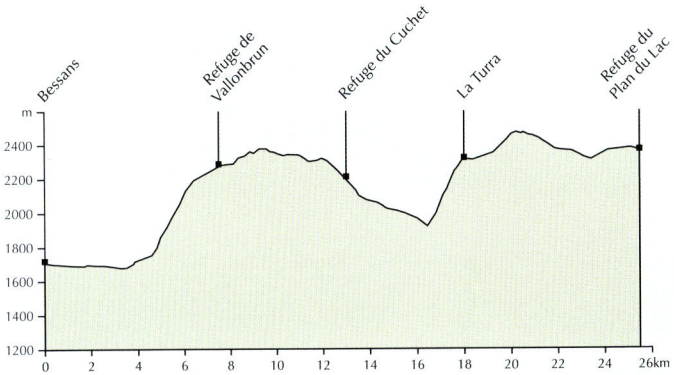

Follow a track down to the **Refuge de Vallonbrun**, at 2270m (refuge, bivouac and restaurant), entering the Parc National de la Vanoise.

Refuge de Vallonbrun to Refuge du Cuchet   1hr 45min, 5.5km, +150m -255m
The GR5 climbs from the refuge up a grassy track to pass a few stone buildings. A path continues uphill, tracing around a steep, stony ravine and crossing the **Ruisseau de Burel**. Climb parallel to a track then cross it to follow a signposted path around a ridge of stony moraine to enter a valley at **Plan de la Cha**, around 2370m.

Cross the **Ruisseau du Diet** and other streams, following the path onwards to reach a junction (where you can descend off route to Lanslevillard in 1hr 30min).

The slope steepens, is rugged in places and is grazed by cattle. The path drops and eventually reaches the **Refuge du Cuchet** on a scenic perch at 2160m (unstaffed refuge with kitchen; if staying, bring your own food, and if using the water, note the instructions on the purifying system). There is the option to descend off route to Lanslebourg in 1hr 30min.

Refuge du Cuchet to La Turra   2hr 30min, 5km, +360m -235m
Don't follow the steep path downhill from the refuge but instead walk along a gentler path, passing well to the right of a couple of chalets. Join a track and turn right to follow it, looping down past a couple more buildings on the way to a forest, the **Bois de Fontanon**. Continue down to a junction with another track at **Pré Vaillant**, at 1920m.

The Refuge de Vallonbrun sits on a grassy terrace high above the Arc valley

Turn right, not up the track but up a path instead. Turn right at a junction further uphill and zigzag from the forest onto flowery slopes, where the trees thin out and juniper creeps across the ground. Climb around a rocky edge and pass above three little chalets to reach **La Turra de Termignon**, at 2290m, from where there is a view of glaciated peaks around the Doron valley in the heart of the Vanoise.

La Turra to Refuge du Plan du Lac   2hr 30min, 7.5km, +270m -200m

Follow the path onwards, as marked, dropping downhill a little then climbing easily, keeping above a couple of little dairy farms, to reach **La Femma**. Follow a track uphill a little then downhill past a couple more farms to reach a road and a car park at **Bellecombe**, at 2307m (refuge, restaurant; Transdev Savoie buses to Termignon, Plan du Lac and Entre Deux Eaux).

Follow a clear path uphill, parallel to the road but on the other side of a limestone ravine. Pass beside a small lake, and if the air is still, enjoy seeing the mountains reflected in the water. There are magnificent views as the path proceeds across the grassy **Plan du Lac** to reach the **Refuge du Plan du Lac** at 2365m (refuge, bivouac, restaurant, Parc National de la Vanoise information; Transdev Savoie buses to Termignon and Entre Deux Eaux).

Start	Refuge du Plan du Lac
Finish	Le Montana
Time	10hr 15min
Distance	29km
Total Ascent	1290m
Total Descent	1475m
Terrain	After crossing a deep valley, a succession of ascents and descents leads across high, boulder-strewn slopes. Later, a fine balcony path offers easier walking.
Maps	3633 ET and 3534 OT
Refreshments	Off route at Entre Deux Eaux. Also Refuge de l'Arpont and Le Montana, but note the gap between them.
Accommodation	Refuge d'Entre Deux Eaux lies off route. Refuge de l'Arpont is halfway through the stage. Le Montana and nearby Refuge de Plan Sec are at the end of the stage.

This is a long and hard day's walk. Anyone who feels it is too much should break at the Refuge de l'Arpont and cover the distance in two easier days. There are often views of glaciers during the day, and the middle part of the route is surprisingly high. Bear in mind that, while paths may be rough and stony at first, traversing high above the Doron, they are much easier later in the day, especially the balcony path overlooking the Arc valley.

Refuge du Plan du Lac to Lacs des Lozières   2hr 30min, 7.5km, +470m -415m

Leave the refuge by walking downhill, roughly parallel to a road. Cross the road beside the **Chapelle St-Barthélémy** and walk down a path, crossing a band of quartzite. This band of quartzite is a prominent feature that is seen later on the other side of the valley. The path winds downhill to rejoin the road at Pont de la Renaudière, at 2045m (Transdev Savoie buses to Termignon; Refuge d'Entre Deux Eaux lies 15min off route and the GR55 is 45min off route).

Turn left, down the road, to cross bridges over two rivers at **Entre Deux Eaux**. Water drawn from the rivers runs through a tunnel to a reservoir at Plan d'Aval. Follow a track past the Chalets de l'Ile at 2000m. Turn left after passing the last

Pointe de la Réchasse
3212m

Pointe du Dard
3206m

Refuge d'Entre Deux Eaux
2120m

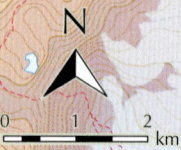

Pont Renat
204

N

Mont de la Para
2337m

La Para

Entre Deux Eaux

Link-to GR5

0   1   2
km

Laes des Lozières
2475m

Refuge du Plan du Lac
2365m

Chape St-Barthé

Ruisseau de la Letta

Ruisseau de Miribel

Dôme de Chasseforêt
3586m

Pointe Lanser
2009

S

Plan du Lac

Refuge de l'Arpont
2309m

Doron de Termignon

Ruisseau de

Dôme de l'Arpont
3599m

Chapelle St-Laurent

Le Mont
2090m

Ruisseau du

Ruisseau du Grand Pyx

Dent Parrachée
3695m

Montafia Dessus
2190m

Ruisseau du Pissa

L'Arc

La Loza
2360m

Termignon
1290m

Refuge de Plan Sec
2330m

Sollières

La Turra
2360m

D1006

Le Plan Amont

Le Montana
2190m

F

Ruisseau Saint-Pierre

Le Plan d'Aval

Mont Froid
2822m

D1006

L'Arc

Aussois

D215

D83

Bramans

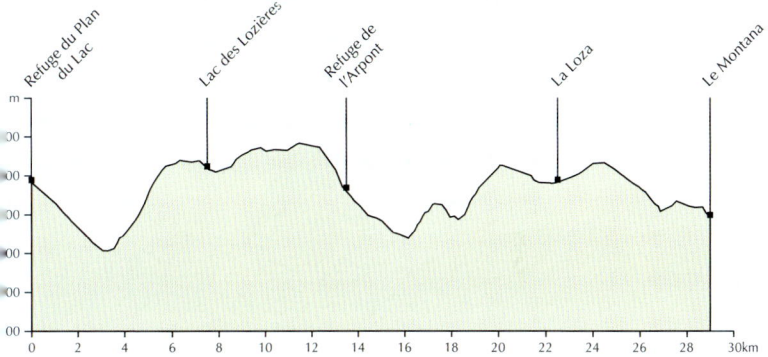

building to follow a vague path, as signposted. Pick up and follow a grassy track, zigzagging up a flowery slope with great views of the surrounding mountains. Pass a couple of ruins and ignore a track to the farm of **La Para**. Eventually, a signpost and a path junction are reached at **Mont de la Para**, at 2337m.

Turn left and keep climbing. Although the bedrock is schist, the mountainside is covered in quartzite fallen from a prominent band above. After passing one huge boulder, quartzite blocks are aligned beside the path. Eventually, the path levels out on a boulder-strewn slope, crossing a couple of slight dips. Curiously banded limestone boulders have fallen from an unstable band further uphill. Spend a while gazing at the reflections of the mountains in the little **Lacs des Lozières**, at 2475m. The lakes fill ice-scooped hollows in the hummocky schist bedrock, overlooked by the dark peak of Roche Ferran and the glaciated Dôme de Chasseforêt.

Lacs des Lozières to Refuge de l'Arpont   2hr, 6km, +155m -270m

Cross a stream and follow the path across glacial moraine comprised largely of quartzite ripped from the valley side. Cross a bridge over a milky glacial stream and follow the path as it winds up a huge tongue of bouldery moraine, this time mainly limestone. Climb from the moraine to see the glacier high above. The path turns a corner overlooking a sheep-grazed pasture. Further along, the schist bedrock is covered in masses of limestone boulders fallen from a peak above. Follow the path across the mountainside then cross a broad valley full of slabs and angular boulders.

155

Tiny walkers follow the GR5 near Le Montana, while dense cloud fills the Arc valley below them

The many streams forming the Ruisseau de Miribel must be forded at around 2530m, and while gradients are gentle, the going is slow. Follow cairns where the line of the path is unclear. After climbing to 2589m, the path crosses a rocky slope where bouquetin may be seen. There is a view down the gorge to Termignon and through Col du Mont-Cenis into Italy. The path eventually descends more steeply, and the **Refuge de l'Arpont**, at 2309m, suddenly comes into view (refuge, bivouac and restaurant).

Refuge de l'Arpont to La Loza   3hr 30min, 9km, +500m -450m

Follow the path down from the refuge, walking on bare schist at times, passing the **Chapelle St-Laurent** and old farm buildings. The path crosses streams and passes below a waterfall. Some path sections are held in place by girders. Pass through alder-scrub woodland then descend to some ruined buildings at **Le Mont**, at 2090m (a path leads off route down to Termignon in 1hr 30min).

Climb uphill to cross a rocky ravine, where a very narrow cleft has been plugged with rock to make a footbridge. Zigzag further uphill, then the path runs almost level for a while. There are views of glaciated peaks on almost all sides. The path zigzags down to a solitary building at **Montafia Dessus**, at 2190m.

The GR5 runs downhill and uphill, still on schist, crossing streams, before zigzagging up a steep slope to run at a gentler gradient. A fine balcony path crosses vast sandstone scree overlooking Termignon. Reach a junction of paths at 2350m then climb a little to reach a crumbling building and a modern hut at **La Loza**, at 2360m (a path leads off route down to Sollières in 2hr 15min).

La Loza to Le Montana   2hr 15min, 6.5km, +165m -340m

A delightful, level, grassy track gives way to a gentle climb up across a steep, grassy, sheep-grazed slope overlooking Bramans. The track traces around a huge limestone ravine overlooked by a crumbling rock tower. Sweeping zigzags lead down a steep, grassy slope to a grassy col and a signpost at **La Turra**, at 2360m.

Turn right to find another zigzag path, and don't shortcut, as the crumbling dolomitic limestone has been badly eroded and required expensive work to stabilise it. Keep straight ahead at a path junction and follow tight, gravelly zigzags down to a stream-bed. Cross over and continue along a narrow terrace path, roughly contouring across a steep and grassy slope, exiting the Parc National de la Vanoise, to reach a chairlift. Turn left, downhill, to reach **Le Montana** at 2190m (hotel/refuge, restaurant; chairlift down to Aussois for all services; tourist information office: tel 04 79 05 99 06 www.aussois.com). Alternatively, keep straight ahead along the GR5 or follow signs for nearby **Refuge de Plan Sec**.

STAGE 14
Le Montana to Modane/Fourneaux

Start	Le Montana
Finish	Modane/Fourneaux
Time	7hr 25min
Distance	18km
Total Ascent	645m
Total Descent	1745m
Terrain	Good tracks and rugged paths across high, rugged slopes. A long descent through forest, ending with a steep and rugged path and urban road-walking.
Maps	3534 OT
Refreshments	Refuge de Plan Sec, Refuge de la Fournache and Refuge de l'Orgère are all slightly off route. Plenty of choice at Modane and Fourneaux.
Accommodation	Refuge de Plan Sec, Refuge de la Fournache and Refuge de l'Orgère are all slightly off route. Hotels and campsite at Fourneaux.

The GR5 finally descends from the Parc National de la Vanoise to Modane. First, there is a rugged circuit around a side-valley containing two hydroelectric reservoirs, then a fine balcony path offers a bird's-eye view of Modane and Fourneaux. A steep, forested descent must be endured before the towns are reached. Few walkers have a kind word to say about Modane and Fourneaux and they are by no means 'tourist' towns, but they provide all necessary services in a business-like manner.

Le Montana to Pont de la Sétéria   1hr 15min, 4km, +150m -125m

If you spent the night at Le Montana then retrace your steps back up to the GR5 and turn left. Pass a signposted path junction to reach a junction of two tracks. Cross the first of these and follow the other one gradually up into a valley, with a fine view down to a reservoir. A path up to the right allows an optional visit to the **Refuge de Plan Sec** at 2330m (refuge, bivouac and restaurant).

The track eventually leads through a cutting in the quartzite bedrock. Leave the path at this point to go down a path on the left to cross a stream. Climb a little and cross another stream, then there is an option to visit the **Refuge de la**

Tête d'Aussois
3126m

Dent
Parrachée
3697m

Ruisseau de Saint-Benoit

Pointe de
l'Échelle
3422m

Refuge de
la Fournache
2340m

Pont de
la Sétéria
2206m

Le Plan
d'Amont

Refuge
de Plan Sec
2330m

Ruisseau de Povaret

Le Rateau
d'Aussois
3128m

Le Plan
d'Aval

Le Montana
2190m

Ruisseau Saint-Pierre

Tête
Noire
2675m

Refuge
de l'Orgère
1945m

Le Barbier

Col du Barbier
2295m

Aussois

GR55

Ruisseau de Saint-Bernard

Chapelle
Notre-Dame
des Neiges

Chalets de
l'Orgère

Bois du
Bourget

D215

D1006

Pierre-Brune
1800m

Avrieux

L'Arc

Ruisseau du Nant

Loutraz
1100m

Fourneaux

Modane

1050m

1070m

A43

Ruisseau de Saint-Antoine

Mont
Rond
2772m

N

0   1   2
km

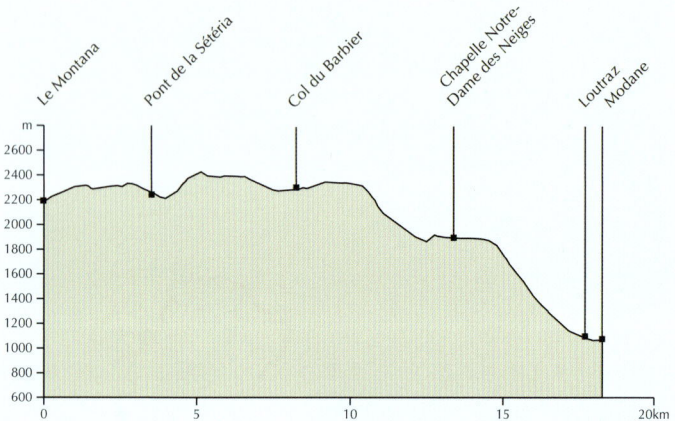

Fournache at 2340m (refuge, bivouac and restaurant).

The GR5 heads down a path, crossing schist bedrock. Keep left at a path junction (the right turn leads off route up to the Refuge de la Parrachée in 30min). The path enjoys good views of the Plan d'Amont reservoir and leads downhill to cross a bridge, **Pont de la Sétéria**, at 2206m, entering the Parc National de la Vanoise.

Pont de la Sétéria to Col du Barbier

2hr, 4.5km, +275m -185m

Head straight up a winding path, on flaky schist bedrock, with great views back to the Dent Parrachée. The path eventually levels out at a junction and signpost. Turn left to descend then climb gently across a boulder-strewn area, where

The GR5 makes a high-level circuit around the hydroelectric reservoir of Plan d'Amont

alpenrose gives way to blueberry cover. There are fine views down to both reservoirs and the village of Aussois, then the path zigzags down a steeper slope before dropping more gently. A gradual ascent crosses slopes of creeping juniper and ankle-twisting quartzite blocks to reach a signpost on **Col du Barbier** at 2295m.

Col du Barbier to Chapelle Notre-Dame des Neiges   2hr 15min, 5km, +170m -520m
Gentle gradients lead across the col then the path climbs again, passing a ruin and sheds. Pass below a new house and later, pass an old building at **Le Barbier**. A splendid balcony path overlooks Modane, and the view across the valley leads the eye to Valfréjus, Mont Thabor and Col de la Vallée Étroite. Zigzag down through a forest, **Bois du Bourget** (water), and follow the path across boulder-scree, where a sign advises against stopping. The path later divides, so climb to the right then follow a soft, pine-needle path to a few buildings on a pasture at the **Chalets de l'Orgère** (water). Follow a track around a grassy valley to a few more chalets and the **Chapelle Notre-Dame des Neiges**, and exit the Parc National de la Vanoise. A choice of two paths leads a short distance uphill and off route for an optional visit to the **Refuge de l'Orgère**, at 1945m (refuge, bivouac and restaurant).

Chapelle Notre-Dame des Neiges to Loutraz   1hr 45min, 4km, +40m -885m
Beyond the chapel, look for a marked and signposted path climbing into a forest. Contour across the slope, avoiding other paths, to emerge on a track in a clearing near a little house at **Pierre Brune**, at 1800m (water). Turn left, down a steep and rugged forest path, watching carefully for GR5 markers at a number of path junctions. Eventually, the path joins a forest track near a bridge over a stream. Continue down the track, which later becomes a road. Turn left down Rue de la Charmette to reach a little chapel and a road junction at **Loutraz**, at 1100m. Choose now whether to descend left to Modane or right to Fourneaux, bearing in mind that these routes don't meet again until Valfréjus (Section 4, Stage 15).

Loutraz to Fourneaux   30min, 1.5km, +5m -40m
Turn right to reach a gymnasium, where a right turn leads along Rue de la Vanoise. Continue down to a junction and turn right along Avenue Emile Charvoz. Cross a bridge, Pont Emile Charvoz, and turn right to follow the main road into **Fourneaux**, at 1050m (all services).

Loutraz to Modane   10min, 0.5km, +10m -30m
Turn left down Rue des Chavières, passing through a staggered crossroads to cross a river. Note La Rizerie, a beautiful building on the right. Go under a railway line

Fort du Sapey is easily missed if you don't look up while passing through Fourneaux

then go straight past a roundabout and along Rue Croix Blanche. This leads to the town hall (*mairie*) in the centre of **Modane**, at 1070m (all services except accommodation). Note that a road-walking route is signposted and waymarked from the *mairie* to Fourneaux.

MODANE/FOURNEAUX

Not a 'classic' Alpine town but a workaday settlement handling road and rail freight in and out of the tunnels between France and Italy. There are some interesting old buildings around town and a full range of services.

Those who start or finish a section of the GR5 here find rapid access by train to and from Lyon and Paris. Those who require accommodation, trains or the tourist information centre should head for Fourneaux rather than Modane. Cars Région Savoie buses run up through the Arc valley to serve many parts of the GR5E (the low-level variant route that starts from Bonneval-sur-Arc): www.cars-region-savoie.fr. Tourist information office (Fourneaux): tel 04 79 05 26 67.

GR55 HIGH-LEVEL ROUTE
(REFUGE D'ENTRE LE LAC TO MODANE/
FOURNEAUX)

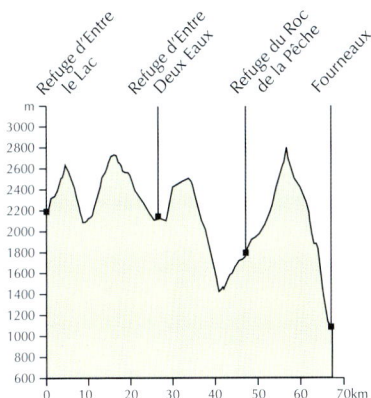

GR55 STAGE 1

Refuge d'Entre le Lac to Refuge d'Entre Deux Eaux

Start	Refuge d'Entre le Lac
Finish	Refuge d'Entre Deux Eaux
Time	9hr 15min
Distance	27km
Total Ascent	1200m
Total Descent	1235m
Terrain	Fairly easy paths over high passes – unless covered by snow, in which case, attention to route-finding is required.
Maps	3532 ET and 3633 ET
Refreshments	Refuge du Col du Palet. Plenty of choice at Val Claret. Refuge de la Leisse. Refuge d'Entre Deux Eaux.
Accommodation	Refuge du Col du Palet. Plenty of choice at Val Claret. Refuge de la Leisse. Refuge d'Entre Deux Eaux.

This alternative route through the Vanoise breaks away from the GR5 on Stage 10 at Tignes le Lac. Most of this stage's walk is in the Parc National de la Vanoise, the exception being around Val Claret, where the urban intrusion is distracting but there is an opportunity to stock up on provisions. The scenery is wonderful over the Col de la Leisse and down through the Vallon de la Leisse, but at this altitude, snow lies well into summer. The heart of the national park is a wildlife haven, so keep an eye open for bouquetin, chamois, marmots and golden eagles.

Refuge d'Entre le Lac to Refuge du Col du Palet   1hr 30min, 4km, +430m -0m

Leave the refuge and follow the signposted path back uphill, across a slope of grass and boulders, to get straight back to a junction with the GR5, then turn right and look ahead to spot the white dome of La Grande Motte. Keep to the right of grassy **Plan de la Grassaz**, away from a little stone chalet. Look out for marmots. Cross a stream-bed and climb more steeply, crossing the outflow and inflow of **Lac du Grattaleu**. Head left at a path junction to reach the **Refuge du Col du Palet** at 2600m (refuge, bivouac and restaurant).

Refuge du Col du Palet to Tignes le Lac   2hr, 5km, +70m -565m

Leave the refuge and either climb straight up a path or take a slightly longer, easier track uphill. Both routes meet to cross the **Col du Palet**, at 2652m, which might be flanked by snow patches late into summer. Enjoy the views of nearby glaciated peaks as you exit the Parc National de la Vanoise.

   The geology around the Col du Palet is quite mixed. On the ascent, the underlying rock is a mixture of limestone and schist. On the col itself, both can be found, while nearby, grey, crumbling humps are rich in gypsum. On the

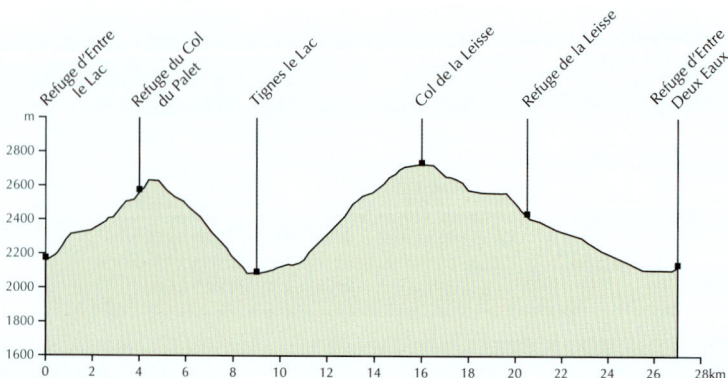

Mont-Blanc
de Peisey
2866m
(S)

Lac de
La Plagne

Refuge d'Entre le Lac
2155m

Plan de la
Grassaz

**Rochers
Rouges**
3003m

Lac du Chevril

Tignes le Lac
2100m

**Pointe du
Chardonnet**
2870m

Lac du Grattaleu

Refuge du
Col du Palet
2600m

Croix
de Lognan
2300m

Col du Palet
2652m

Lac de Tignes

Val Claret

**Pas de
La Tovière**
2695m

Bollin/Fresse

**Rocher de la
Petite Balme**
2779m

Col de Fresse
2576m

**Dôme de
Pramecou**
3081m

Col de la Leisse
2758m

N

0   1   2 km

**La Grande
Motte**
3657m

Lac des
Nettes

**La Grande
Casse**
3855m

Plan des
Nettes

Torrent de la Leisse

Refuge de
la Leisse
2487m

**Pointe de
la Sana**
3435m

VALLON DE LA LEISSE

**Pont de
la Croé-Vie**
2099m

e de
hasse

2m

(F)

Draie des Fés

GR5

Refuge d'Entre Deux Eaux
2120m

Pont de la
Renaudière
1597m

Torrent de la Rocheure

Refuge du
Plan du Lac
2365m

GR5

**Pointe de
Lanserlia**
2009m

Ruisseau de F

Looking back from Col du Palet to the Refuge du Col du Palet

way downhill, the limestone is dolomitic and full of tiny holes. Pass a couple of dolines, or solution hollows, one of which contains a small pool. When a track is reached, climb a short way up it and pass under a chairlift, then follow a path further downhill to the Tichot *télésiège* station, at 2469m.

Keep to the left of the chairlift and follow a path across a track. The Tignes and Val Claret conurbations are evident below, and the high-rise buildings seem quite incongruous so close to a national park. After passing tall poles stuck into the mountainside, the route reaches a viewpoint at **Croix de Lognan**, at 2300m.

Walk down into a little valley at Combe des Militaires to reach a junction of paths. Keep left to follow the GR5 down to Tignes le Lac. (Turn right for a shortcut down to Val Claret, passing the Destination Glacier attraction then climbing, as signposted, towards apartments, to join the GR55.) Follow the path across two tracks and zigzag down to a busy road. Cross the road to reach the shore of **Lac de Tignes** and either turn left to visit nearby **Tignes le Lac**, at 2100m (all services), or turn right to follow the GR55 along the lakeshore path towards Val Claret.

TIGNES LE LAC

This high-altitude resort thrives on the fact that it can offer all-year-round skiing, courtesy of the Glacier de la Grande Motte. In the summer months, it sells itself as a sporting and family resort. Surprisingly, much of the land nearby is designated as the Réserve Naturelle de la Tignes-Champagny, and presumably, this limits further development.

A full range of services is available in the town, and at nearby Val Claret, with free buses, or *navettes gratuites*, linking both sites. Belle Savoie Express buses run to and from Tignes le Lac and Bourg-St-Maurice: tel 04 80 00 70 00 www.altibus.com. Tourist information office: tel 04 79 40 04 40 www.tignes.net.

Walkers cross snow patches on their way from Val Claret to Col de la Leisse

Tignes le Lac to Col de la Leisse
2hr 30min, 7km, +665m -15m

The lakeshore path leads to a footbridge. Cross it and turn right to follow a river upstream, soon walking parallel to a main road, which leads to a roundabout. Turn left before you reach the roundabout and walk parallel to another road, which rises and curves around Val Claret (all services). Turn left at a cinema to follow the Route du Golf. Don't go through a tunnel but instead follow a path to the right of it, passing the last few apartment blocks in the resort, linking with the shortcut path that climbs from the Destination Glacier attraction.

VAL CLARET

This high-rise resort is surrounded by the Réserve Naturelle de la Tignes-Champagny, and presumably, this limits further development. A full range of services is available, with a free bus, or *navette gratuite*, linking with nearby Tignes le Lac.

Watch carefully for signposts and markers for the GR55, taking care to find a small river and follow a path upstream, ensuring you are not drawn onto a parallel cycle path. The path soon climbs from the river to reach the **Bollin/Fresse chairlift station** (nearby restaurant). Follow the pylons of the Télésiège Fresse uphill, as marked, and as height is gained, urban views are lost.

A post bearing rules and regulations is reached on entering the Parc National de la Vanoise. The scenery is stunning, and the marked path leads gradually uphill, while La Grande Motte looks striking with its glacial cap. Snow patches lie well into the summer and may obscure the path, and as the **Col de la Leisse** is broad and hummocky, it could be a confusing place in mist. The highest point is at 2758m and bears a signpost.

Col de la Leisse to Refuge de la Leisse   1hr 30min, 4.5km, +5m -285m

The path wanders through a bleak landscape and is marked by cairns. Lovely lakes come into view, and the path stays well to the left of them, descending gently to the outflow of **Lac des Nettes**. The area is strewn with rubble and only very lightly vegetated, sporting a few brave flowers. Cross a slight hump and head down into a grassier part of the valley. Keep to the right-hand side of **Plan des Nettes**, which was the site of a reservoir built in 1953, until its dam was demolished in 2012. Cross extensive scree and pass the site of the dam, then turn a corner to see the next part of the valley. The **Refuge de la Leisse** is reached in a charming situation at 2487m (refuge, bivouac and restaurant).

Refuge de la Leisse to Refuge d'Entre Deux Eaux   1hr 45min, 6.5km, +40m -400m

The GR55 doubles back, a short way from the refuge, to descend, winding downhill to cross a footbridge (also used by marmots!). There is only one path down through the grassy, boulder-strewn **Vallon de la Leisse**. Simply enjoy the grandeur of the place throughout the gradual descent, until you reach the arched stone bridge of **Pont de la Croé Vie**, at 2099m. The GR55 crosses the bridge, but don't cross it if you require accommodation. Instead, follow the path downstream to a huddle of buildings. Keep left at a junction for the **Refuge d'Entre Deux Eaux**, at 2120m (refuge, bivouac and restaurant). You can detour 15min off route if you wish to link with the GR5 or Transdev Savoie buses to Termignon, to link with the low-level GR5E.

GR55 STAGE 2

Refuge d'Entre Deux Eaux to Refuge du Roc de la Pêche

Start	Refuge d'Entre Deux Eaux
Finish	Refuge du Roc de la Pêche
Time	7hr 15min
Distance	21km
Total Ascent	1020m
Total Descent	1230m
Terrain	A relatively easy climb over a high mountain pass. A steep descent is followed by a long climb on clear tracks.
Maps	3532 ET and 3633 ET
Refreshments	Refuge du Col de la Vanoise. Refuge des Barmettes. Restaurant at Les Fontanettes. Plenty of choice at Pralognan. Restaurants at Les Prioux and Refuge du Roc de la Pêche.
Accommodation	Refuge du Col de la Vanoise. Refuge des Barmettes. Plenty of choice at Pralognan. Refuge Le Repoju at Les Prioux and Refuge du Roc de la Pêche.

Col de la Leisse and Col de la Vanoise have been used since the Bronze Age for passage though these high mountains. The traverse is wonderfully scenic, and for a high-level route, the walking is relatively easy, with refuges along the way. The descent from Col de la Vanoise passes dramatic scenery and eventually leads to the village of Pralognan. Good valley tracks lead back into the mountains by way of Refuge du Roc de la Pêche. Alternatively, this entire day's walk could be switched for Stage 13 of the main GR5 route.

Refuge d'Entre Deux Eaux to Refuge du Col de la Vanoise 2hr 30min, 6km, +435m -40m

Leave the refuge and retrace your steps back into the Vallon de la Leisse to reach a path junction at the arched stone bridge of **Pont de la Croé Vie** at 2099m. Turn left and cross the bridge, then follow a zigzag path up a rough and rocky slope that is covered in patches of alpenrose and juniper. Look out for bouquetin, which frequent this area. Schist and quartzite will be noticed, and a path junction is reached at **Voûtes du Clapier Blanc** at 2300m. Turn right to continue uphill, passing a monument, to reach an old blockhouse at 2439m.

Grande Motte
3656m

Ruisseau de Fontabert

VALLON DE LA LEISSE

Pointe de Lanserlia
2009m

Torrent de la Leisse

Refuge d'Entre Deux Eaux
2120m

Pont de la Renaudière
1597m

Pont de la Croé-Vie
2099m

La Grande Casse
3855m

Refuge du Plan du Lac
2365m

GR5

Voûtes du Clapier Blanc
2300m

Dalle des Fés

Ruisseau de la Vanoise

Pointe de la Réchasse
3212m

Lac Rond

Refuge du Col de la Vanoise
2518m

Ruisseau de Termignon

GR5

Ruisseau de Mirabel

Lac Long

Pointe des Volnets
3247m

Lac des Vaches

Col de la Vanoise
2522m

Pointe du Creux Noir
3154m

Pont du Chanton

Chalets de la Glière
2060m

Pointe du Dard
3206m

Dôme de Chasseforêt
3586m

N

km

2

1

0

Refuge des Barmettes
2010m

Fontanettes

Ruisseau d'Isertan

Dôme de l'Arpont

Mont Bochor
2023m

Pic de la Vieille Femme
2738m

Le Pommier Blanc
2513m

Doron de Chavière

Pralognan
1418m

Pont de Gerlon
1592m

Les Prioux
1715m

D915

de Pralognan

Aiguille d'Août
2555m

Petit Mont Blanc
2677m

Refuge du Roc de la Pêche
1911m

S

F

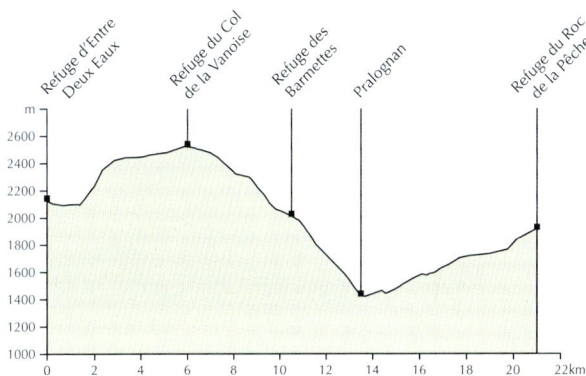

The path rises less steeply and soon runs almost level. Cross stepping stones over **Ruisseau de la Vanoise** and enjoy an easy walk upstream. Pass one shallow lake after another, with views of soaring glaciated peaks all around. All of a sudden, after passing **Lac Rond**, the second highest refuge in this guidebook comes into view, the **Refuge du Col de la Vanoise**, at 2518m (refuge, bivouac and restaurant).

Refuge du Col de la Vanoise to Refuge des Barmettes   1hr 15min, 4.5km, +5m -510m

Keep to the right-hand side of the refuge, picking up a rugged track and following it past **Lac Long**, admiring rock walls rising nearby. Turn left at a fork, where

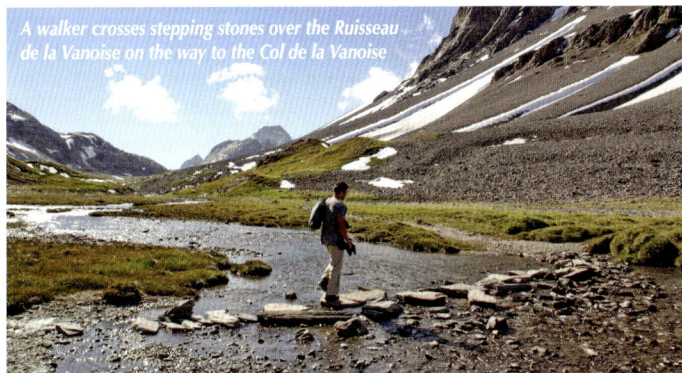

A walker crosses stepping stones over the Ruisseau de la Vanoise on the way to the Col de la Vanoise

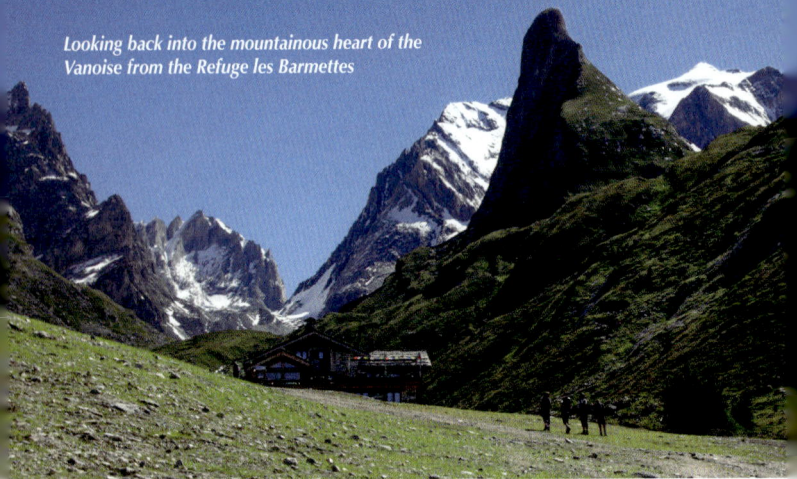
Looking back into the mountainous heart of the Vanoise from the Refuge les Barmettes

a shortcut avoids a bend in the track. The descent becomes quite stony and leads to the shallow **Lac des Vaches**, at 2319m. Walk straight through the middle of the lake, using a rock-slab causeway. Descend further, either by following the track or shortcutting the bends where trodden paths allow, and exit the Parc National de la Vanoise. Cross the **Pont du Chanton** over a stream, pausing to admire the mountains rising all around, then continue down past the **Chalets de la Glière**, at 2060m. A walled track leads onwards, crossing Pont de la Glière to reach the **Refuge des Barmettes** at 2010m (refuge and restaurant).

Refuge des Barmettes to Pralognan   1hr 15min, 3km, +45m -640m

The track continues downhill but is intertwined with a ski piste and a chairlift, so leave it as directed and follow a path down through a forest. Don't follow the track, except where marked, and always keep to the right-hand side of the piste. Continue down to a car park at **Les Fontanettes**, at 1650m (restaurant).

Keep to the left of the restaurant then keep left again down a rugged 'street'. When you reach a road bend, avoid the first path on the left, which leads to the Cascade de la Fraîche, and take the second path down to the left. On the way down the forested slope it is worth stepping left as signposted for a viewpoint, to enjoy a fine view from Rocher de la Fraîche, revealing Pralognan surrounded by mountains.

Zigzag downhill and pass a chapel at Les Bieux, then continue down to another chapel on Place du Baroz. The Hôtel de la Vanoise is reached further downhill, where the GR55 turns left, while most of the village of **Pralognan** lies to the right, at 1418m (all services; Belle Savoie Express buses link Pralognan with Moûtiers: www.altibus.com; free buses, or *navettes gratuites*, link Pralognan with Les Fontanettes and Les Prioux; tourist information office: tel 04 79 08 79 08 www.pralognan.com).

Pralognan to Refuge du Roc de la Pêche   **2hr 15min, 7.5km, +535m -40m**

Turn left at the hotel to leave Pralognan then turn right at the next junction to cross a bridge at Dou des Ponts. Turn left, as signposted for Isertan. Follow the tarmac road to its end and turn right along a track, or a slightly higher forest path could be followed instead. Walk either along the edge of a campsite or just inside the forest. The track beside the campsite swings right, so turn left up a forest track, walking upstream beside **Doron de Chavière** to pass above the Pont de Chollière. The forest track climbs onwards, apart from one downhill stretch, and eventually reaches a car park. Turn right to cross a bridge, **Pont de Gerlon**, at 1592m.

Turn left to continue upstream along another track. Climb past a water intake at the Prise d'Eau de Chavière, where water is piped to a hydro-electric station. The track continues up to a stone-built hamlet at **Les Prioux**, at 1715m, passing the Refuge Le Repoju (refuge and restaurant).

Follow the track straight through the hamlet to reach the river beyond, but don't cross it. Instead, follow a riverside path upstream to a footbridge, Passerelle des Anciens, and cross at that point. Turn right to continue along a road to reach a car park. Follow a track onwards then, when it forks, keep right to cross a culvert bridge at Pont de la Pêche. Zigzag uphill, climbing steeply at times, until a crest is crossed. Turn left to pass a little chapel and reach the **Refuge du Roc de la Pêche** at 1911m (refuge, hire tent and restaurant).

Patches of snow lie late into the season near the Refuge du Col de la Vanoise

GR55 STAGE 3
Refuge du Roc de la Pêche to Modane/Fourneaux

Start	Refuge du Roc de la Pêche
Finish	Modane/Fourneaux
Time	7hr 10min
Distance	19km
Total Ascent	900m
Total Descent	1730m
Terrain	A long track and a rugged path lead to a high col. A descent from mountains to pasture gives way to forest and urban road-walking.
Maps	3633 ET
Refreshments	*Buvette* at Alpage de Ritord. Restaurants at Refuge de Péclet-Polset and Chalet d'Alpage de Polset. Plenty at Modane/Fourneaux.
Accommodation	Refuge de Péclet-Polset. Chalet d'Alpage de Polset. Hotels and campsite at Fourneaux.

The Col de Chavière is the highest point on the GR55 and the second highest point reached in this guidebook. The steep and stony slopes may be covered with extensive patches of snow, even late into summer, and views are extensive on clear days. A gradual descent to Modane/Fourneaux sees the mountainsides give way to pleasant pastures at Polset, then there is a steep and convoluted descent through forest. Modane has a full range of services, except accommodation (which is available at nearby Fourneaux), and is an important transport hub in the Arc valley.

Refuge du Roc de la Pêche to Refuge de Péclet-Polset **2hr, 5.5km, +515m -0m**
The track beyond the refuge undulates across a pasture, with a view of the gla-ciated peak of Péclet-Polset. When a fork is reached, a detour left leads to the **Alpage de Ritord**, at 1971m (cheese and buvette). Keep right to stay on the GR55, which climbs past ruins at Chavière, entering the Parc National de la Vanoise. Although views of Péclet-Polset are lost, an impressive range of saw-tooth peaks rises across the valley.

Le Pommier Blanc
2513m

Refuge du Roc
de la Pêche
1911m

Ⓢ

N

0   1   2
km

Alpage de Ritord
1971m

Mollaret
d'en bas

*Pointe de
Chevrière*
3057m

Refuge de Péclet-Polset
2474m

*Pointe de
l'Observatoire*
3015m

Ruisseau de Saint-Benoît

*Aiguille
de Polset*
3528m

*Pointe de
Thorens*
3262m

Col de Chavière
2796m

*Pointe de
l'Échelle*
3422m

GR5

*Le Plan
d'Amont*

2504m

Pointe Renod
3380m

Le Grand
Planay

Ruisseau de Saint-Bernard

Ruisseau de Povaret

*Tête
Noire*
2675m

*Le Rateau
d'Aussois*
3128m

*Le Plan
d'Aval*

Source
du Vin

Refuge de l'Orgère
1945m

GR5

D215

L'Estiva

Bois du
Bourget

Polset

Pierre
Brune
1800m

Avrieux

La
Perrière

D1006

Loutraz
1100m

L'Arc

Fourneaux

Ⓕ

Modane
1070m

1050m

Ⓕ

A43

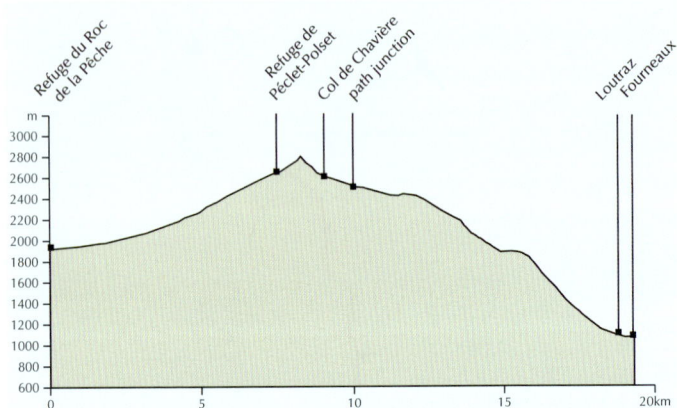

Pass a cabin at **Mollaret d'en bas** then later pass a ruin and keep climbing. The track traces around a hollow then zigzags uphill past a small pool. Watch out on the right for the appearance of a refuge from behind a rock bar. Only turn right if you intend to visit the **Refuge de Péclet-Polset** at 2474m (refuge and restaurant); otherwise, keep left to continue.

The Refuge de Péclet-Polset sits in a remote area of the Vanoise and is passed by the GR55

Refuge de Péclet-Polset to Col de Chavière   1hr 15min, 2.5km, +365m -0m

The GR55 follows a narrow path that meanders up and along a grassy, bouldery moraine and proves reasonably easy underfoot. Later, it climbs on crumbly schist, and there are fine views back down the valley. Broken, barren, limestone slabs come next, and cairns help to identify the route, but bear in mind that large snow patches lie late into summer in this area. Broken quartzite forms a boulder-scree then more schist proves loose underfoot on the final steep climb to the **Col de Chavière**, at 2796m. This is the second highest point reached in this guidebook, with a view back to Mont Blanc and ahead to Monte Viso.

Col de Chavière to path junction   45min, 2km, +10m -295m

The far side of the col is steep and stony but less likely to carry large snow patches. The path winds about as it descends and eventually levels out before climbing gently onto a grassy hump studded with huge boulders. A path junction is reached at **2504m**, where a decision needs to be made. The GR55 turns right while a variant route turns left, with both routes meeting later to continue descending to Modane/Fourneaux.

Path junction to Loutraz via GR55   3hr, 8.5km, +0m -1405m

Turn right to follow the GR55 down through the boulder-strewn pasture of **Le Grand Plannay**. Clearly, the area wasn't always so peaceful, as the shattered, rusting remains of military shell-cases testify. Pass a restored cabin and enjoy a view of three waterfalls side-by-side across the valley. Pass the **Source du Vin** (water only, not wine!). Enter a forest, where the path contours across steep and flowery slopes, then drop downhill to emerge in a pleasant valley dotted with restored buildings at Polset, at 1840m (restaurant).

Continue down from the hamlet and watch for a path shortcutting down to a road. Cross the road and continue down a forest track. The rock alongside is generally hard gneiss, and the track is often flanked by pines, although there are still views. This is an old road, partly stone-paved, winding down past a few houses at La Perrière before zigzagging down a steep, forested slope.

Cross a bridge over a stream and continue down the track, which later becomes a road. Turn left down Rue de la Charmette to reach a little chapel and a road junction at **Loutraz**, at 1100m. Choose whether to descend left to Modane or right to Fourneaux, bearing in mind that these routes don't meet again until Valfréjus (Section 4, Stage 15).

Variant: path junction to Loutraz   3hr, 8km, +110m, -1525m

Turn left to follow the variant route and climb a little past some big boulders. The path descends gently across the flanks of **Tête Noire** then climbs gently along a broad, inclined, grassy terrace. Descend again and pass ruins at **L'Estiva**. Zigzag down though forest to land on a road at the **Refuge de l'Orgère**, at 1945m (refuge, bivouac and restaurant), leaving the Parc National de la Vanoise.

Walk down the road and turn left, down a path, then turn right, along the main GR5, to continue through the forest. Contour across the slope, avoiding other paths, to emerge on a track in a clearing near a little house at **Pierre Brune**, at 1800m (water). Turn left, down a steep and rugged forest path, watching carefully for GR5 markers at a number of path junctions. Eventually, the path joins a forest track near a bridge over a stream. Continue down the track, which later becomes a road. Turn left down Rue de la Charmette to reach a little chapel and a road junction at **Loutraz**, at 1100m. Choose now whether to descend left to Modane or right to Fourneaux, bearing in mind that these routes don't meet again until Valfréjus (Section 4, Stage 15).

Loutraz to Fourneaux
30min, 1.5km, +0m -50m

Turn right to reach a gymnasium, where a right turn leads along Rue de la Vanoise. Continue down to a junction and turn right along Avenue Emile Charvoz. Cross a bridge, Pont Emile Charvoz, and turn right to follow the main road into **Fourneaux**, at 1050m (all services, see GR5 Stage 14).

Loutraz to Modane
10min, 0.5km, +10m -30m

Turn left down Rue des Chavières, passing through a staggered crossroads to cross a river. Note La Rizerie, a beautiful building on the right. Go under a railway line then go straight past a roundabout and along Rue Croix Blanche. This leads to the town hall (*mairie*) in the centre of **Modane**, at 1070m (all services except accommodation). Note that a road-walking route is signposted and waymarked from the *mairie* to Fourneaux.

MODANE/FOURNEAUX

Not a 'classic' Alpine town but a workaday settlement handling road and rail freight in and out of the tunnels between France and Italy. There are some interesting old buildings around town and a full range of services.

Those who start or finish a section of the GR5 here find rapid access by train to and from Lyon and Paris. Those who require accommodation, trains or the tourist information centre should head for Fourneaux rather than Modane. Cars Région Savoie buses run up through the Arc valley to serve many parts of the GR5E (the low-level variant route that starts from Bonneval-sur-Arc): www.cars-region-savoie.fr. Tourist information office (Fourneaux): tel 04 79 05 26 67.

GR5E LOW-LEVEL ROUTE (BONNEVAL-SUR-ARC TO MODANE/ FOURNEAUX)

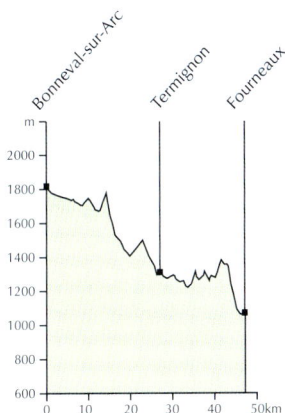

GR5E STAGE 1
Bonneval-sur-Arc to Termignon

Start	Bonneval-sur-Arc
Finish	Termignon
Time	6hr 45min
Distance	27km
Total Ascent	370m
Total Descent	880m
Terrain	A gentle, valley walk along easy riverside tracks, forest tracks, field tracks and roads. Mostly downhill but some climbing.
Maps	3633 ET
Refreshments	Plenty of choice at Bessans, Lanslevillard, Lanslebourg and Termignon.
Accommodation	*Gîte d'étape* at Le Villaron. Hotels and *gîte* at Bessans. Campsite at Les Chardonnettes. Hotels and campsite at Lanslevillard. Hotels at Lanslebourg. Hotel and campsite at Termignon.

The GR5E leaves Bonneval-sur-Arc along an easy, riverside track, pulling away from the river to pass through fields, woods and the hamlet of Le Villaron. After exploring Bessans, the route often follows forest tracks, climbing high past Chantelouve. After descending through fields, the trail reaches Lanslevillard and Lanslebourg, continuing to Termignon.

Note that, in addition to the usual GR signposts and waymarks, trail furniture and large logs are painted yellow at both ends to mark the route. The GR5E is also named at frequent intervals as the Chemin du Petit Bonheur.

Bonneval-sur-Arc to Bessans   2hr, 8.5km, +90m -180m

Follow a narrow road straight through the rustic Bonneval-sur-Arc, admiring old buildings and passing the church. Leave the village and turn right at a small wayside shrine, following a clear track through hay meadows. This runs roughly parallel to a river, **L'Arc**, although little is seen of it due to trees and bushes. The track eventually leads to a few stone cabins then a short, rugged path crosses a rocky hump to reach the overhanging **Rocher du Château**. Neolithic art is carved on the rock face but is difficult to discern.

Another track continues through meadows to reach a road at Chapelle St-Bernard. Walk up the road into the little hamlet of **Le Villaron**, at 1740m (gîte d'étape and water). Keep left to pass the *gîte*, where the road gives way to a track through fields, later running close to L'Arc again. Pass the Carrefour Alpage du Vallon, at 1734m, where the main GR5 joins and runs concurrent with the GR5E and GR5 downstream to a bridge. The GR5E crosses the bridge to **Bessans**, at 1710m (all services; Cars Région Savoie buses to Bonneval-sur-Arc and Modane/

Following a nature trail (sentier nature) gently uphill after leaving Bessans

Fourneaux: www.cars-region-savoie.fr; tourist information office: tel 04 79 05 96 52 www.haute-maurienne-vanoise.com).

Bessans to Lanslevillard   **2hr 30min, 9.5km, +140m -370m**

Leave the central square as signposted for the GR5E to Escalier de Soliet. Walk through a crossroads and turn left at a large crucifix in the middle of the road. Follow the road uphill to reach a nature trail (*sentier nature*) signpost. The road gives way to a sunken track running gently up through fields. Turn left to cross the main road, follow a grassy track and turn right to reach a footbridge over the **Torrent du Ribon**. Cross over and turn right, then turn left to walk beside a former main road, now closed. Pick up a grassy track running parallel to the road, which rises before heading gently downhill beside a forest. Turn right at a badly signposted junction and walk downhill to an open, grassy space at **Les Chardonnettes**, at 1680m (nearby campsite).

Turn left to follow a gravel track through mixed forest, staying on the main track as marked and signposted, avoiding other tracks. This later climbs through the forest, through a meadow and through more forest then drops steeply past a few little houses at **Chantelouve d'en Haut**, at 1770m (water).

Follow the track back into forest, cross a stream and go down some curious wooden steps. Keep walking downhill and turn right, as signposted, at **Le Châtel**. The track leaves the forest and winds down past Chapelle St-Étienne. Keep following the track down through fields to reach a junction at La Lauzière, at 1515m, then keep left to reach the top end of the large village of **Lanslevillard** (all services). Simply follow a road down through the centre to reach a church at 1480m.

Lanslevillard to Lanslebourg-Mont-Cenis   **45min, 2.5km, +20m -100m**

Leave Lanslevillard by following Rue des Rochers away from the church but almost immediately, turn left down Chemin des Chenevers. At the bottom of the

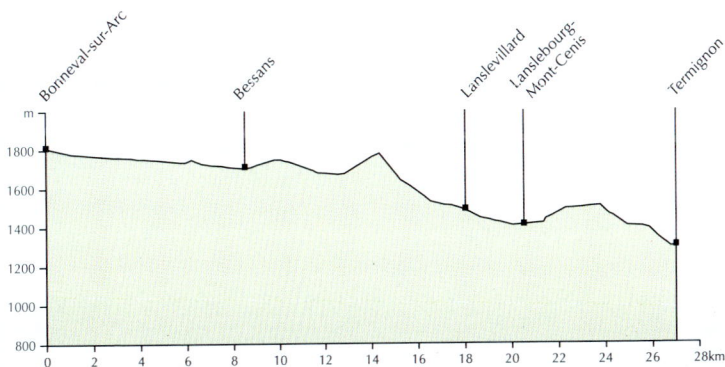

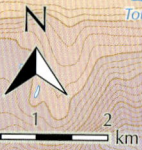

VALLON DE LA LENTA

L'Arc

Tralenta

S Bonneval-sur-Arc
1800m

Pointe de Méan-Martin
3330m

Chalets des Roches
2453m

Pont du Vallon
2242m

Ruisseau du Vallon

GR5

L'Arc

D902

Le Mollard

Rocher du Château

Pointe Est du Grand Fond ▲
3419m

Ruisseau de Pis

Le Villaron
1740m

Bessans
1710m

D902

Le Rebon

Ruisseau de Chatelard

Torrent d'Avérole

Pointe de Tierce
2973m

D902

GR5

Les Chardonnettes
1680m

Ruisseau de l'Arsels

Torrent du Ribon

L'Arc

Chantelouve d'en Haut
1770m

Pointe de Charbonnel
3751m

Ruisseau du Châtel

Signal du Mont Cenis
3377m

Pointe de Ronce
3612m

road, keep left to walk down a grassy path. Turn left to follow the main road to a nearby roundabout. Turn left again, as signposted for Lanslebourg. Turn left again, as signposted for the GR5E, along and down a quiet road. A signpost points up another road at Le Plan des Champs, then a gravel track is followed downhill among trees. This leads to a road running beside L'Arc, which in turn leads to a bridge. Pass it as signposted and reach another bridge. Only cross the bridge if you wish to go into the centre of Lanslebourg-Mont-Cenis, at 1400m (all services).

LANSLEBOURG-MONT-CENIS

Hannibal is reputed to have passed through here in AD218, crossing Col du Mont-Cenis to fight the Romans on their own soil. For centuries, the col was a major transport route between France and the Piémont, and Napoleon had the first real road over it constructed in 1805. Traffic is much reduced these days, following the construction of rail and road tunnels between Modane and Bardonecchia. Since 1967, Lanslebourg, Lanslevillard and other nearby villages have been collectively referred to as Val Cenis. They offer a full range of services.

Cars Région Savoie buses run to Bonneval-sur-Arc and Modane/Fourneaux: www.cars-region-savoie.fr. Tourist information office: tel 04 79 05 99 06 www.valcenis.com.

Lanslebourg-Mont-Cenis to Termignon   1hr 30min, 6.5km, +120m -230m

Cross the Mont Cenis road and follow a minor road under a nearby chairlift. Walk down the road until a signpost marks a forest track climbing to the left. There are a couple of sharp bends; otherwise, keep straight ahead at all junctions. The track climbs gently to a signposted junction at Carrefour du Revet, at 1494m. Keep straight ahead after **Le Mélézet**, passing a signpost at 1520m. Watch for views of the glaciated Dent Parrachée.

Keep right at a track junction at 1490m and follow a couple of sharp bends on the descent. The track leaves the forest to descend gently through fields. Turn right, down a road, to reach a car park. The GR5E continues through the car park, but this is far enough for the day, so turn right and follow a road downhill and cross a bridge. Turn right and walk up Rue Impériale into the centre of **Termignon**, at 1290m (all services; Cars Région Savoie buses to Bonneval-sur-Arc and Modane/Fourneaux: www.cars-region-savoie.fr; Transdev Savoie buses to Entre Deux Eaux, to link with the main GR5 and high-level GR55; tourist information office: tel 04 79 05 99 06 www.valcenis.com).

Start	Termignon
Finish	Modane/Fourneaux
Time	5hr 45min
Distance	21.5km
Total Ascent	425m
Total Descent	670m
Terrain	Easy roads and tracks through fields and forest, finishing with a steep descent on a forest path then urban road-walking.
Maps	3633 ET and 3634 OT
Refreshments	Restaurants at Le Verney, Bramans and Fort Marie-Thérèse. Plenty of choice at La Norma, Modane and Fourneaux.
Accommodation	Hotel at Bramans. Plenty of choice at La Norma and Fourneaux.

After leaving Termignon, the route runs mainly through grassy meadows and forests, often with views of the mountains surrounding the Arc valley. The imposing Fort Victor-Emmanuel is seen across the valley while the Redoute Marie-Thérèse is closer at hand. A gradual ascent leads to the resort village of La Norma. After descending, trekkers need to decide whether to link with the main route of the GR5 at Modane or walk to neighbouring Fourneaux for accommodation.

Termignon to Bramans   2hr, 8.5km, +155m -200m

To leave Termignon, follow Rue Impériale, cross a bridge and follow a road up to a car park to rejoin the GR5E. Follow a track out of the car park and down through fields looking down on a gravel pit beside a river. The track runs through forest and more fields then passes beneath a marble cliff, where there is a prominent tower of rock, with small lakes nearby at **Grotte des Balmes**. Follow the road past a campsite and turn left, up into the village of **Sollières L'Envers**, at 1275m, where there is an archaeological museum.

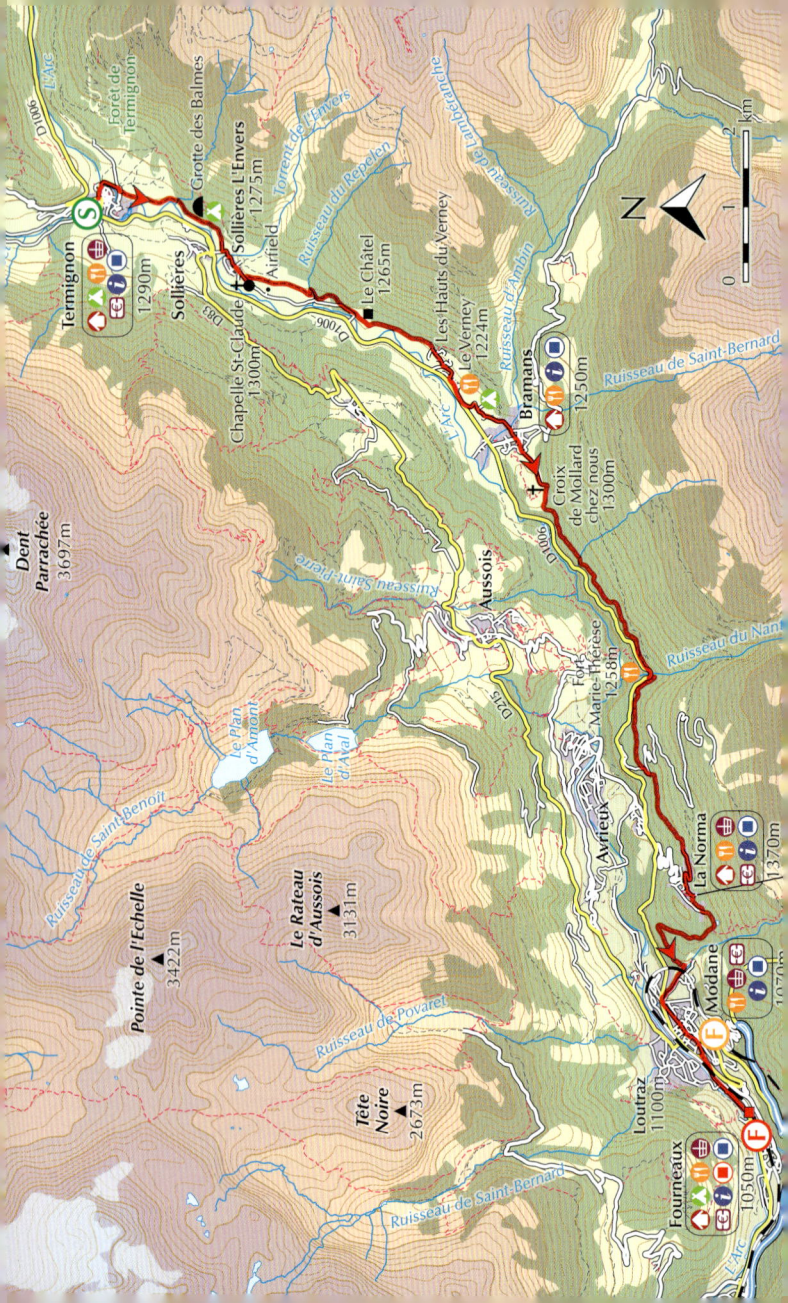

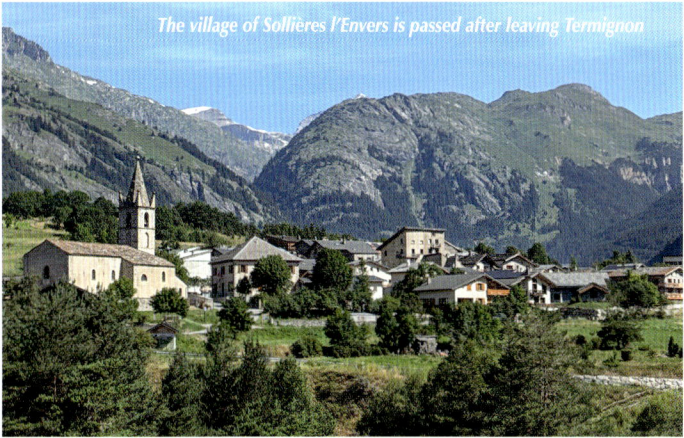

The village of Sollières l'Envers is passed after leaving Termignon

Walk straight through the village by road and out the other side. After pass-ing **Chapelle St-Claude** at 1300m, turn left, up a track. This rises and falls gen-tly through fields, passing a small **airfield**. Head down through a patch of forest towards a quarry but turn left as signposted, along another track. As soon as a road is reached, turn left then left again, up a track. Pass **Le Châtel**, at 1265m, and continue down a walled track with good views of the valley.

Continue along a road called Chemin du Châtel to reach the little hamlet of **Les Hauts du Verney**. Walk down Route du Mont Froid and turn left, down Route

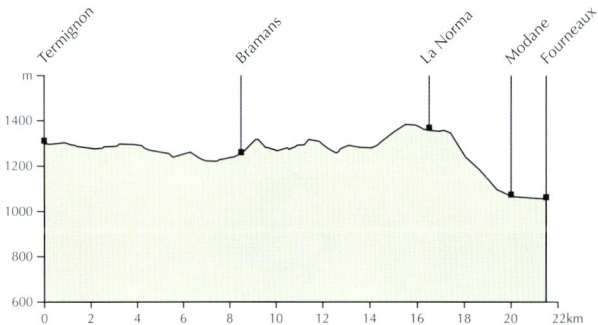

The imposing Fort Victor-Emmanuel is seen dominating the valley

des Chasseurs Alpins. Turn left again to enter the village of **Le Verney**, at 1224m (bar, boulangerie; Cars Région Savoie buses to Bonneval-sur-Arc and Modane/Fourneaux: www.cars-region-savoie.fr). Follow Rue des Diligences all the way through the village, but keep off the main road to rise gently towards a church spire. Take a shortcut through a bend to reach a church (campsite).

Follow a path beside a road to Le Moulin and note a mill wheel in passing. Cross two girder-work bridges, looking upstream to see a ravine cut into the marble bedrock. Walk straight along the road into the village of **Bramans**, at 1250m (hotel, restaurant; Cars Région Savoie buses to Bonneval-sur-Arc and Modane/Fourneaux: www.cars-region-savoie.fr; tourist information office, tel 04 79 05 03 45 www.valcenis.com).

Bramans to La Norma   2hr 15min, 8km, +270m -145m

Leave the town hall (*mairie*) in Bramans and walk straight through the village along Rue de la Combe, then Rue du Canton leaves the village, and walkers climb until the tarmac ends. Follow a track cut into the marble bedrock on a gentle col at **Croix de Mollard Chez Nous**, at 1300m.

The track runs down through forest and open spaces then generally climbs, steeply at times. There are a few mountain and valley views before the track runs down to a busy main road near **Fort Marie-Thérèse**, at 1258m (early 19th-century fort and restaurant).

Cross the Pont du Nant Ste-Anne then follow a zigzag track uphill. Keep right, along a fairly level track, with views between trees of Fort Victor-Emmanuel. When the track descends steeply from a junction, keep left, as signposted, at Chemin d'Avrieux, at 1280m (right leads off route to Avrieux in 40min for chambres d'hôte, restaurants and Cars Région Savoie buses to Bonneval-sur-Arc and Modane/Fourneaux: www.cars-region-savoie.fr). Later, keep left at another junction, as signposted for La Norma. The track climbs and undulates, passing a marble sculpture, to reach a road. Follow the road uphill to a sharp bend and continue straight ahead along another road. When this road makes a sharp bend at another marble sculpture, continue up a forest track. The track becomes a road at some chalets and heads down into the village of **La Norma**, at 1370m (all services).

LA NORMA

La Norma is primarily a family sport resort but it also provides for passing walkers. The GR5E is sparsely marked through the village but if in doubt, ask someone the way to the *aquapark* to get back on course.

Cars Région Savoie buses run to Modane and Fourneaux: www.cars-region-savoie.fr. Tourist information office: tel 04 79 05 99 16 www.la-norma.fr.

La Norma to Modane   1hr, 3.5km, +0m -295m

Walk through the pedestrianised commercial centre to find a *télécabine* station then turn right then left to pass a yellow-painted log marker and follow a gritty path down between chalets. Avoid a car park and spot a nearby signpost. Turn right, along a forest track, as signposted for Modane, following the Sentier de la Forêt d'Erica. Pass through a park containing marble sculptures and turn right, down a path, as marked, beside an aquapark enclosed by a fence.

Turn right, alongside the fence, then right again, as signposted for Modane, down a forest path. Unseen cliffs are protected by a wooden fence, and there is a sudden viewpoint overlooking Modane deep in the valley. Follow a gently graded forest path as signposted. Avoid shortcuts and stay on the marked path throughout the descent. The forest thins out as the path goes down through a rock cutting, into a ravine. The GR5E used to cross a concrete ford but this has been damaged, so turn right to follow a path downstream instead, landing beside a busy road. Turn left to cross a bridge then follow the quiet Rue Gambetta into town, not the main road, walking to the town hall (*mairie*) in the centre of **Modane**, at 1070m (all services, except accommodation).

Modane to Fourneaux   30min, 1.5km, +0m -30m

Signposts point in all directions, indicating the way back along the GR5E and GR55. While the GR5 can be followed straight uphill from Modane, a variant route runs via Fourneaux. If accommodation is needed then follow quiet roads as signposted, linking with the main road leading to the railway station in neighbouring **Fourneaux**, at 1050m (all services, see GR5 Stage 14).

MODANE/FOURNEAUX

Not a 'classic' Alpine town but a workaday settlement handling road and rail freight in and out of the tunnels between France and Italy. There are some interesting old buildings around town and a full range of services.

Those who start or finish a section of the GR5 here find rapid access by train to and from Lyon and Paris. Those who require accommodation, trains or the tourist information centre should head for Fourneaux rather than Modane. Cars Région Savoie buses run up through the Arc valley to serve many parts of the GR5E (the low-level variant route that starts from Bonneval-sur-Arc): www.cars-region-savoie.fr. Tourist information office (Fourneaux): tel 04 79 05 26 67.

SECTION 4:
MODANE/
FOURNEAUX TO
CEILLAC

Crumbling slopes of conglomerate have to be crossed on the way down into the Vallée de la Clarée (Stage 16)

GR5

GR5E

GR5S

Lac du
Mont Cenis

(S) Modane

Fourneaux (15)

(S)

Refuge du
Mont Thabor

(16)

Col de la
Vallée Étroite

Bardonnecchia

**Mont
Thabor**

Col des Thures

Névache (17) Roubion

ITALY

*La Grande
Peyrolle*

Col du Granon

Montgenèvre

Briançon (18)

Villard
St-Pancrace

FRANCE

Col des Ayes (19) **Brunissard**

Ville-Vieille

Château-Queyras

N

Col Fromage

0   5   10
km

Mont-Dauphin

(F) Ceillac

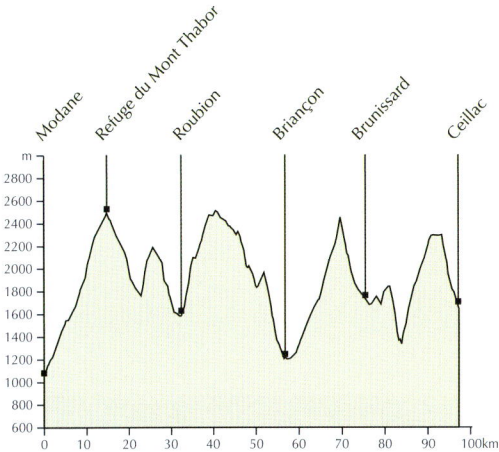

A choice of routes is available between Modane/Fourneaux and Valfréjus on Stage 15. On the Col de la Vallée Étroite, on Stage 16, the departmental boundary is crossed between Savoie and Hautes-Alpes, and Mediterranean influences begin to creep in. Once over Col des Thures,

A view of the little Lac de Cristol from the rugged col of Porte de Cristol (Stage 17)

the GR5 drops into the Vallée de la Clarée for an easy interlude.

On Stage 17, the GR5 continues to Briançon along what was originally the GR5C variant. (The GR5 main route formerly ran through Montgenèvre.) After climbing from the Vallée de la Clarée, a ridge route is followed by a forested descent to Briançon. There are few big towns along the course of the GR5 but Briançon is well worth exploring if time can be spared.

The GR5 leaves Briançon and climbs to Col des Ayes, where it enters the Parc Naturel Régional du Queyras. This well-forested region specialises in the production of woodwork crafts and timber. Fine villages and the iconic Fort Queyras are passed before

Stage	Place	Altitude	Walking time	Distance
15	**Modane/Fourneaux**	**1050m**	**0hr 00min**	**0km**
15	Valfréjus	1560m	2hr 00min	6km
15	Les Tavernes	1620m	0hr 15min	1km
15	**Refuge du Mont Thabor**	**2502m**	**3hr 15min**	**8km**
16	Les Granges de la Vallée Étroite	1770m	2hr 15min	7.5km
16	**Roubion**	**1585m**	**3hr 15min**	**10km**
17	Col du Granon	2413m	3hr 30min	10km
17	Cité Vauban	1330m	4hr 15min	13km
17	**Briançon**	**1180m**	**0hr 30min**	**1.5km**
18	Sachas	1240m	1hr 00min	2.5km
18	Chalets des Ayes	1711m	1hr 30min	5km
18	L'Izoard	1850m	3hr 00min	9.5km
18	**Brunissard**	**1746m**	**0hr 30min**	**1.5km**
19	La Chalp	1684m	0hr 15min	1km
19	Château-Queyras	1365m	2hr 30min	8.5km
19	**Ceillac**	**1650m**	**5hr 30min**	**13.5km**

the route crosses Col Fromage and descends to Ceillac in the heart of the park. This entire section is never very far from the Franco-Italian border, while valleys head west to converge on the distant town and transport hub of Gap.

Trekkers tackling the GR5 over a series of trips should check transport details carefully on the latter part of this section. While Modane/Fourneaux and Briançon are excellent transport hubs, Brunissard and Ceillac have limited bus links to nearby towns. If you're planning to break a trek along the GR5, check transport details well in advance.

Legend

- ⬆ refuge/hut/gîte d'étape
- 🔴 hotel
- 🟡 home stay
- ⌂ unmanned hut/bothy
- 🟢 camping
- ✳ bivouac
- 🟠 restaurant/refreshments
- 🔵 shop/groceries
- ATM
- 🛈 TIC
- 🔴 train
- 🔵 bus
- 🔵 lift/cable car

Facilities

refuge/hut	hotel	camping	bivouac	restaurant	shop/groceries	ATM	TIC	train	bus
	●	●		●	●	●	●	●	●
	●			●	●	●	●		●
●				●					
●				●					
●			●	●					
●				●					●
				●					
	●			●	●				●
	●			●	●	●	●	●	●
●	●			●					●
				●					
		●		●					
●	●			●					●
●	●			●					●
				●					●
●		●		●	●	●	●		●

STAGE 15
Modane/Fourneaux to Refuge du Mont Thabor

Start	Modane/Fourneaux
Finish	Refuge du Mont Thabor
Time	5hr 30min
Distance	15km
Total Ascent	1520m
Total Descent	70m
Terrain	A choice of forested ascents then a long walk up through a valley, where a steep track and easier paths cross grassy slopes.
Maps	3535 OT
Refreshments	Restaurants at Valfréjus. Refuge du Mont Thabor.
Accommodation	Hotels at Valfréjus and *gîte d'étape* nearby. Refuge du Mont Thabor.

There are two ways up to Valfréjus: the main GR5 from Modane and a variant route from Fourneaux. The route from Modane is longer in terms of distance and time but is also more gently graded than the steep climb from Fourneaux. Either way, the GR5 continues towards Col de la Vallée Étroite and is quite gentle towards the top. While some will cross the col and keep walking, others will be happy to divert a little off route to stay at the Refuge du Mont Thabor.

Fourneaux to Valfréjus
1hr 30min, 4km, +510m -30m

Start from the railway station in Fourneaux, at 1050m, where a signpost lists walking destinations. Walk along the main road to the town hall, or *mairie*, and turn left as signposted. Follow a road to the railway line and turn right to find a footbridge. Cross over the line and turn right, along a road, then left, up Rue des Cités Moulin, to reach a car park by a church (water). Follow a winding track up to the towering supports of the **Viaduc de Charmaix**. Turn left, along a path going under the viaduct and into woodland.

Climb straight through an intersection of paths into mixed forest. Keep climbing and branch left at a path junction. The path climbs steeply to a track, where another left turn is made. Another path heads up to the left, and as more height

D215

L'Arc

Loutraz
1100m

Fourneaux
1050m

D1006

A43

S

Modane
1070m

Le Saut
1340m

Viaduc du
Charmaix

Sanctuaire
Notre Dame
du Charmaix
1506m

Ruisseau de Saint-Antoine

Forêt de
Fourneaux

Pic Noir
2874m

Mont
Rond
2772m

Valfréjus
1560m

La Belle
Plinier
3086m

Pointe des Sarrasins
2963m

Les Tavernes
1620m

Les Herbiers

FRANCE

Le Lavoir
1900m

Ruisseau du Charmaix

Cime du
Grand Vallon
3129m

La Loza

Le Mounioz
2745m

Torrent de Pierre Froide

La
Replanette

Le Grand
Argentier
3042m

F

Refuge du
Mont Thabor
2502m

Col de la
Vallée Étroite
2434m

ITALY

Cime de la Planette
3104m

N

e Grand Séru
2888m

0   1   2
km

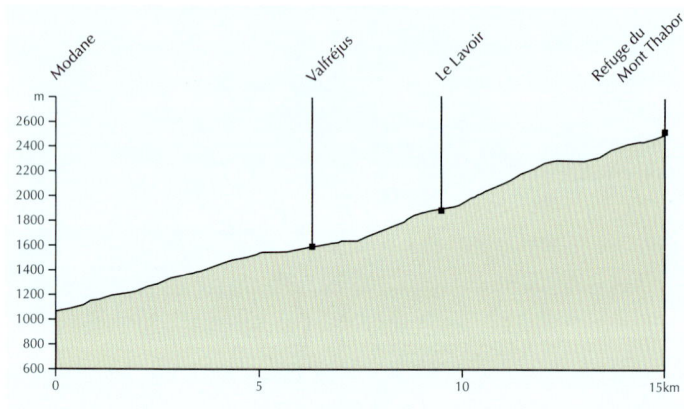

is gained, there are views back to Fourneaux and across the valley to Valfréjus. When a higher track is reached, turn left and follow it downhill. Cross a bridge over the **Ruisseau du Charmaix** and follow a track up to a road on the outskirts of **Valfréjus** (all services; Cars Région Savoie buses to Modane/Fourneaux: www. cars-region-savoie.fr; tourist information office: tel 04 79 05 99 16 www.valfrejus. com), rejoining the main GR5.

Modane to Valfréjus (main GR5)   2hr, 6km, +540m -55m

Start at the town hall, or *mairie*, in the centre of Modane, at 1070m, where a sign-post is laden with walking destinations. Face the building, keep to the right-hand side and follow a road up to a junction. Turn left, along Rue de la Liberté, which leads close to a church. Turn right, up Rue du Charmaix, and continue up Rue du Fréjus. Reach a cross and a small shrine (the first of several), which is the start of a pilgrim route, the Pélerinage du Charmaix. Turn right, along Rue de la Touvière, then turn left to leave the road, following a path enclosed by trees and bushes.

Go under a railway line then go under a road. A grassy track climbs to reach a junction with another track. A signpost points up a path, which climbs to a road. Cross the road to follow steep, narrow, gritty paths on a forested slope criss-crossed by storm drains. Walk parallel to the main road serving the Tunel de Fréjus. A narrow tarmac road goes under the main road, later turning left then right and giving way to a forest track.

Follow the track uphill, climbing steeply, to a road bend at **Le Saut**, at 1340m. Walk up the road, turning left and right at other hairpin bends. Follow another forest track from the next bend, climbing steeply while watching for two shortcut zigzag paths, to rejoin the road at a higher level. Follow yet another track, which crosses a bridge over a gorge to reach a chapel, the **Sanctuaire Notre Dame du Charmaix**, at 1506m. The chapel dates from 1401 and was built to house a 5th-century statue of the Virgin.

Follow the winding track up to a road then turn right and walk straight towards the resort village of **Valfréjus**, at 1560m (all services; Cars Région Savoie buses to Modane/Fourneaux: www.cars-region-savoie.fr; tourist information office: tel 04 79 05 99 16 www.valfrejus.com). Either walk into the centre for facilities or keep right to follow a road that mostly bypasses the village.

Valfréjus to Le Lavoir   1hr 30min, 3.5km, +380m -10m

Follow the road around two hairpin bends and leave Valfréjus, watching carefully to pick up a track parallel to the road to reach **Les Tavernes**, at 1620m (gîte d'étape). Continue along the road and turn right, down a track, to cross a wooden bridge. Follow the track up past a few houses at **Les Herbiers**, climbing through a forest, the Forêt Domaniale de la Belle Plinier. One bendy part of the track can be shortcut by using a narrow path. The track eventually crosses a bridge to reach a dirt road beneath the imposing Fort du Lavoir. Walk up the road and keep straight ahead at a junction to reach a car park beside a hydro-electric intake dam at **Le Lavoir**, at 1900m (cheese for sale off route).

As the GR5 climbs above Valfréjus, there are views back through the valley to the Vanoise

The Refuge du Mont Thabor is a little off route from the Col de la Vallée Étroite

Le Lavoir to Refuge du Mont Thabor

2hr, 5.5km, +600m -5m

Follow a winding track up a slope of alder-scrub woodland to reach a higher hydro-electric intake dam. Branch left at a track junction at **La Loza**, as signposted for the GR5. The track climbs to another signposted junction, where the GR5 turns right – although keeping straight ahead works just as well and seems to be more popular with trekkers.

The track gives way to an easy path at the solitary stone cabin of **La Replanette**. Continue climbing, on grassy slopes, to reach another signposted junction, where there is a view of Mont Thabor at the head of the valley and a view back to the Vanoise beyond the mouth of the valley. Little buildings and ruins dot the land-scape, and the highest building in view is the Refuge du Mont Thabor. The best way to approach the refuge is to walk almost to the top of **Col de la Vallée Étroite**, at 2434m. Turn right at a signpost just before you reach the col and follow a clear path that skirts around the foot of bouldery quartzite scree. A short climb leads to the **Refuge du Mont Thabor**, at 2502m (refuge and restaurant). The refuge is very popular and if a bed can't be secured then it is necessary to continue down into La Vallée Étroite.

STAGE 16
Refuge du Mont Thabor to Roubion

Start	Refuge du Mont Thabor
Finish	Roubion
Time	5hr 30min
Distance	17.5km
Total Ascent	440m
Total Descent	1350m
Terrain	Gentle walking down through a valley, with increasing forest cover. A steep climb to a grassy col then a rugged descent to valley tracks and roads.
Maps	3535 OT
Refreshments	Restaurants in La Vallée Étroite, at Roubion and at nearby Névache (off route).
Accommodation	Refuges in La Vallée Étroite. *Auberge* and *gîte d'étape* at Roubion. Plenty of choice around Névache (off route).

The main GR5 route crosses the Col de la Vallée Étroite, leading from Savoie to Hautes-Alpes, and this col was, until the mid-20th century, the frontier between France and Italy. Despite France's annexation of La Vallée Étroite, the easiest road access is from Italy, and Italian is usually spoken in the valley. A forested climb leads to the broad, grassy Col des Thures, from where the GR5 descends to Roubion in the Vallée de la Clarée.

Refuge du Mont Thabor to Les Granges de la Vallée Étroite 2hr 15min, 7.5km, +5m -740m

Leave the refuge and retrace your steps along the path skirting the foot of bouldery quartzite scree. Turn right at a signpost to cross the gentle **Col de la Vallée Étroite**, at 2434m. The col used to be the Franco-Italian border, and the Italian name is Passo di Valle Stretta, but since 1945, it has been the departmental boundary between Savoie and Hautes-Alpes.

A path runs gently down cattle-grazed slopes in the higher part of the valley. After a more rugged stretch on broken quartzite, cross a stream and continue along an easy path. Enjoy views of the surrounding mountains and follow a little stream down past a tiny lake. A grassy stretch leads to a cliff edge, so look right to

Le
Mounioz
2745m

Refuge du
Mont-Thabor
2502m

Le Cheval
Blanc
3020m

Col de la
Vallée Étroite
2434m

Le Grand
Argentier
3042m

Mont Thabor
3178m

Cime de la Planette
3104m

le Grand Séru
2888m

Roche Bernaude
3222m

Pointe Balthazar
3153m

ITALY

Pointe Melchior
2948m

Pont de
la Fonderie
1910m

FRANCE

Pointe Gaspard
2808m

Pic du
Lac Blanc
2980m

Les Granges
de la Vallée Étroite
1770m

N

0   1   2
km

Col des Thures
2194m

L' Aiguille
Rouge
2545m

Chalet des Thures
2106m

La Demoiselle

Chapelle
des Âmes
1623m

Névache

Roubion

Le Cros 1585m

La Clarée

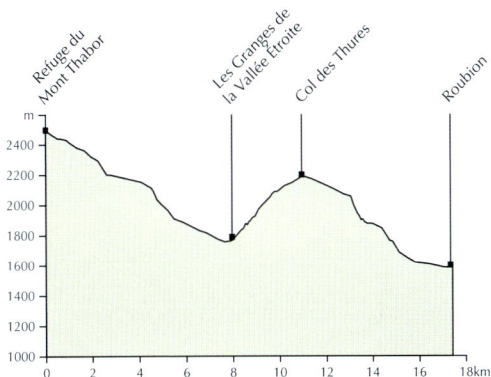

find the path picking its way down a loose and rocky slope. Sparse larches grow near the gravelly path, which winds down to **Pont de la Fonderie**, at 1910m.

A clear track leads downstream, parallel to the **Ruisseau de la Vallée Étroite**, although trees often hide the river from view. Keep straight ahead at track junctions. When a house is reached, step to the left to follow a path downhill, short-cutting down to the track at a lower level. Walk straight onwards, past fields and houses, to reach the hamlet of **Les Granges de la Vallée Étroite**, at 1770m (refuges, bivouac and restaurants). The three prominent mountains above the hamlet are the 'Three Wise Men': Pointe Balthazar, Pointe Melchior and Pointe Gaspard. The GR5 passes the Rifugio i Re Magi then turns right to climb a track to the Rifugio Tre Alpini.

Les Granges de la Vallée Étroite to Col des Thures   1hr 15min, 3.5km, +435m -10m
Climb straight up a field track, turning left across a stream-bed to enter a forest. Zigzag uphill, passing from limestone to quartzite. Views become splendid as the larches thin out giving way to grassy slopes. Cross over the gentle **Col des Thures**, at 2194m, to pass a small lake. Again, this was formerly the Franco-Italian border before La Vallée Étroite was annexed by France in 1945. Views stretch across La Vallée de la Clarée to the mountains beyond.

Col des Thures to Roubion   2hr, 6.5km, +0m -600m
Grooved paths leave the col, heading gently down to the solitary **Chalet des Thures**, at 2106m (water). Turn left before you reach the building and walk to a path junction. Keep right to follow the GR5, which is a level path along the top of

La Vallée Étroite was entirely within Italy until it was annexed by France in 1945

crumbling cliffs of coarse conglomerate. Take a winding path that drops suddenly down those same cliffs into a pine forest. Keep left at a path junction near the imposing rock tower of **La Demoiselle**.

The path traverses a steep, forested slope then zigzags downhill. Eventually, turn left, as signposted for Roubion. Walk down a track beside a river to reach a road. Turn right to cross a wooden bridge and follow the road past the Centre des Vacancies and some houses to reach the tiny **Chapelle des Âmes** at 1623m. Follow the road onwards through the village of **Roubion** (auberge and restaurant) and turn right along a road running parallel to a river, **La Clarée**, passing the Gîte les Mélézets (gîte d'étape and restaurant) at around 1585m. If all the accommodation near Roubion is full, regular shuttle buses run up and down the valley, passing other lodgings in the nearby villages of Névache and Plampinet. Resalp buses link Névache and Roubion with Briançon: tel 04 92 20 47 50 www. autocars-resalp.com.

Start	Roubion
Finish	Briançon
Time	8hr 15min
Distance	24.5km
Total Ascent	1160m
Total Descent	1550m
Terrain	A forested ascent to a lake, a climb to a rugged col, then easy walking along tracks. A choice between a fairly easy, forested descent or a rugged, exposed ridge walk with a steep and rocky descent. Urban walking to finish.
Maps	3535 OT and 3536 OT
Refreshments	Café at Col du Granon. Plenty of choice in Cité Vauban and Briançon.
Accommodation	Plenty of choice in Cité Vauban and Briançon.

The GR5 route throughout this day was formerly a variant route known as the GR5C, which is still noted on some signposts. (The main route originally ran from Plampinet to Montgenèvre to reach Briançon.) The route passes a couple of scenic mountain lakes and reaches a military site on Col du Granon. Originally, the route ran along the high, rocky, exposed ridge of Crête de Peyrolle but this is now offered as a variant route, and the main route takes a convoluted course across forested slopes before descending past splendid fortifications around Cité Vauban to reach Briançon.

Roubion to GR5/GR57 junction   1hr, 2.5km, +500m -0m

Leave the road between Roubion and Névache by crossing Pont de Fortville over **La Clarée**, at 1584m. Walk straight ahead along a track (water) then climb through terraced fields into forest. Watch for a path signposted to the right, which soon starts zigzagging uphill. Wider bends feature as the trees thin out, with views of La Vallée de la Clarée. Limestone gives way to quartzite before a signposted **junction** is reached at 2093m. The GR57 heads left and the GR5 heads right.

ITALY

Névache Le Cros Chapelle
des Âmes
1623m
Roubion

Sommet du Guiau
2654m

1585m

S

La Clarée

GR5/GR57 Junction
2093m

Ruisseau de Cristol

Lac de Cristol

FRANCE

N

Porte de
Cristol
2483m

La
Gardiole
2753m

Le Grand Area
2869m

Col des Cibières
2525m

0   1   2
km

Torrent de Granon

Col du Granon
2413m

Col de Barteaux
2380m

Val-des-
Prés

Croix
du Pied

Croix de la Cime
2606m

La Salle-
les-Alpes

La Grande Peyrolle
2645m

Le Gros
Feu

La Guisane

Serre des Aigles
2567m

Saint-
Chaffrey

D1091

Bois de
l'Ours

Serre Lan
1848m

Croix
de Toulouse
1973m

Font de
Bon Repos

Sommet
du Prorel
2566m

Fort des Salettes
1452m

Briançon

Cité Vauban
1330m

1180m

F

La Durance

D902

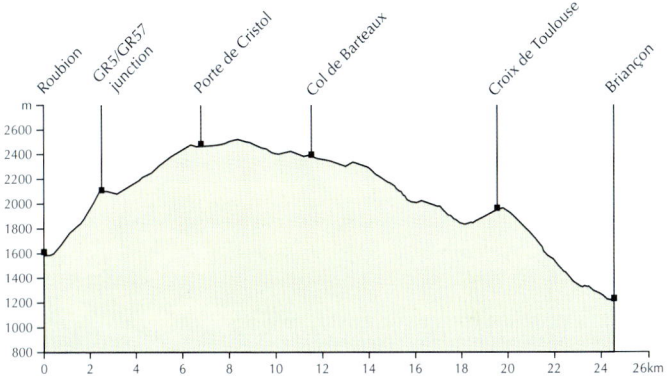

GR5/GR57 junction to Porte de Cristol   1hr 30min, 4km, +440m -45m

Keep right and cross a shoulder, then drop gently through larches to reach the **Ruisseau de Cristol**. Don't cross a footbridge but instead follow the path upstream, leaving dense forest to climb gentle, grassy, sparsely forested slopes to the lovely lake of **Lac de Cristol**, at 2245m. Watch carefully for markers, as the route doesn't follow the lakeshore path but rather turns left just before reaching the lake. Climb across grassy slopes and a variety of hard sandstones and grit-stones to reach the rugged col of **Porte de Cristol**, at 2483m, from where there is a view back across La Vallée de la Clarée to the distant Vanoise.

Porte de Cristol to Col de Barteaux   1hr 15min, 5km, +30m -135m

Drop down a short, rugged path and continue straight ahead along a track, as sign-posted for Col du Granon. Keep left at a junction with another track and climb gently around the slopes of **La Gardiole**. When another junction is reached, turn sharp left, up a track, and zigzag almost as far as **Col des Cibières**, at 2525m. Turn right just before you reach the col, following a clear path as marked, generally downhill, to join a track, which leads to a road and car park on **Col du Granon** at 2413m (café and nearby barracks, which housed soldiers training for mountain warfare).

Follow a path as marked, climbing a little from the car park and passing close to a fine viewpoint for the glaciated Écrins. The path undulates and later passes well to the left of two cabins to reach **Col de Barteaux**, at 2380m. Either turn right to follow the GR5 downhill or keep straight ahead, climbing along a path marked with yellow paint flashes, to follow a rugged, high-level variant route.

Fortifications abound around Cité Vauban and Briançon

Col de Barteaux to Croix de Toulouse   3hr, 8km, +185m -595m

For the main route, turn right to follow a path down to a vehicle track, quickly turning left, as signposted, along a path which generally descends gently across the mountainside then climb past **Croix du Pied**. The path crosses the bed of the **Torrent de Ste-Elisabeth** and descends into forest, becoming more convoluted. Watch for a signposted junction at **Le Gros Feu** and eventually, link with a track in **Bois de l'Ours** that leads to a huddle of buildings at **Serre Lan**, at 1848m (water).

    Turn left to follow a clear track, which climbs gradually, across a forested slope and meadows. Reach a junction with the variant route then pass ruined buildings to reach **Croix de Toulouse**, at 1973m. There is a splendid bird's-eye view of Briançon and surrounding fortifications, with a valley leading the eye to Col des Ayes.

Croix de Toulouse to Briançon   1hr 30min, 5km, +5m -775m

A via ferrata drops straight down towards Briançon, but ordinary walkers will follow the path, zigzagging downhill, passing the **Font de Bon Repos** (water) on one bend. Eventually, the zigzag path lands beside the **Fort des Salettes**, at 1452m. This is occasionally open for visits, and there are views of other forts around Briançon.

    Walk down a track towards a cliff used by rock climbers. Watch for a path down to the left then, after taking it, continue straight down a track. Walk down a minor road to reach a busy main road. Cross over to reach fortified ramparts near the Porte de Pignerol and enter **Cité Vauban**, at 1330m (all services, being part of Briançon). Walk down through the walled city and leave via Porte d'Embrun, turning right.

    Turn left, down Chemin Vieux, as marked, and turn left again after a school. Go down a stepped path on a well-wooded slope, watching for markers at junctions, in

208

La Parc de la Schappe. At the bottom, turn right and keep to the right of a car park. Cross a bridge over a river, **La Durance**, then turn right to reach a main road and a roundabout, the Rond-Point du Queyras, in the heart of **Briançon**, at 1180m.

Variant route: Col de Barteaux to Croix de Toulouse   3hr, 7.5km, +470m -875m

A well-worn, crunchy, quartzite path climbs steeply uphill. Walk along the rugged crest of Crête de Peyrolle or alongside it, either as the path dictates or your ability permits. Pass a cross on **Croix de la Cime** at 2606m. There is a view of the Écrins, the distant Vanoise and Monte Viso in Italy. Walk down to a col, still on quartzite, then climb and outflank a dramatic overhanging crest of limestone. The narrow path heads from col to col rather than summit to summit. After passing **La Grande Peyrolle** and dropping to a col, keep close to the rocky crest or even walk along it to reach the final summit on the ridge, **Serre des Aigles**, at 2567m.

The descent is very steep and rocky, so follow the marked path faithfully. The surface can be bare rock or loose stones, so take care throughout. After this initial nasty stretch, a better path zigzags down past a few pines to reach a col and a derelict blockhouse. Climb past the building on its left-hand side then follow a well-engineered path downhill. Sometimes it has been cut into the limestone and sometimes it features a built-up edge. The gradient is gentle, but pines press in on both sides at times. Zigzag downhill to a track near a wooden building and a transmitter mast. Follow the track down to some ruined stone buildings then turn left, along the main GR5, up to **Croix de Toulouse** at 1973m.

BRIANÇON

The Guigues family, who were the first to use the name (later title) Dauphin, dominated a fortified hilltop site from the 11th century but lost power in the 15th century. The town of Briançon is known from the 13th century and appears to have been planned and built in one fell swoop with its regular street pattern. Massive fortified walls were built in the late 17th century under the direction of Sébastien Le Prestre, Marquis of Vauban and Marshal of France. Forts continued to be built after his death, into the 18th century, and Briançon became a major garrison town. It is one of the highest towns of its size in Europe, surpassed only by Davos in Switzerland.

A full range of services are available and the town is a transport hub. Altigo buses link Briançon with nearby villages. There are bus and rail services to Gap and Valence, for Paris. Direct bus services run to Grenoble, www.autocars-resalp.com, and Marseille, https://zou.maregionsud.fr. Tourist information office: tel 04 92 24 98 98 www.serre-chevalier.com.

STAGE 18
Briançon to Brunissard

Start	Briançon
Finish	Brunissard
Time	6hr
Distance	18.5km
Total Ascent	1295m
Total Descent	740m
Terrain	Town suburbs give way to fields and forest, with a long and gradual climb to a high col. Good paths and tracks lead downhill.
Maps	3536 OT and 3537 ET
Refreshments	Off route at Villard St-Pancrace. *Buvette* at Chalets des Ayes. Restaurants at Brunissard.
Accommodation	Off route at Villard St-Pancrace. Campsite near Brunissard. *Chambres d'hôtes, gîte d'étape* and apartments in Brunissard.

The GR5 takes a fairly direct route as it leaves Briançon, striving to avoid the busiest roads in the suburbs on the way to Villard St-Pancrace. After climbing above the village, a lengthy dirt road leads through a forested valley to Chalets des Ayes. A forest path climbs higher, then trees give way to open slopes on the final approach to Col des Ayes. The GR5 enters the Parc Naturel Régional du Queyras, enjoying remarkable scenery on the way down to Brunissard.

Briançon to Villard St-Pancrace   **1hr, 2.5km, +75m -5m**

Leave the Rond-Point du Queyras in Briançon as signposted for Col de l'Izoard then turn right, down Route des Toulousannes. Reach a roundabout, where a road is signposted for Villard St-Pancrace. Follow the road to another roundabout and continue straight ahead, past the Hotel/Pension St-Antoine.

The road later crosses the **Pont de Cervières**, at 1200m, then continue onwards as marked, passing houses and fields on the way towards **Villard St-Pancrace** and its suburb of Sachas, at 1240m (gîte d'étape, chambres d'hôte, bar and post office

Briançon
1180m

Cité Vauban
1330m

Le Chenaillet
2650m

Sommet
des Anges
2459m

Pont-
de-Cervières
1200m

La Cerveyrette

D902

Chapelle
St-Laurent

Cervières

Villard
St-Pancrace

Torrent des Ayes

N

0   1   2 km

Chalets des Ayes
1711m

Torrent de l'Orceyrette

Bois des
Ayes

Torrent des Ayes

Chalets de
Vers le Col
2163m

Pic de
Beauduis
2843m

Clos
la Cime
2732m

Col d'Izoard
2362m

Pic de Peyre
Eyraute
2903m

Col des Ayes
2477m

Pra Premier
2050m

Camping
de l'Izoard
1850m

D902

Pic du Haut
Mouriare
2808m

L'Eychaillon
2142m

Torrent de la Rivière

Brunissard
1746m

Pic du Cros
2695m

La Chalp

Sommet de
Catinat
2107m

Arvieux

D902

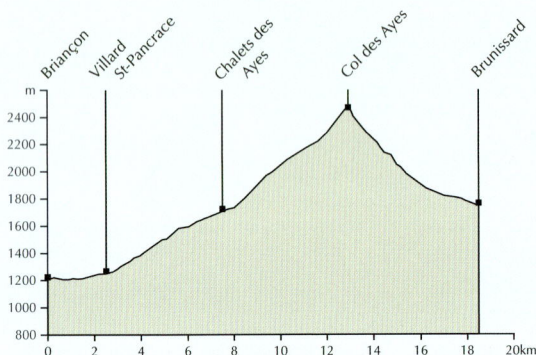

off route; Altigo buses to Briançon). Turn left, along Rue des Ayes, then turn right to cross a bridge over a river.

Villard St-Pancrace to Chalets des Ayes   1hr 30min, 5km, +465m -5m
Walk straight up a path, Chemin du Serre (mountain centre and buvette off route), and continue up a road to pass **Chapelle St-Laurent**. The road zigzags up to a junction signposted both left and right for Les Ayes. Turn left, along a blocked-off dirt road reserved for walkers and cyclists. This climbs straight through a forested valley drained by the **Torrent des Ayes**, eventually reaching a junction with another road. Turn left and pass a sheer cliff, which is popular with rock climbers. Continue along the road, following the river upstream to a little chapel then keeping right to pass the **Chalets des Ayes**, at 1711m (buvette).

Chalets des Ayes to Col des Ayes   1hr 30min, 5km, +755m -0m
Turn left, off the road, to go up a track then take a path to the left of the highest chalet. Walk up through a field and climb steeply into the **Bois des Ayes**. The trees are mixed and dense at first then later dominated by larch, but there are views as height is gained, and the gradient eases. Turn left, up a track, and as the last few pines thin out, grassy slopes rise around the scattered **Chalets de Vers le Col**, at 2163m. Just before the end of the track, a path climbs to the left. Follow it up grassy slopes, crossing limestone and quartzite scree, aiming for **Col des Ayes**, at 2477m. There are views back to Briançon and the Écrins and ahead to Monte Viso in Italy. The Parc Naturel Régional du Queyras is entered.

A stony path shortcuts a dirt road on the descent from Col des Ayes to Pra Premier

Col des Ayes to Brunissard   2hr, 6km, +0m -730m

Zigzag down a path on a slope covered in wiry tufts of grass, noting a transition underfoot from quartzite back to limestone. The path overlooks a lovely grassy valley containing a few chalets overlooked by mountains. Land on a dirt road beside some cabins at **L'Eychaillon**, at 2142m (water). Turn left, downhill, and the scene changes dramatically, revealing a looming cliff overlooking a flat, grassy area, a small lake and a cabin. The dirt road zigzags down a scree slope, but walkers can shortcut part way down, reaching a gravel car park beside the grass at **Pra Premier**, at 2050m, where there is information about via ferrata routes.

Continue down the dirt road, shortcutting down to the right, along a path, to another car park on a tarmac road. Walk down the road a little and use another shortcut, signposted 'Via Ferrata'. Afterwards, stay on the road, passing **Camping de l'Izoard**, at 1850m (campsite and café, with tents and vans for hire). Follow a path parallel to the road to reach a village surrounded by meadows. Walk down Route des Ayes to reach a junction with a main road at **Brunissard** at 1746m (gîte d'étape, apartments, restaurants; free buses, or *navettes gratuites*, link Brunissard with Château-Queyras, Ville-Vieille and Ceillac).

STAGE 19
Brunissard to Ceillac

Start	Brunissard
Finish	Ceillac
Time	8hr 15min
Distance	23km
Total Ascent	1335m
Total Descent	1430m
Terrain	Roads, tracks and forest paths, with a few open slopes. Mostly gently graded but with some steep ascents and descents.
Maps	3537 ET
Refreshments	Restaurants at La Chalp, Arvieux (off route), Château-Queyras and Ceillac.
Accommodation	Plenty of choice at La Chalp and off route at Arvieux and Ville-Vieille. *Gîtes d'étape* and campsite at Ceillac.

Leaving Brunissard, views stretch to Col Fromage and almost as far as Col Girardin, so two days of the GR5 are visible. Those wishing to explore Fort Queyras properly should break at that point, even though it is short of the day's halfway point. Unfortunately, there are no lodgings but a bus can be used to reach nearby Ville-Vieille and other villages. A long, forested valley climbs steeply at first, continuing fairly easily to Col Fromage. The descent to Ceillac is along good paths and tracks.

Brunissard to Lac de Roue   1hr 30min, 5.5km, +255m -150m

Follow the main road downhill from Brunissard to the neighbouring village of **La Chalp** (hotel, chambres d'hôte, gîte d'étape, restaurants; free buses, or *navettes gratuites*, link La Chalp with Château-Queyras, Ville-Vieille and Ceillac). Turn left at La Ferme de l'Izoard to follow a road uphill. Turn right at a junction to walk down a road, passing old houses. Turn right at another junction, passing only one house before turning left, up a path. The path undulates across a forested slope, with a glimpse down to the village of Arvieux. Drop down to a farm road and walk up between the buildings at **Les Maisons** at 1693m.

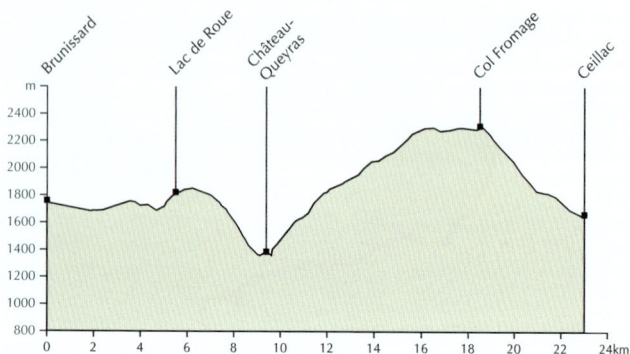

ARVIEUX

The village of Arvieux is 20min off route from Les Maisons, offering a hotel, bank with ATM, shop, restaurant and tourist information office: tel 04 92 46 75 76 https://lequeyras.com. Free buses, or *navettes gratuites*, link Arvieux with Brunissard, Château-Queyras, Ville-Vieille and Ceillac.

The iconic Fort Queyras was strengthened by Vauban in 1692

Walk straight up a track to pass fields but watch for a winding path climbing to the left. Turn right at a junction with another path then cross a track at a higher level, just to cut out a bend. When the track is joined again, turn right and follow it to a junction close to the little **Lac de Roue** at 1850m.

Lac de Roue to Château-Queyras   1hr 15min, 4km, +35m -520m
Pass the outflow of the lake and follow the GR5 markers indicating a forest track. Climb a little, avoiding other paths to the right and left, then descend gently, among pines. Watch out where the path crosses, joins or leaves a rugged, bull-dozed track. Later, the path drops steeply, and after passing a cliff-edge viewpoint for Fort Queyras, it becomes loose and stony. Zigzag down to a busy road and turn left to follow it, keeping an eye on the traffic as you approach the village of **Château-Queyras**, at 1365m (restaurant).

Walk down a narrow road as signposted, past the town hall (*mairie*), to reach a church (water). Turn right, and if time can be spared, visit the Espace Géologique in an old crypt to learn how the Alps were formed.

FORT QUEYRAS

The stump of rock filling the valley was first fortified in 1260. Fortifications were strengthened by the great engineer Sébastien Le Prestre, Marquis of Vauban and Marshal of France, in 1692 and now present an iconic and instantly recognisable picture. If the day is broken at this point, there will be time to enjoy a decent exploration: see www.fortqueyras.fr.

The village has a restaurant but lacks accommodation. Free buses, or *navettes gratuites*, link Château-Queyras with Brunissard, Arvieux, Ville-Vieille and Ceillac, which all offer more services.

Château-Queyras to Col Fromage   4hr, 9km, +1045m -110m
Walk through a car park and cross a bridge over a river, **Le Guil**. Climb straight up a steep, stone-paved path to reach a grassy slope, where an easy path soon gives way to a steep, stony, uneven forest path. There is a good view back to Fort Queyras. Climb through a pine forest and divert left, up to a road. Climb round one bend and walk up to the next bend. Leave the road to follow a path, clipping a higher road bend, to climb up to a track junction near a couple of buildings at **Le Pré Premier** at 1760m.

Take the higher track but later step off to the right, along a path. The valley appears densely forested with larch, but the path actually wanders from meadow to meadow. There is a view back to the striking Grand Pic de Rochebrune and

Col Fromage is broad and is crossed by easy paths on the way to Ceillac

ahead to Pointe de la Selle. Pass a wooden cabin at Pré Faure, at 1950m, and keep climbing, through larch forest. Follow the river and cross over it, catching a view of Pointe de la Selle again, now revealed as towering twin peaks. Reach an open space at **Fontaine Rouge**, at 2125m (water).

Follow a path up a grassy slope, where the trees become rather sparse. There are sudden turns to the right then left (possible water). Pass an area of pits, where gypsum was mined. The path is trodden to white powder as it passes above the appropriately named **Ravin de Ruine Blanche**. Pines give way to grassy slopes and limestone scree as the path approaches the broad **Col Fromage**, at 2301m. Views ahead include the snow-streaked Pics de la Font Sancte but Col Girardin is just out of sight.

Col Fromage to Ceillac   1hr 30min, 4.5km, +0m -650m

Follow a path straight downhill, zigzagging past larches. Crumbling dolomitic limestone gives way to crumbling quartzite, so the path is gravelly all the way down. There are fine views from the head of the Vallon du Cristillan down to Ceillac. The path finally lands on a track near a few houses at **Le Villard**, at 1840m.

Turn right, along the track, then later, watch for a wooden cross on the left and follow a path that winds down to a road. Turn right, down the road, and walk straight into the centre of **Ceillac**, to Place Philippe Lamour, near the church and town hall (*mairie*), at 1650m (gîtes d'étape, post office, ATM, shops, bars, restaurants and nearby campsites; free buses, or *navettes gratuites*, to Ville-Vieille, Château-Queyras and Brunissard; tourist information office: tel 04 92 45 05 74 https://lequeyras.com). This is the woodworking centre of the Queyras, and Philippe Lamour was the originator of the Parc Naturel Régional du Queyras.

SECTION 5:
CEILLAC TO
ST-DALMAS

S 20 Ceillac

Guillestre

Col Girardin

21 Maljasset

Fouillouse

St-Paul-
sur-Ubaye

Col de Mallemort

Meyronnes

Larche 22

Col de la Madeleine

ITALY

Barcelonnette

Pas de la Cavale

Col de la Bonette

23 Bousieyas

Col de la Colombière

St-Dalmas
le Selvage

Col d'Anelle

St-Étienne de Tinée

Auron 24

FRANCE

Col du Blainon

Roya

Isola

Mont
Mounier

Refuge
de Longon

25

St-Sauveur
sur Tinée

St-Dalm

N

0   5   10

GR5

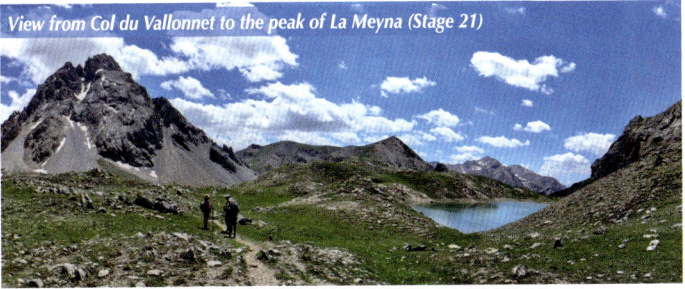
View from Col du Vallonnet to the peak of La Meyna (Stage 21)

Beyond Ceillac, the GR5 leaves the Parc Naturel Régional du Queyras, and the Hautes-Alpes, and enters the Alpes de Haute-Provence as it crosses the Col Girardin on Stage 20. The last few peaks that boast obvious, permanent snow and ice cover lie nearby. The route descends into the deep Ubaye valley and has to follow a road. Beyond Fouillouse, the GR5 runs concurrently with the popular GR56, or Tour de l'Ubaye, passing from one col to another to reach Larche on Stage 21, close to the Franco-Italian frontier.

After leaving Larche, walkers enjoy a spectacular trek through the northern part of the scenic and rugged Parc National du Mercantour. The route crosses the steep and rocky Pas de la Cavale, leaving the Alpes de Haute-Provence to enter the Alpes Maritimes on Stage 22. Ahead lies the long and complex Vallée de la Tinée,

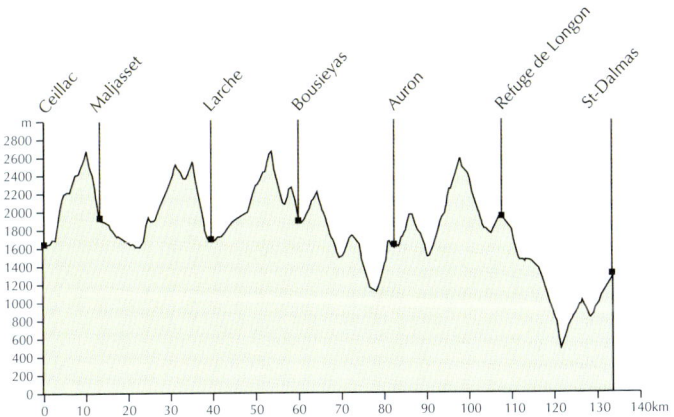

221

where the mountains have a habit of generating sudden and spectacular summer afternoon thunderstorms, so keep an eye on the weather.

The GR5 parts company with the GR56 on Col de la Colombière on Stage 23 and heads down to St-Dalmas le Selvage, then over to St-Étienne de Tinée. Don't imagine that the route has abandoned the mountains due to these forays into the valley, since there is still

plenty of climbing before the end of the trail on the shore of the Mediterranean.

For those covering the GR5 in sections, St-Étienne de Tinée and Auron have regular bus services linking directly with Nice – a name that suggests that the end draws near, yet the route still has to climb over the shoulder of the formidable Mont Mounier.

Stage	Place	Altitude	Walking time	Distance
20	Ceillac	1650m	0hr 00min	0km
20	*Pied de Mélézet*	*1639m*	*1hr 00min/3km to turn off, +5min off main route*	
20	Maljasset	1910m	5hr 45min	11km
21	*St Paul sur Ubaye*	*1625m*	*2hr 00min/9km to turn off, +1hr off route*	
21	Fouillouse	1907m	1hr 00min	3km
21	Larche	1680m	5hr 15min	13.5km
22	Pont Rouge	1907m	1hr 30min	5.5km
22	Bousieyas	1883m	6hr 15min	15km
23	St-Dalmas le Selvage	1500m	3hr 30min	9km
23	St-Étienne de Tinée	1144m	2hr 45min	7.5km
23	Chapelle St-Maur	1200m	0hr 45min	2km
23	Auron	1602m	2hr 00min	3.5km
24	Roya	1500m	3hr 30min	8km
24	Refuge de Longon	1883m	7hr 45min	19km
25	Roure	1096m	3hr 15min	9km
25	St-Sauveur sur Tinée	496m	1hr 30min	4km
25	Rimplas	1016m	2hr 30min	4.5km
25	La Bolline	995m	1hr 30min	4km
25	St-Dalmas	1290m	1hr 00min	3km

Summer heat can make the valley towns and villages seem like furnaces, but the same heat also draws moisture from the sea, leading to afternoon thunderstorms. After a descent to St-Sauveur sur Tinée, a long and gradual climb passes a number of villages to reach St-Dalmas. A decision needs to be made at this point whether to walk directly to Nice on the GR5 or switch to the more scenic and exciting, but also longer and more difficult, GR52 to Garavan/Menton.

Legend

- ♠ refuge/hut/gîte d'étape
- ◯ hotel
- ◯ home stay
- ⌂ unmanned hut/bothy
- ◉ camping
- ✳ bivouac
- ◉ restaurant/refreshments
- ◉ shop/groceries
- ◉ ATM
- ➊ TIC
- ◉ train
- ◉ bus
- ◉ lift/cable car

Facilities							
refuge	hotel	camping/bivouac	restaurant	shop	ATM	TIC	train/bus
♠			◉	◉	◉	➊	◉
	◯		◉				
♠	◯		◉				
♠	◯	◉	◉	◉		➊	◉
♠	◯	✳	◉	◉			
♠		◉	◉	◉			◉
							◉
♠	◯	✳	◉				
♠	◯		◉	◉		➊	◉
♠	◯	◉	◉	◉	◉	➊	◉
							◉
	◯	◉	◉	◉	◉	➊	◉
♠		✳	◉				
♠			◉	◉			
♠							◉
♠	◯	◉	◉	◉	◉		◉
	◯		◉				◉
	◯		◉	◉			◉
♠	◯	◉	◉	◉			◉

STAGE 20
Ceillac to La Barge/Maljasset

Start	Ceillac
Finish	La Barge/Maljasset
Time	6hr 45min
Distance	14km
Total Ascent	1060m
Total Descent	800m
Terrain	A steep climb up a forested slope then easier climbing past a couple of lakes. Another steep climb to a col then a steep and stony descent into a deep valley.
Maps	3537 ET and 3637 OT
Refreshments	Restaurants at Pied du Mélézet and off route at Maljasset.
Accommodation	Campsites near Pied du Mélézet. Hotel at Pied du Mélézet. Refuge, *gîte d'étape* and *maison d'hôte* off route at Maljasset.

This is a short day's walk but it involves steep slopes and crosses one of the highest cols on the GR5. A decision needs to be made on the descent. Either head off route to Maljasset for food, drink and accommodation or stay on the GR5 to descend to La Barge. The problem with the latter choice is that there are no services, so a detour to Maljasset may be required anyway. The only other options involve extending the walk as far as St-Paul-sur-Ubaye or Fouillouse.

Ceillac to Lac Miroir   2hr 30min, 5.5km, +580m -10m

Leave Place Philippe Lamour in the centre of Ceillac. Go behind the town hall (*mairie*) and follow a river downstream, then follow the narrow Rue du Sarret, keeping straight ahead along Rue de la Gravière. Turn left, along the main road that bypasses the village, then turn right, across a bridge over the **Torrent du Mélézet**, and immediately turn left. A grassy track, the Chemin des Contes et Legends, passes wooden sculptures as it runs upstream. Follow the river past two campsites – Les Moutets and Les Mélèzes. Later, turn right, as signposted, at **Pied du Mélézet**, at 1639m (hotel and restaurant off route).

The path zigzags up a steep slope of larch, passing brittle outcrops of sedimentary rock, with occasional views back into the valley. The forest is denser at a

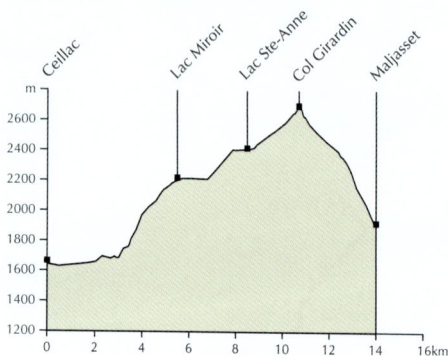

higher level, then the path climbs alongside the foaming cascade of **Ruisseau de la Pisse** before crossing it at a footbridge. Emerge on a grassy pasture, with stunning views of the grey, serrated, snow-streaked peaks of Crête des Veyres, before reaching the popular little **Lac Miroir**, at 2214m.

Lac Miroir to Lac Ste-Anne   1hr 30min, 3km, +195m -0m

The lake, if still, mirrors the peaks beautifully. Pass the outflow, which drains into a limestone fissure, then cross a slight rise. The path heads downhill, so keep right at a junction to climb again. Pass well to the right of a *bergerie* at **Les Preynasses**, in a sparsely forested area. Climb towards a ski piste and follow a path and a track

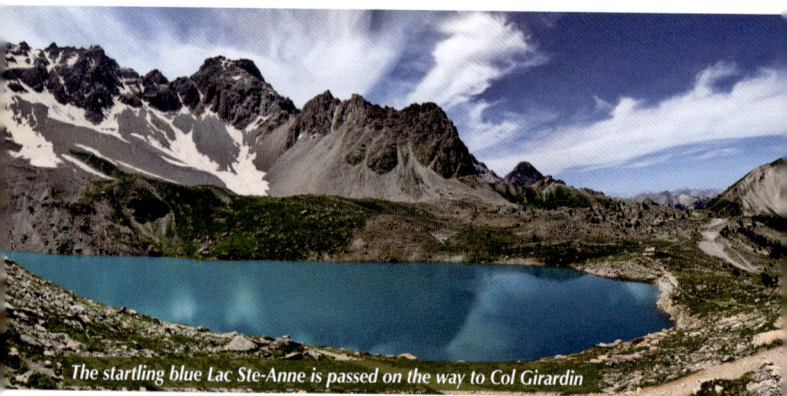

The startling blue Lac Ste-Anne is passed on the way to Col Girardin

uphill, beside a chairlift. Continue around hummocky moraine to reach a chapel overlooking **Lac Ste-Anne**, at 2415m.

Lac Ste-Anne to Col Girardin
1hr, 2km, +280m -0m

There is no outflow, so cross the lowest point near the lake and follow a path up a slope of bouldery moraine. Slopes of lustrous, friable scree lie beyond, sparsely tufted with vegetation, and a path zigzags up to **Col Girardin** at 2699m. This marks the departmental boundary between Hautes-Alpes and Alpes de Haute-Provence, and also the exit from the Parc Naturel Régional du Queyras.

Col Girardin to La Barge/Maljasset
1hr 45min, 4km, +5m -790m

Initially, the path downhill is a series of steep, worn, slippery zigzags. It becomes a delightful grassy path, although this, in turn, leads to a prominent tongue of bouldery moraine. Continue down the path and watch out on the right for the tiny, stone-built **Cabane de Girardin** and its modern counterpart tucked in among rocks frequented by marmots. Follow another gentle, grassy path and don't be tempted along a cairned path. Walk down to a signposted path junction in the Ravin des Séchoirs, at 2388m. At this point, a decision has to be made as to whether to descend along the GR5 to La Barge or descend a variant route to Maljasset.

Turn right for La Barge, climbing for a while, but only to outflank an awkward cliff. The descent crosses a steep and fairly well-vegetated slope, later dropping in tight, steep zigzags, passing occasional larches. There are views of stone, slab rooftops before the zigzag path finally lands on a road. Turn right to reach the little hamlet of **La Barge** and its tiny chapel, at 1875m (water but no other facilities).

For Maljasset, turn left, as signposted and marked with a boulder painted 'Maljasset'. The path looks pleasant and easy but it gradually steepens on a loose and stony slope, which requires care. The path is marked throughout with yellow paint flashes. The first sight of the hamlet is almost an aerial view, revealing a huddle of houses and a chapel standing alone among fields. Pass a few larches before finally landing on a road at **Maljasset**, at 1910m (refuge, gîte d'étape, maison d'hôte and restaurants).

STAGE 21
La Barge/Maljasset to Larche

Start	La Barge/Maljasset
Finish	Larche
Time	8hr 15min
Distance	25.5km
Total Ascent	1245m
Total Descent	1475m
Terrain	A long road-walk, followed by a steep, forested climb and a gradual ascent through a valley. Two high cols are linked by a good path and track. A largely grassy descent leads to Larche.
Maps	3537 ET and 3637 OT
Refreshments	Restaurants off route at St-Paul-sur-Ubaye, and at Fouillouse and Larche.
Accommodation	Lodgings off route at St-Paul-sur-Ubaye. *Gîte d'étape*, *chambres* and bivouac at Fouillouse. Refuge, *gîte d'étape* and campsite at Larche.

Lying between the Parc Naturel Régional du Queyras and Parc National du Mercantour, the scenery in these parts is by no means diminished for being excluded from the neighbouring parks. The only drawback is the long road-walk through the Vallon de Maurin, and it takes time for the route to get back into the mountains. Once you begin crossing high cols again, interesting ruined military sites are seen. One fort was built at 2772m, on top of Tête de Viraysse.

Maljasset to Le Châtelet   2hr, 9km, +10m -300m
Leave Maljasset and walk along the road, passing a point where the GR5 comes down from the mountainside. Continue through the little hamlet of **La Barge**, noting its tiny chapel, at 1875m (water). Follow the road down through a forested part of the valley, with views of soaring rocky peaks and the **L'Ubaye** river from time to time.

Cross a road bridge then turn left and follow a rugged path between the road and the river, later passing a hydro-electric plant. Continue between the road

Pic de Panestrel 3258m

La Mortice Nord 3187m

Maljasset 1910m

La Barge 1875m

Torrent des Houerts

L'Ubaye

La Gélinasse 2854m

N

FRANCE

0   1   2
km

Le Grand Caire 2923m

Le Pont Voûté 1656m

St-Antoine

Pointe de l'Aval 3325m

Le Bec Roux 3013m

Le Châtelet 1625m

Le Pont Châtelet

Brec de Chambeyron 3389m

Fouillouse 1907m

Pralouyer

L'Ubaye

Riou de Fouillouse

ITALY

Fort de Plate Lombarde

Buc de Nubiera 3215m

St-Paul-sur-Ubaye

Tête de Adrechenouns 2896m

Tête de la Courbe 3089m

Col du Vallonnet 2524m

Rocca Blanca 3193m

Monte Sautron 3166m

FRANCE

La Meyna 3067m

Baraquements de Viraysse

Col de Mallemort 2558m

L'Ubayette

Torrent Rouchouze

D900

La Tête Dure 2629m

Larche 1680m

F

Tête de Siguret 3032m

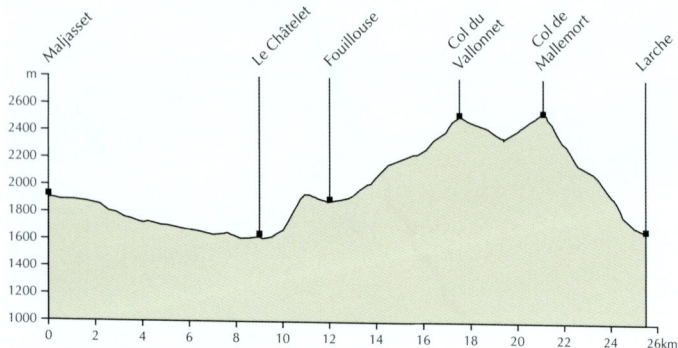

and the river, later rejoining the road to cross **Le Pont Voûté**, at 1656m. Shortly after the bridge, step off the road and walk on a grassy slope between the road

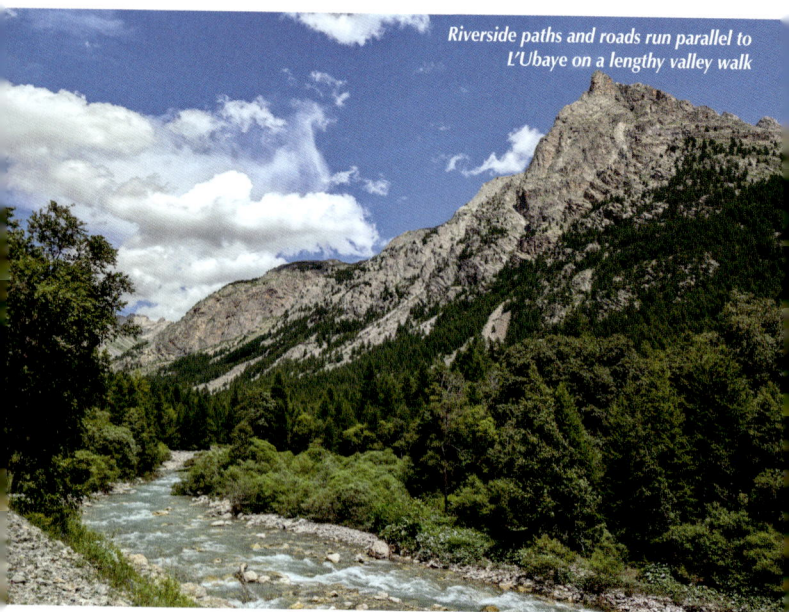

Riverside paths and roads run parallel to L'Ubaye on a lengthy valley walk

and river. Follow marker posts, which lead across a stream, below a road bridge. Climb briefly, through a wood, to reach houses and a chapel at **St-Antoine**.

Pass the buildings by road then step down onto another path, leaving the road before a bridge. Again, walk between the road and the river, crossing a stream below a road bridge. Pass some pines, and the path links with a track. The track leads gently up to the road at a restored lime kiln, or *four à chaux*. Follow the road onwards to a junction at **Le Châtelet**, at 1625m (road access to **St-Paul-sur-Ubaye**).

ST-PAUL-SUR-UBAYE

St-Paul-sur-Ubaye lies off route in an area where services are sparse. The commune is in several parts, and it may be necessary to walk for over an hour to fulfil a particular need. Heading down the road, the first settlement is La Grande Sérenne, with a bar restaurant. Next is Petite Sérenne, followed by Pont de l'Estrech, where there are *chambres d'hôte*. The greatest bulk of services is at St-Paul-sur-Ubaye: hotel, *chambres d'hôte, gîte d'étape*, shop, post office, restaurants, campsite, museum and free bus, or *navette gratuite*, to Barcelonnette. Tourist information office: tel 04 92 81 04 71 www.ubaye.com.

Le Châtelet to Fouillouse
1hr, 3km, +410m -120m

Turn left, up a road hacked from rock and signposted for Fouillouse. Cross **Le Pont Châtelet**, which spans a deep and narrow rocky gorge. The bridge was proposed in 1875 as a wooden span but was completed in stone in 1882, arching 27m across and 108m above the river. It was mined in 1944 but resisted the explosion and was repaired in 1945. Continue through a tunnel, and after enjoying a view down the Ubaye valley, turn left, up a path. Climb steeply and cross an access road serving a house at La Meire. Keep climbing, among pines, until a path junction is reached at Les Vistes, where there is a fine valley view. Turn right to traverse around the head of a ravine then walk down in loops to land on a road at the small village of **Fouillouse**, at 1907m (gîte d'étape, chambres d'hôte, restaurants, shop and bivouac).

Fouillouse to Col du Vallonnet
2hr, 5.5km, +625m -10m

While walking through Fouillouse, look out for 19th-century water troughs carved out of huge blocks of stone. Larger ones – up to 4m long – can be found in the Ubaye valley. Walk past a chapel and simply follow a track onwards, climbing roughly parallel to a river, **Riou de Fouillouse**. Larches proliferate around

Pralouyer but they don't obscure views, and there are many grassy slopes. Reach a little cabin and turn right to follow a path past the concrete ruin of **Fort de Plate Lombarde**. The path is gentle and easy, keeping well to the left of a farm cabin. Climb a little before crossing a footbridge, then climb again, watching for marmots. A steeper climb, up a sandstone slope dotted with alpenrose, leads to the boulder-strewn **Col du Vallonnet**, at 2524m. There is a view of Col de Mallemort, to the right of the striking peak of La Meyna.

Col du Vallonnet to Col de Mallemort   1hr 15min, 3.5km, +200m -170m

Walk down a gentle path, which soon follows a sluggish stream. There are two signposted path junctions: keep right at the first and left at the second, confirming each move by looking for markers. The path crosses bouldery, sheep-grazed moraine to reach a track, which is actually an old military road. Turn left to follow it up to the ruined **Baraquements de Viraysse** (basic shelter). Follow a well-graded path in sweeping zigzags above the fort to reach the **Col de Mallemort**, at 2558m. A well-graded, zigzag military path could be followed off route to the ruined Batterie de Viraysse on the 2772m summit of Tête de Viraysse.

Col de Mallemort to Larche   2hr, 4.5km, +0m -875m

Follow a winding path down from the col which is stony where the grass cover is sparse but delightful where there is complete grass cover. There is a brief view ahead along the GR5 to Pas de la Cavale. Pass a few larches and keep straight ahead at two signposted path junctions. Larche is nearly always in view during the descent. French, Italian and European flags draw attention to a Second World War military site. The last part of the path is steep and stony, zigzagging down a slope dotted with juniper and thorn bushes and crossing brittle shale. Join a track, which leads easily down beside a stream, then continue along a road into **Larche**, at 1680m (gîtes d'étape, restaurants, post office, shop, nearby campsite/shop; free bus, or *navette gratuite*, to Pont Rouge and Barcelonnette).

LARCHE

There is a long history of travel over Col de Larche (in Italian, Colla della Maddalena), between Provence and Piémont. Shepherds who frequented high pastures in the summer drove their flocks to Piémont before the onset of winter. The establishment of a border in the region led to times of strife. The village was destroyed by German and Italian troops in 1944 and has been completely rebuilt. Oddly, the only feature to survive the destruction was the 1914–18 war memorial.

STAGE 22
Larche to Bousieyas

Start	Larche
Finish	Bousieyas
Time	7hr 45min
Distance	20.5km
Total Ascent	1205m
Total Descent	1005m
Terrain	Roads, tracks and paths climb through a valley, becoming more rugged, up to a high col. After a steep and rocky descent, a lower grassy col is crossed then a final, easy descent follows.
Maps	3538 ET and 3639 OT
Refreshments	Campsite restaurant after Larche. Restaurants at Bousieyas.
Accommodation	Campsite after Larche. *Gîtes d'étape, chambres d'hôte* and bivouac at Bousieyas.

Leaving Larche, the GR5 enters the Parc National du Mercantour in grand style, climbing through the Vallon de Lauzanier. Great slabs of sandstone and limestone hide charming little lakes, then the route crosses the rocky Pas de la Cavale. From this point onwards, the GR5 is confined to the large and complex Vallée de la Tinée all the way to Nice. The whole day's walk runs close to the Franco-Italian border, and old military sites are evident.

Larche to Pont Rouge   1hr 30min, 5.5km, +245m -20m
Leave Larche via the main road in the direction of Italy but fork right, along a minor road, to pass the Gîte Auberge du Lauzanier. Pass **Camping des Marmottes** (campsite, cabins, shop and restaurant). Later, a grassy track on the left is signposted as the GR5, leading gently up to a small **cemetery**. Walk down a winding grassy track and cross a bridge over **L'Ubayette**. Turn left to follow a road, which eventually rises to a car park at **Pont Rouge** at 1907m (free bus, or *navette gratuite*, to Larche and Barcelonnette). The car park is often busy with visitors from both France and Italy.

Larche
1680m

La Tête Dure
2629m

Camping
des Marmottes

Cime des Palets
2686m

Cemetery

Pointe
de la Signora
2774m

L'Orrenaye

Col de la Madeleine
1991m

Bec de l'Aigle
2815m

FRANCE

Pont Rouge
1907m

L'Ubayette

SS21

Tête de Fer
2885m

N

0   1   2
km

VAL FOURANE

Monte Ventasuso
2712m

ITALY

Tête de
Parassac
2777m

L'Ubayette

Lac du Lauzanier
2284m

FRANCE

Rocher des
Trois Évêques
2868m

Lac de
Derrière la Croix

Pas de la Cavale
2671m

Lacs
d'Agnel

Le Castel de la Tour
2778m

SALSO MORÉNO

Ravin
de la Tour

Camp des
Fourches

Cima del Bal
2831m

Col des Fourches
2261m

Pointe des
Chaudrède
2732m

Bousieyas
1883m

La Tinée

Tête de

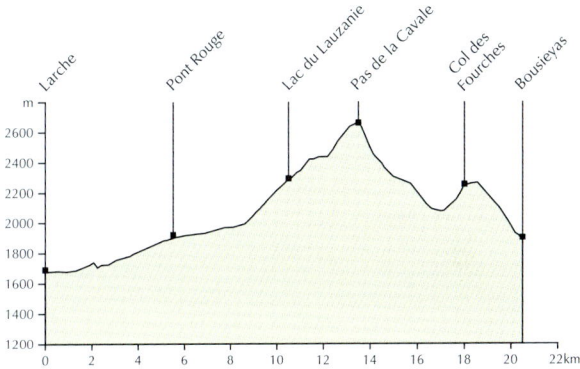

Pont Rouge to Lac du Lauzanier   1hr 45min, 5km, +385m -5m

Enter the Parc National du Mercantour and follow a track into **Val Fourane**, where the scenery is impressive. The track runs gently up through the valley then narrows and steepens to become a largely reconstructed path. Climb beside a stream flanked by lush vegetation to reach the lovely **Lac du Lauzanier**, at 2284m, overlooked by a little chapel.

Lac du Lauzanier to Pas de la Cavale   1hr 30min, 3km, +385m -0m

Keep well to the right of the lake to follow a well-trodden path further up through the Vallon du Lauzanier, heading towards slabby mountains. If walking here after wet weather, the mud can be thick and sticky, so take care while crossing the limestone slabs afterwards. Pass a vigorous spring then climb beside limestone slabs. Cross a river at a huge boulder and keep climbing.

The path splits and rejoins, so either keep left, on the GR5, or right to visit nearby Lac de Derrière la Croix at 2428m. Zigzag uphill and follow the path from a grassy slope onto boulder scree, which is easy if taken steadily, to reach the impressively rocky **Pas de la Cavale** at 2671m. This is the departmental boundary between Alpes de Haute-Provence and Alpes Maritimes, with views ahead to Col de la Colombière, Auron and Mont Mounier.

Pas de la Cavale to Col des Fourches   2hr, 4.5km, +185m -595m

Take care descending from the col as the limestone is badly fractured and blocks of rock could fall. The path traverses narrow ledges and runs down boulder-scree to reach grassy slopes grazed by sheep and goats. Looking back, it is impossible to trace the path! The whole area is shaped by unstable geology, with crumbling black shale along Les Roubines Nègres and crater-like dolines (solution hollows) in the dolomitic limestone near the little Lacs d'Agnel.

The gradient eases and the grass may be dotted with delightful pale crocuses. The valley was named Salso Moréno when it was occupied by Spanish troops from 1744 to 1747. Cross a broad and bouldery stream-bed around 2100m and pass a little cabin (shelter). The path later crosses **Ravin de la Tour** and climbs a steep slope to pass concrete casemates – bunkers in which guns were mounted. Cross the gentle **Col des Fourches**, at 2261m.

Col des Fourches to Bousieyas   1hr, 2.5km, +5m -385m

Follow an easy, grassy track to ruined barracks at **Camp des Fourches**. Built in the 1890s, the barracks housed soldiers known as 'Les Diables Bleus', who patrolled the border between France and Italy. Halfway through the barracks, turn left to cross a road, and continue downhill as marked. (The road climbs to Col de la Bonette, the highest road pass in Western Europe at 2802m.)

A grassy path flanked by sandstone boulders winds downhill, and there is a view across the valley to Col de la Colombière. Cross the road again then later, cross it twice in quick succession to cut out a bend. Continue down a grooved path, where boulders have been pushed to one side, catching a glimpse of a hamlet below. Step down a series of old terraces and later, pass a house, keeping to the right, then turn left, down the road. Turn right, down a path that leads to stone steps in the tin-roofed hamlet of **Bousieyas**, at 1883m (gîtes d'étape, chambres d'hôte, restaurants and bivouac). This is the highest hamlet in the Alpes Maritimes, intended to be inhabited in the summer and abandoned in the winter.

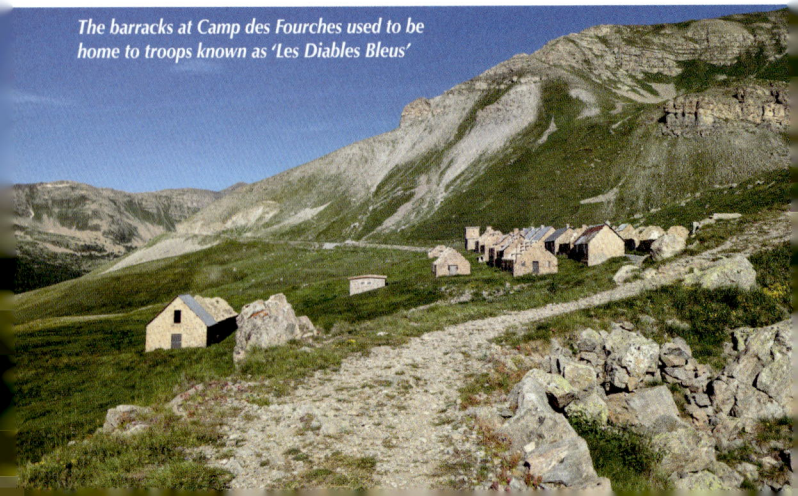

The barracks at Camp des Fourches used to be home to troops known as 'Les Diables Bleus'

Start	Bousieyas
Finish	Auron
Time	9hr
Distance	22km
Total Ascent	1200m
Total Descent	1480m
Terrain	Easy tracks and paths climb to a high col, but the descent is narrow and stony. More easy tracks and paths then cross another col, then after a descent into a valley, a steep and stony forest path climbs to Auron.
Maps	3639 OT
Refreshments	Restaurants at St-Dalmas le Selvage, St-Étienne de Tinée and Auron.
Accommodation	*Gîte d'étape, chambres d'hôte* and bivouac at St-Dalmas le Selvage. Plenty of choice at St-Étienne de Tinée, including a campsite. Hotels and campsite at Auron.

Mediterranean influences become pronounced during the day. Col de la Colombière is high, but the descent to St-Dalmas le Selvage features broom, lavender and large, bright-green lizards not seen so far on the GR5. After a gentle traverse of Col d'Anelle, the descent to St-Étienne de Tinée leads deep into La Vallée de la Tinée, which could be very hot during summer afternoons. If this is the case, the steep and stony ascent to Auron could be quite tiring and it might be better to leave it until the cool of the following morning.

Bousieyas to Col de la Colombière   1hr 30min, 4km, +375m -25m

Leave Bousieyas by walking down a road from the church, following a sharp left bend then turning sharp right, down a track. Cross a bridge over **La Tinée** and climb gradually, through larch forest, with occasional views back to the hamlet. Ford **Le Rio** and keep climbing, until the track is almost level and grassy. A path is marked up to the right, zigzagging up the forested slope, crossing the track again and again to emerge from the trees onto a grassy gap at 2123m.

Le Castel de la Tour
2778m

Cima del Bal
2831m

ITALY

Bousiéyas
1883m

S

L'Alpe
2512m

FRANCE

D64

La Tinée

Pointe de Colombart
2642m

Tête de
Vinaigre
2394m

Cime de
la Blanche
2534m

Col de la
Colombière
2237m

Torrent de Vens

Claï Inférieur
2590m

C
Supé
298

La Tinée

Le Rio

Vallon de
la Combe

Rochepin

St-Dalmas le Selvage
1500m

Col d'Anelle
1739m

Anelle
1650m

Ublan

St-Étienne de Tin
1144m

Torrent de Ténibres

Torrent de Chalorgues

Bec de
Marseille
2744m

L'Ardon

M2205

Chapelle St-Maur
1200m

La Ti

Sommet d'Auron
1929m

Cime de Bouchiet
2202m

F

Auron
1602m

N

0   1   2
km

Cime du
Chavalet
2452m

Las
Donnas
2475m

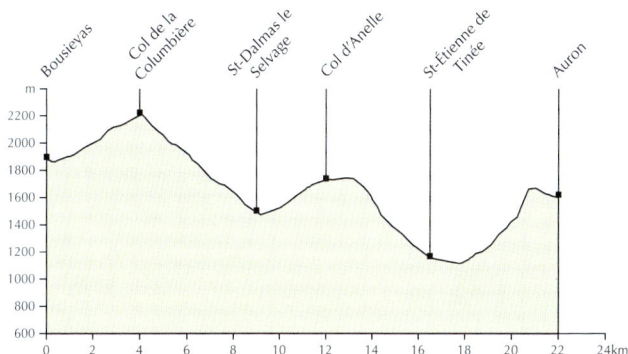

Follow the track as it climbs easily across limestone boulder-scree overlooking slopes grazed by sheep and goats. Avoid a final zigzag by using a shortcut path straight to **Col de la Colombière**, at 2237m. There is a view ahead along the GR5 to Mont Mounier.

Col de la Colombière to St-Dalmas le Selvage   2hr, 5km, +5m -740m
Leave the track on the col and walk down a winding, stony path. This narrow path contours across steep slopes and wanders in and out of ravines. Dolomitic limestone gives way to glistening mica schist. Cabins at **Rochepin** could easily pass unnoticed where the path makes a sharp right turn. Traverse around more

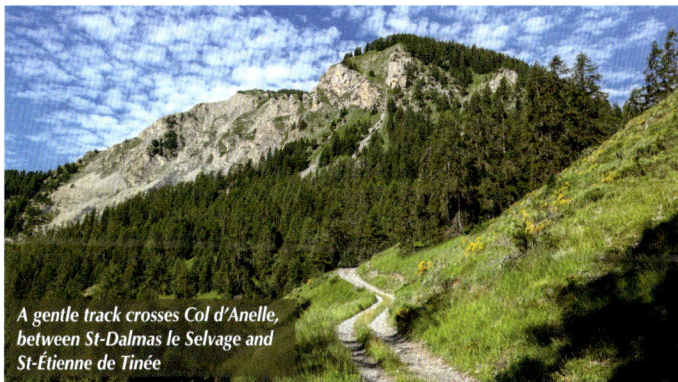

A gentle track crosses Col d'Anelle, between St-Dalmas le Selvage and St-Étienne de Tinée

Walkers approach tightly huddled houses in the little village of St-Dalmas le Selvage

crumbling ravines to land on dolomitic limestone in the **Vallon de la Combe** and exit the Parc National du Mercantour.

Feathery clumps of grass and thorny scrub lend a Mediterranean air to the valley. Continue along the path, which, further downhill, has been hacked from a limestone cliff. Wander down past little terraces and vegetable plots then walk straight down a road into the compact village of **St-Dalmas le Selvage**, at 1500m (gîtes d'étape, chambres d'hôte, shop, post office and restaurants; Lignes d'Azur bus to St-Étienne de Tinée and Auron: www.lignesdazur.com; tourist information office: tel 04 93 02 46 40 http://saintdalmaslesevage.fr). This is the highest village in the Alpes Maritimes, and 'selvage' is derived from 'sylvatica', meaning forested.

St-Dalmas le Selvage to Col d'Anelle   1hr, 3km, +270m -30m
Leave the village via the tourist office and notice the decorated front of the church. A grassy path winds down to a bridge over a river. Cross over and follow a track uphill, forking right at a junction. The track crosses a stream and is quite bendy as it climbs through larch forest. Watch out for a couple of marked paths that offer shortcuts then pass a couple of buildings before reaching **Col d'Anelle** at 1739m (possible water). There is a view ahead to Mont Mounier.

Col d'Anelle to St-Étienne de Tinée   1hr 45min, 4.5km, +15m -575m
Follow the track over the col, bending left as signposted for St-Étienne and descending slightly. Climb again to reach farm buildings, slightly higher than the col at 1745m. Turn right, down a path, passing a building, to descend beside terraced fields. There is a view from the bottom of La Vallée de la Tinée to the top of Mont Mounier. Continue down to a clear track at **Anelle**, at 1650m.

Turn right to follow the track downhill in sweeping zigzags, on a slope of sparse pines, broom and tall grass. Signposts indicate where a path shortcuts down to a lower stretch of the track, with St-Étienne clearly in view. Turn left, along the track, then turn right, down another path. Cross a track and continue down the path, accompanied by a gurgling water channel. Land on a dirt road and turn right to find another path, flanked by box trees, leading down past a couple of houses near **Ublan**.

Cross a road twice to avoid a bend then keep to the left of a house called Le Rocher to walk down a rough, boulder-paved path. Keep straight ahead at a junction then turn left, along a road, to reach a chapel. Turn right, along the road, then turn left, down Rue du Val Gelé. Turn right at a chapel and follow Rue Droite past an orchard. The street narrows as it runs close to the centre of **St-Étienne de Tinée**, at 1144m (all services; Lignes d'Azur bus to St-Dalmas le Selvage, Auron, St-Sauveur sur Tinée and Nice: www.lignesdazur.com; tourist information office: tel 04 93 02 46 40 https://saintetiennedetinee.fr). The town is full of four and five-storey buildings, with a landmark church steeple and several little chapels from the 15th–18th centuries.

St-Étienne de Tinée to Auron   2hr 45min, 5.5km, +565m -110m

Follow Rue Droite onwards through town and out into the country. It is signposted as the old road to Nice. Keep right at a junction beside a water trough. Walk down and then up a road then later, turn right, as signposted for Auron, up a path flanked by walls and trees. Turn right, up a track, to reach the main road then turn left to reach a roundabout at Chapelle St-Maur at 1200m (Lignes d'Azur bus to St-Dalmas le Selvage, Auron and Nice: www.lignesdazur.com).

Follow the main road uphill, as signposted for Auron, but only as far as can be seen from the roundabout. Step up to the right to follow a narrow path to a track. Turn left to climb steeply up the track, keeping right to climb even more steeply up a broad and stony forest path. Little wayside shrines are passed, and the path drifts to the left, across the forested slope. Climb steep zigzags on loose stones, then at a higher level, keep right at a path junction to reach a dusty dirt road at 1700m.

Turn left, along the dirt road, to quickly link with a tarmac road. This is the winding Chemin du Puy d'Auron, which can be followed all the way down to the tourist office near the centre of **Auron**, at 1602m (all services; Lignes d'Azur bus to St-Étienne de Tinée, St-Sauveur sur Tinée and Nice: www.lignesdazur.com; tourist information office: tel 04 93 23 02 66 https://ete.auron.com). This modern ski resort features a few old buildings and is also a popular family sport resort offering plenty of summer activities, particularly mountain biking.

STAGE 24
Auron to Refuge de Longon

Start	Auron
Finish	Refuge de Longon
Time	11hr 15min
Distance	27km
Total Ascent	1775m
Total Descent	1500m
Terrain	A forested climb and a grassy descent to Roya then a long climb up a rugged valley to cross the broad flanks of Mont Mounier. After crossing a valley, the route climbs through Les Portes de Longon.
Maps	3639 OT, 3640 OT and 3641 ET
Refreshments	Restaurants at Roya and Refuge de Longon.
Accommodation	*Gîte d'étape* at Roya. Refuge de Longon.

This is a long day's walk, and those who are unsure about their ability should adapt the schedule. Anyone who spent a night in St-Étienne de Tinée, for example, could spend the following night at Roya then enjoy an easier walk over Mont Mounier to the Refuge de Longon. Mont Mounier, which once bore an observatory on its summit, is a broad, exposed, stony mountain. It is the last big mountain on the GR5 and is often caught by the afternoon storms afflicting the Alpes-Maritimes.

Auron to Col du Blainon   2hr, 4km, +410m -0m

Leave Auron as signposted beside the tourist office. A huge, rubble embankment fills the valley, so follow its rim to join a road. Turn left, along the road, then turn left again to follow a dirt road up to a car park. Exit left and walk down past a restaurant. Turn right at the Blainon chairlift at **Ubac** to follow a track up beside a golf driving range. Turn left, up a path that climbs beneath the chairlift and leads into forest.

The path becomes convoluted but is clearly marked and gently graded. Avoid a path down to the left and keep climbing to pass a viewpoint on the **Belvédère des Chamois**, at 1810m. Climb to a broad track – a ski piste – and turn left up it, but quickly leave it, as marked, and climb roughly parallel to it, along a forest

A tiny belltower beside the ruined St-Sébastien, on the way down to the little village of Roya

path. Cross the piste at a higher level then climb until trees give way to the grassy **Col du Blainon**, at 2014m. Views stretch across the Vallée de Tinée to the high peaks of the Parc National du Mercantour, with Mont Mounier ahead.

Col du Blainon to Roya   1hr 30min, 4km, +40m -550m
Follow a narrow path down past a timber cabin then a stone cabin, then the ruined **St-Sébastien** and its little belltower. Pass several half-timber, half-stone buildings, including a few in ruins. Rose bushes, along with clumps of lavender,

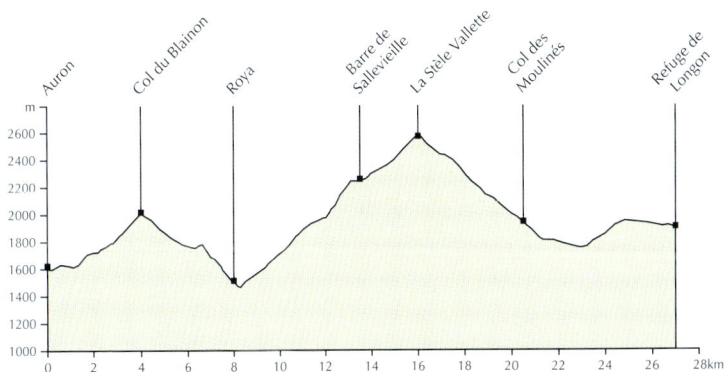

Auron
1602m

Cime du
Chavalet
2452m

Las
Donnas
2475m

Sommet du
Colombier
2180m

Clôt Giordan

Ubac

Belvédère
des Chamois
1810m

Col du Blainon
2014m

St-Sébastien

Roya
1500m

Barres de Roya

VALLON DE SALLEVIEILLE

Cime Nègre
2553m

Barre de
Sallevieille

Col de
Crousette
2480m

Mont Mounier
2817m

La Stèle Vallette
2587m

Mont
Démant
2473m

Col du
Refuge

Le Démant

Vallon de la
Gourgette
1800m

Vignols

Vacherie de
Roubion

Col des
Moulinés
1982m

Les Portes
de Longor

Montag
Haute
2341m

FRANCE

La Tinée

M2205

N

0   1   2
km

flank grassy terraces. Cross a bouldery stream-bed at **Clôt Giordan** and climb a little, then follow a path signposted for Roya. This later winds down a stony groove, with views of the village below. Watch for big, bright-green lizards in the undergrowth on the way down to a road. Don't follow the road but instead shortcut down a path and pass between buildings to reach a church in **Roya**, at 1500m (gîte d'étape, restaurant and bivouac).

Roya to Barre de Sallevieille   2hr 30min, 5.5km, +775m -40m

Keep to the right of the church to follow a rugged path downhill. Cross two footbridges over two rivers, at 1465m, entering the Parc National du Mercantour. Zigzag up a forested slope then climb at a gentler gradient as the trees thin out to offer fine valley views. Pass the **Barres de Roya**, where limestone cliffs in a gorge look like drystone walling. Continue up into a boulder-strewn part of the valley, cross a footbridge and continue climbing.

Follow the path carefully in the **Vallon de Sallevieille**, since it has been rerouted to run closer to the river and is marked with a line of upright stones. Zigzag uphill to outflank a long line of cliffs at **Barre de Sallevieille**, passing through a breach to find a gentle, grassy valley.

Barre de Sallevieille to La Stèle Vallette   1hr 15min, 2.5km, +350m -0m

Cross a narrow stream, and although there are plenty of cliffs in view, the path climbs grassy slopes and makes an easy traverse of boulder-scree to reach **Col de Crousette** at 2480m. Don't go down the other side of the col but instead follow a well-trodden, rough and stony path up across a scree slope. Turn left just before you reach a small, white, marble memorial known as **La Stèle Vallette**, at 2587m, on a mountain crest. Wide-ranging views stretch back to the Queyras and ahead across La Vallée de la Tinée

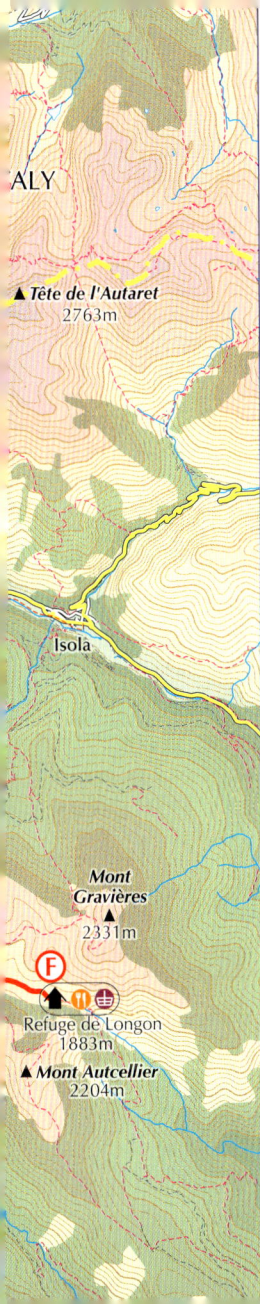

to the Franco-Italian border and to the distant Mediterranean. It is possible to make a bid for the 2817m summit of Mont Mounier but it adds another 2hr to what is already a long day.

La Stèle Vallette to Col des Moulinés   1hr 45min, 4.5km, +0m -610m

Walk a short way along the rocky crest before turning right, then turn sharply right to follow a path downhill. The line of the path is very clear across the rounded slopes of **Mont Démant**, crossing stony ground dotted with sparse clumps of grass and flowers, particularly blue gentians, to reach cairns and a signpost.

Branch left and note how the limestone bedrock is like paving underfoot. The path winds downhill in lazy loops to a gentle, grassy gap. There is a view from here of Mont Mounier and the awesome Barre Sud du Mounier. Descend to **Col du Refuge** and briefly leave the national park to pass below a stump of limestone, then re-enter the park on the grassy **Col des Moulinés** at 1982m. There is a view beyond the hamlet of Vignols to the 'hanging valley' of Les Portes de Longon.

Col des Moulinés to Refuge de Longon   2hr 15min, 6.5km, +200m -300m

Follow a path downhill across scree slopes, passing a few larches. Drop to the right, along a winding path, and cross **Le Démant** at 1810m. The path crosses another river nearby then climbs gently, across old grassy terraces. Pass above a long, low cattle shed, the **Vacherie de Roubion**, and pass below a series of intriguing rocky towers, where the dolomitic limestone weathers into dramatic landforms. First, cross a stream-bed and then a nearby stream in Vallon de la Gourgette, at 1800m. (The hamlet of **Vignols** is off route but has no services.)

Climb a zigzag path to cross scree slopes below a cliff. Climb closer to crumbling cliffs and cross a stream in a ravine to enter the hanging valley of **Les Portes de Longon**. A gentle track is followed but it peters out in a flat, grassy area overlooked by a chalet, around 1950m. Don't be drawn off course to the chalet but stay low and enjoy easy walking through the grassy valley. Pass a stone pillar and exit the Parc National du Mercantour. Continue onwards, and the path leads down to the isolated **Refuge de Longon** at 1883m (refuge, restaurant, small shop, dairy and cheese production).

STAGE 25
Refuge de Longon to St-Dalmas

Start	Refuge de Longon
Finish	St-Dalmas
Time	9hr 45min
Distance	24.5km
Total Ascent	1065m
Total Descent	1660m
Terrain	A long traverse of a deep, forested valley, following good paths and tracks from village to village.
Maps	3641 ET
Refreshments	Restaurants at St-Sauveur sur Tinée, Rimplas, La Bolline and St-Dalmas.
Accommodation	*Gîte d'étape* at Roure. Hotel, *gîte* and campsite at St-Sauveur sur Tinée. Hotel at Rimplas. Hotel and *chambres d'hôte* at La Bolline. *Chambres d'hôte* at La Roche. Hotel, *chambres d'hôte*, *gîtes d'étape* and campsite at St-Dalmas.

This whole day's walk involves crossing the deep and mostly forested Vallée de la Tinée. The initial descent uses a rugged mule path and a gentle forest track. The next part, from Roure to St-Sauveur sur Tinée, uses an old mule path pre-dating the long and looping vehicular road. The ascent from St-Sauveur to Rimplas follows a track that has been hacked from crumbling slate, then old paths and tracks continue from village to village to climb to St-Dalmas.

Refuge de Longon to Roure
3hr 15min, 9km, +45m -835m

Walk down through the valley from the refuge, passing the ruins of an old *vacherie* (cowshed) that was destroyed by an avalanche, to enter larch forest. A steep and winding descent leads to a footbridge below the fine waterfall at **Pissous**. The surrounding rock is sandstone and gritstone altered by metamorphism. Keep walking down through forest, keeping straight ahead at a path junction and later turning a prominent corner around **Crête Autcellier**.

Continue downhill and cross a footbridge over **Ruisseau de l'Arcane**, which runs through a ravine cut into soft sandstone. The path cuts across a forested

slope then passes grassy terraces dotted with old cabins, some in ruins, at **Rougios**, at 1467m. Turn right, as directed, at the last cabin and step up to a forest road. Turn left to follow it, with occasional views revealing the depth of La Vallée de la Tinée.

The forest road becomes a tarmac road at a small car park at **La Barre**, at 1373m, from where the Mediterranean can be seen in the distance. Step down to the left and follow a path parallel to the road, crossing blocks of purple slate. Later, cross the road near a bend. An optional detour to the right leads to the nearby **Arboretum Marcel Kroenlein**.

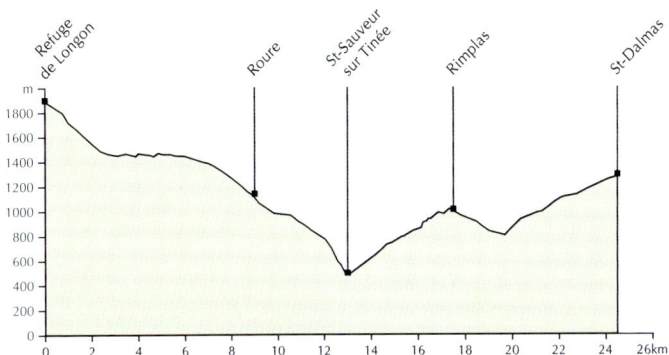

Continue along a rugged, stone-paved path, as marked. Pass a few houses, then the path cuts across the road twice to avoid bends. Keep to the left of a small football pitch (water) to walk down to a chapel. Turn left, down the road, past a house, then right to shortcut down to a lower bend. Drop straight down beside a church, keeping to its left-hand side, to reach the village of **Roure** at 1096m (gîte d'étape, apartment, chalet, dome tent; occasional bus to St-Sauveur sur Tinée).

Roure to St-Sauveur sur Tinée 1hr 30min, 4km, +0m -595m

Walk down steps from the church to reach the town hall (*mairie*). Walk past a wash-place and turn sharp right, down more steps, to pass a cog-wheel contraption that once operated a cable car connecting Roure with St-Sauveur. A stone-paved path leads down past the lowest houses, then a slate-strewn path continues down old terraces to reach a road. Turn right, down the road, to reach a sharp bend then drop straight down a path to zigzag past more terraces, landing on the road at a lower level.

Cross over and continue down the path, which becomes well wooded with oak, chestnut and the occasional fig tree. Zigzag downhill but watch for a signpost at a junction, and turn left to continue. Cross a concrete water conduit then cross the road again. Follow the path down to the road but step to the right to find its continuation. Wind down to cross the road yet again then walk down one last stretch of path to land on a road beside a graveyard in the Quartier St-Blaise. Walk straight ahead to cross a road bridge into **St-Sauveur sur Tinée**, at 496m (hotel, gîte d'étape, campsite, shop, restaurant, post office, ATM; Lignes d'Azur bus to St-Étienne de Tinée, Auron and Nice: www.lignesdazur.com).

St-Sauveur sur Tinée to Rimplas   2hr 30min, 4.5km, +525m -10m

Follow the main road straight through town. Immediately on leaving the town, climb a steep road on the left. The road turns sharply left, then shortly afterwards, a narrow, rugged path on the right climbs uphill. Pass a bend in the road and climb further, keeping left of **Chapelle St-Roch**. Climb above the chapel to follow a concrete track onwards, past grassy terraces, oaks and chestnut trees.

Wind uphill until the track ends then continue along a path rising gently across wooded slopes. Another broader track is reached, so keep climbing, enjoying valley views, but beware of the crumbling slate on the left, which has a habit of collapsing. The slate suddenly gives way to quartzite, followed by a series of limestone, sandstone and shale beds. The track gives way to a road as it enters the village of **Rimplas**, at 1016m (hotel and restaurant; Lignes d'Azur bus to La Bolline, La Roche and St-Dalmas: www.lignesdazur.com). This long-established fortified site was once known as Magdalena and is located on the Route du Sel, or Salt Route.

Rimplas to St-Dalmas   2hr 30min, 7km, +495m -220m

The GR5 passes the village by road, but it is better to walk through the narrow, stone-paved streets. Leave, via the road, to pass below a chapel, then go down steps on the right and continue straight ahead, down a stony path across a rocky slope covered in maquis. There is a fine view of the forested Vallon de Bramatam and the villages that will be passed later.

The path becomes a track, leading to a bend on another track. Head downhill and step to the left before you reach another bend, to follow a narrow path. Descend across a scrubby slope, passing a couple of houses before crossing a narrow stone bridge in a wooded valley. Reach a road at a hairpin bend and walk downhill. Leave the road at the next bend, stepping off to the right of a private track.

A narrow path runs along a terrace, then a left turn along another path leads into a wooded valley. Cross a narrow, stone bridge and climb to a junction. Turn left, up an old, cobbled track, passing gnarled chestnuts and hazels in dense woods. The track climbs past orchards, reaching a road end near large buildings.

A series of easy roads, tracks and paths leads from village to village from Rimplas to St-Dalmas

Climb a grassy track to reach a road junction near a church at **La Bolline**, at 995m (hotel, chambres d'hôte, shop, restaurants; Lignes d'Azur bus to La Roche and St-Dalmas: www.lignesdazur.com).

Climb the steepest road from the junction, Route des Gailles, and turn right at a crossroads. Turn left to reach the main road again at the top of another village, **La Roche**, at 1120m (Lignes d'Azur bus to St-Dalmas: www.lignesdazur.com). Turn right, along the main road, then quickly right again, down a minor road, Chemin du Savelet. Later, turn left and walk up another quiet road to cross the main road twice, as signposted, cutting out lengthy bends. When the main road is reached again via a track, turn right to follow it past a campsite to reach **St-Dalmas**, at 1290m (chambres d'hôte, gîte d'étape, campsite, restaurants, shop, museum; Lignes d'Azur bus to Nice: www.lignesdazur.com).

There is an option at St-Dalmas to switch from the GR5 to the GR52, to finish at Garavan/Menton instead of Nice. For full details, see Section 6.

SECTION 6:
ST-DALMAS TO NICE OR
GARAVAN/MENTON

*The GR52 mostly runs through forest as it crosses Col de
Salèse on the way to Le Boréon (GR52 Stage 1)*

Towards the end of this prolonged Alpine trek, one last major decision has to be made. The main GR5 traverses the last few rugged hills to reach the big, brash, bustling city of Nice. Alternatively, the adventure can be extended by switching to the longer, tougher and more mountainous GR52 through the Parc National du Mercantour. Put simply, the trek can finish with three relatively easy days of walking, or six days of harder walking, including some particularly tough mountainsides.

The **GR5 main route** leaves St-Dalmas to follow a long, rocky, forested, arid mountain ridge to Utelle (Stage 26). If this seems daunting, there is an option to break halfway at Les Granges de la Brasque. Beyond Utelle, a final mountain mule path is followed by the crossing of the deep and dramatic Gorges de la Vésubie. Climbing from the gorge, only a few hills are passed on the way from Levens to Aspremont (Stage 27).

Beyond Aspremont, only a final hill remains before the GR5 leads through the streets of Nice, and in high summer the city can feel like a furnace (Stage 28). The end of the GR5 is reached on the Promenade des Anglais, beside the Mediterranean Sea. While some trekkers will be ready to go home, others will be keen to spend time exploring the city, which is a place of great architecture, culture and history. It's worth climbing onto the Colline du Château to look back towards the Alps, remembering the long and arduous trek that brought you to this place.

The **GR52 Grande Traversée du Mercantour** offers a particularly rugged, exciting and scenic alternative to the GR5. After leaving St-Dalmas and climbing to Col du Barn (GR52 Stage 1), it becomes clear that the mountains ahead are formidable, and indeed, some particularly steep and rocky slopes might seem tougher than any experienced on the main

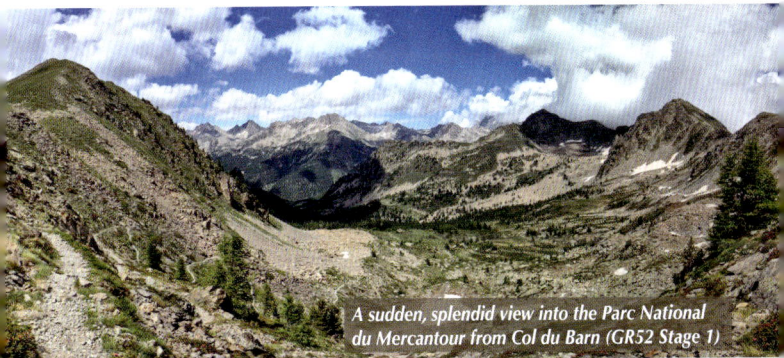

A sudden, splendid view into the Parc National du Mercantour from Col du Barn (GR52 Stage 1)

ITALY

N

0   5   10
km

Col du Barn

Le Boréon

Col de Fenestre

GR52 2

St-Sauveur sur Tinée

GR52 1

GR52 3   Refuge de Nice

S   St-Martin-Vésubie

26

St-Dalmas

GR52 4   Refuge des Merveilles

FRANCE

Camp d'Argent

GR52 5

Pointe de Ventabren

▲ *Le Brec d'Utelle*

Utelle   27

Levens

Sospel

GR52 6

ITALY

Le Grand Mont
▲

28   Aspremont

F

Garavan/ Menton

Ventim

MONACO

F

NICE

Mediterranean Sea

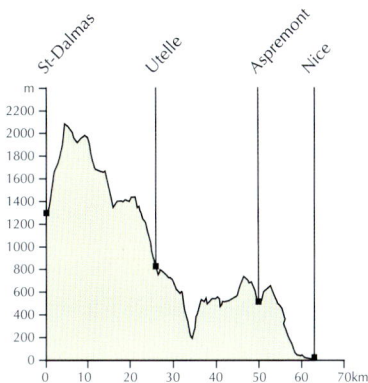

GR5 trail. After leaving the hamlet of Le Boréon (GR52 Stage 2), most services in the mountains revolve around isolated refuges, which can become very busy. Wildlife abounds, and bouquetin and chamois will often tolerate close approaches. There are wolves in the area too, although these are seldom seen, being extremely shy of human contact after centuries of persecution.

One of the most remarkable places along the GR52 is La Vallée des Merveilles (GR52 Stage 3), where Bronze Age artists hammered thousands of rock carvings, or petroglyphs, onto glacially polished rock faces. There used to be a very long stage from La Vallée des Merveilles to Sospel, but the route was later diverted to take advantage of accommodation at Camp d'Argent (GR52

Stages 4 & 5). Military sites can be studied on this part of the trail.

Sospel is the only town on the trail, and it has a long history of serving travellers from the time when salt was transported along the Route du Sel, far into the Alps. After passing through the town, one final mountain crest is traversed before a steep and stony descent to the twin towns of Garavan and Menton (GR52 Stage 6). The trail ends on the shore of the Mediterranean, on a tiny scrap of beach close to the port. There are excellent transport options for those trekkers who wish to go straight home, but there are also many historical sites worth exploring, and Nice is also within easy reach if its history and culture is also going to be appreciated.

Stage	Place	Altitude	Walking time	Distance
26	**St-Dalmas**	**1290m**	**0hr 00min**	**0km**
26	Les Granges de la Brasque	1680m	4hr 30min	12km
26	**Utelle**	**821m**	**5hr 30min**	**14km**
27	Gorges de la Vésubie	180m	3hr 15min	8.5km
27	Levens	550m	1hr 45min	3.5km
27	Les Grands Prés	540m	0hr 30min	2km
27	Ste-Claire	520m	1hr 00min	3km
27	**Aspremont**	**500m**	**2hr 15min**	**7km**
28	Aire St-Michel	316m	2hr 00min	6.5km
28	Place Alexandre Médicin	47m	1hr 00min	3km
28	**Nice**	**0m**	**1hr 15min**	**4km**

GR52

Stage	Place	Altitude	Walking time	Distance
1	**St-Dalmas**	**1290m**	**0hr 00min**	**0km**
1	**Le Boréon**	**1500m**	**9hr 15min**	**21km**
2	Restaurant L'Alpage	1620m	1hr 00min	2.5km
2	Refuge de la Cougourde	2100m	1hr 30min	4km
2	La Madone de Fenestre	1903m	3hr 30min	6km
2	**Refuge de Nice**	**2232m**	**5hr 00min**	**6km**
3	**Refuge des Merveilles**	**2130m**	**6hr 00min**	**9.5km**
4	**Camp d'Argent**	**1750m**	**6hr 00min**	**13km**
5	**Sospel**	**350m**	**9hr 00min**	**22km**
6	*La Ferme St-Bernard*	*820m*	*4hr 30min, 9.5km to turn off, +20min off main route*	
6	**Garavan/Menton**	**0m**	**5hr 15min**	**8km**

♠ refuge/hut/gîte d'étape ◯ hotel ◯ home stay ⌂ unmanned hut/bothy
🌲 camping ✳ bivouac 🍴 restaurant/refreshments 🏪 shop/groceries
🏧 ATM ℹ TIC 🚉 train 🚌 bus 🚠 lift/cable car

Facilities								
refuge	hotel	camping	restaurant	shop				bus
refuge		bivouac	restaurant					
refuge	hotel		restaurant	shop				
								bus
	hotel		restaurant	shop		TIC		bus
	hotel		restaurant					bus
								bus
	home stay		restaurant	shop				bus
	hotel		restaurant					bus
			restaurant	shop				bus
	hotel		restaurant	shop	ATM	TIC	train	bus

Facilities								
refuge	hotel	camping	restaurant	shop				bus
refuge	hotel	bivouac	restaurant					bus
			restaurant					
refuge			restaurant					
refuge			restaurant					bus
refuge			restaurant					
refuge		bivouac	restaurant					
refuge	hotel	camping	restaurant					
	hotel		restaurant	shop		TIC	train	bus
refuge		camping	restaurant					
	hotel		restaurant	shop	ATM	TIC	train	bus

257

GR5 MAIN ROUTE

STAGE 26
St-Dalmas to Utelle

Start	St-Dalmas
Finish	Utelle
Time	10hr
Distance	26km
Total Ascent	1160m
Total Descent	1630m
Terrain	Climb forested and open mountainsides, using paths, tracks and later, roads. Rugged paths towards the end of the stage are usually well graded, even if they cross steep and rocky slopes.
Maps	3641 ET
Refreshments	Meals at Les Granges de la Brasque. Restaurant at Utelle.
Accommodation	Cabins and bivouac at Les Granges de la Brasque. *Gîte d'étape* and farm *auberge* at Utelle.

This is a long day's walk – although it looks much longer on maps – and the only way to break the distance is to stay in cabins at Les Granges de la Brasque, close to the halfway point. Most of the climbing comes early in the stage, and most of the paths and tracks are fairly easy. Even if the mountainsides are steep and rugged, the paths across their flanks have been well engineered and are easy to follow. The hilltop village of Utelle remains hidden until the final descent.

St-Dalmas to Col des Deux Caïres   2hr, 4km, +630m -5m

Leave St-Dalmas by walking up the main road, branching right opposite the church, then turn right, along Rue de la Madone. Turn left to find signposts pointing along the Impasse des Naïges. Climb a steep and stony track into forest to reach a track junction. Take a path climbing straight up a fairly open slope then head into dense forest, where larches hang heavy with skeins of lichen. Climb through another clearing and turn right at a signposted path junction. Pass a

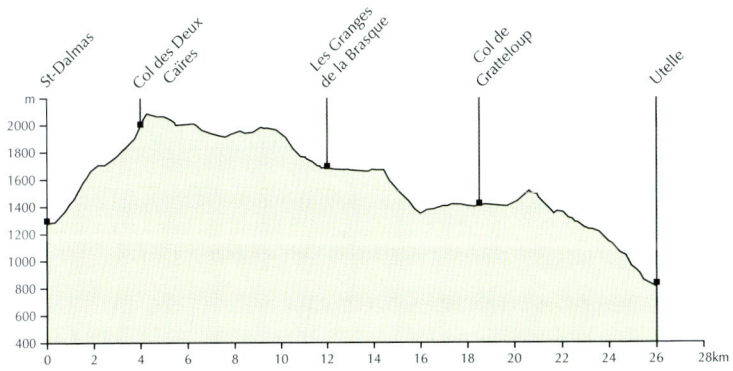

Baus de la Frema
2246m

La Roche

St-Dalmas
1290m

St-Martin-Vésubie

Col du Varaire
1710m

Mont Viroulet
1860m

Col des Deux-Caires
1921m

Le Caire Gros
2087m

Tête de Clans
2081m

Mont Chalancha
2102m

La Vésubie

N

0   1   2
km

Pointe de Sérenton
1836m

Le Pertus
1968m

Baisse de la Combe
1910m

Col de la Trous
1982m

Mont Tournairet
2018m

Les Granges de la Brasque
1680m

Tete d'Albéras
1474m

map continues on page 260

Tête d'Antripas
1550m

le Monal

Col d'Andrion
1690m

St-Dalmas

Col des Deux Caires

Les Granges de la Brasque

Col de Gratteloup

Utelle

m
2000
1800
1600
1400
1200
1000
800
600
400

0   2   4   6   8   10   12   14   16   18   20   22   24   26   28km

ruined cabin and later, drop a little to the forested **Col du Varaire** at 1710m. Keep right to follow the route as marked and signposted, climbing along a winding path in dense forest, to emerge on the open **Col des Deux Caïres** at 1921m.

Col des Deux Caïres to Les Granges de la Brasque 2hr 30min, 8km, +285m -520m
Turn left, as signposted, and climb steeply to the summit of **Le Caïre Gros**, at 2087m, from where the view stretches to the suburbs of Nice, and the

Mediterranean. Follow the crest of the mountain over the gentle summit of **Tête de Clans**, at 2081m. Further along the crest, zigzag downhill and traverse the sparsely forested slopes of **Mont Chalancha**. The well-engineered path turns a corner and drops to a col at **Le Pertus**, at 1968m, which is dominated by a huge stump of limestone. Follow the path around the next slope and head down to a lower col at **Baisse de la Combe**, at 1910m.

The path climbs across a forested slope then runs along a crest. Note a transition from limestone to sandstone underfoot, then the path drops downhill a little. Turn left at a signposted junction and zigzag uphill, crossing a shoulder on **Mont Tournairet** to reach **Col de la Trous** at 1982m. Immediately after crossing the col, turn left, down a grassy track, and look out for a brief view of the suburbs of Nice, and the Mediterranean.

Branch right, as marked, to follow a path down to a bend in a track. Walk down the track but watch for a right turn down a path to shortcut many bends. Follow the track again but make a couple more minor shortcuts. Pass a barrier and join a tarmac road near a ruined chapel. Turn right to pass a series of old barracks at **Les Granges de la Brasque**, at 1680m (cabins, bivouac and meals; water further along the road).

Les Granges de la Brasque to Col de Gratteloup   2hr 30min, 6.5km, +115m -385m

The road climbs gently to **Col d'Andrion**, at 1690m. On reaching a junction of the road and a track, step down to the right. A winding path runs down a forested slope to reach a road. Turn right, along the road, but watch for a path down to the left; this leads down to a road bend. Walk down the road but watch for another path leading down to a lower road bend. Again, walk down the road and watch for a path on the left, this time winding down to a junction of tracks on **Col des Fournés** at 1356m.

Don't follow any of the tracks but instead step straight up onto a path marked and signposted as the GR5. This becomes an old forest track, which climbs gently and reverts to a path. Emerge on a stony slope covered in juniper, box and lavender to see the dome of Le Brec d'Utelle ahead. Enter forest again and roughly contour across the gentle **Col de Gratteloup**, at 1412m.

Col de Gratteloup to Utelle   3hr, 7.5km, +130m -720m

Continue along the forest path to emerge on a grassy slope at **Les Pras**. Branch right at a vague, grassy path junction, as signposted for Utelle. Head back into forest with a juniper and box understorey then climb steeply, up grassy terraces reverting to forest. Cut across a steep and rocky slope to reach a rocky col at **Le Petit Brec**.

The former fortified village of Utelle sits on a hilltop high above the Gorges de la Vésubie

The path winds steeply uphill, like stone steps, then climbs a well-built ramp up a cliff face. Cross the rocky gap of Brèche du Brec, at 1520m, close to the summit of **Le Brec d'Utelle**. There is a view back to Mont Mounier and ahead to the suburbs of Nice, and the Mediterranean. Turn a corner on bare limestone and zigzag down a stony path into a forest to reach a col at 1370m. Keep right to pass through the forest, briefly crossing a slope with open views.

Emerge on a well-defined crest and make a sharp left turn at a path junction. Descend across a steep and rugged slope, sometimes cutting across cliffs. A couple of narrow stretches, formerly protected by chains, have footbridges to carry the path onwards. Despite the steepness of the slope, the path heads gently and easily to **Col du Castel Ginesté** at 1220m. There is a view ahead to La Madone d'Utelle.

Look back to Le Castel Ginesté on the descent, which is surrounded by tiered cliffs. The path becomes more rugged underfoot, passing through mixed woods on a steep and rocky slope. There are glimpses of Utelle when the path turns prominent corners. Later, the village is seen to much better effect, huddled on its hilltop, as the path zigzags down crumbling layers of rock, under sparse pines. A signposted path junction is reached, where turning right leads up to La Madone d'Utelle, so turn left to walk down a concrete road then cross over a tarmac road to the left of a restaurant. The road leads straight into the centre of **Utelle**, at 821m (gîte d'étape, farm auberge, restaurant, shop and post office). The close-knit hilltop village was fortified against Saracen raiders.

Start	Utelle
Finish	Aspremont
Time	8hr 45min
Distance	24km
Total Ascent	870m
Total Descent	1190m
Terrain	Rugged paths traverse wooded and rocky slopes. A deep valley is crossed from village to village, as the surrounding hills decrease in height.
Maps	3741 ET and 3742 OT
Refreshments	Restaurants at Levens, Les Grands Prés and Aspremont.
Accommodation	Hotels near Levens and at Les Grands Prés and Airbnb at Aspremont.

The route from Utelle follows a partly paved path across limestone slopes and cliffs, passing areas of oaks and pines with bushy juniper, box and aromatic shrubs. After passing Cros d'Utelle and dropping into the Gorges de la Vésubie, one of the lowest points reached on the GR5, a steep climb leads to the fortified hilltop village of Levens and later, to the fortified hilltop village of Aspremont.

Utelle to Cros d'Utelle   3hr, 7.5km, +115m -600m

Leave the central Place de la Republique in Utelle, following Rue Emile Passeroni, which ends with a flight of steps down to a footbridge. The path is narrow as it climbs then it enjoys views into a deep valley. Rough-paved surfaces and steps lead gently down across a steep, limestone slope dotted with box, juniper and evergreen oaks. Cross a small, stone bridge in **Vallon d'Aclap**, passing through woods, where old terraces are full of oaks and chestnut trees. The path climbs a little then descends to **Chapelle St-Antoine**, at 673m. Dating from 1686, the chapel is open and offers shelter.

Follow a terrace through an oak wood then zigzag down around **Vallon de la Rosièra**, passing pines, evergreen oaks, junipers, broom and other scrub. The path contours across a cliff, where a dozen metal steps have been fixed, then descends in zigzags. There are always fine valley views, although the surroundings become more wooded. Fork left, as signposted, down a stony path, then walk along an olive terrace and pass to the left of a chapel to enter the upper part of the village of **Cros d'Utelle**, at 330m (water).

Cros d'Utelle to Levens

2hr, 4.5km, +360m -150m

Go underneath part of a house called L'Auberge. Walk down steps and watch for markers to avoid a long and bendy road. Cross the road to continue downhill as the path gets rougher near the bottom. Reach a junction with a main road, deep in the **Gorges de la Vésubie** (Lignes d'Azur bus to Nice: www.lignesdazur.com).

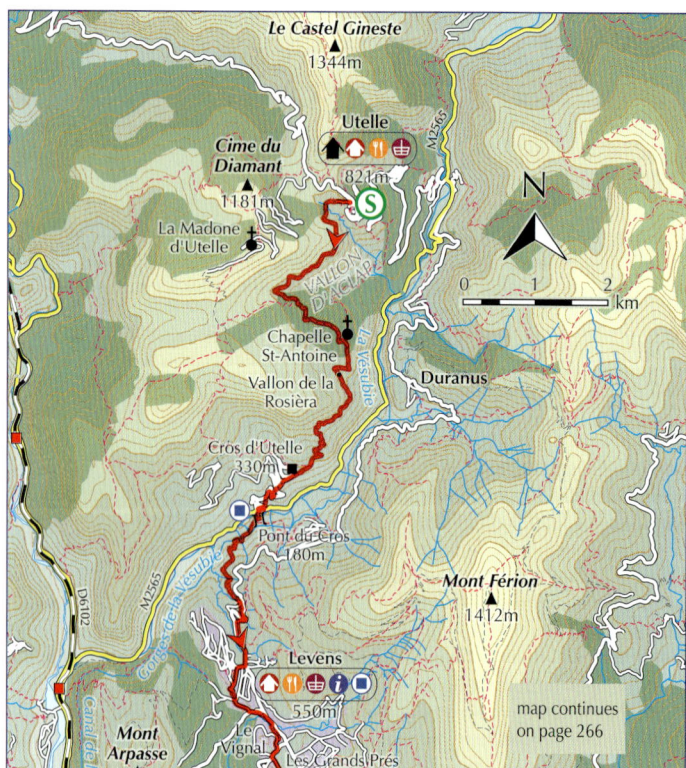

map continues on page 266

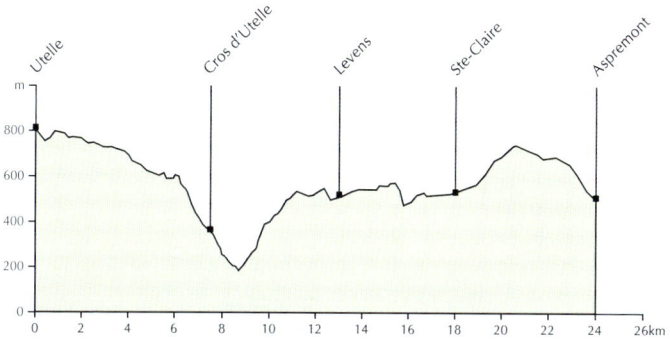

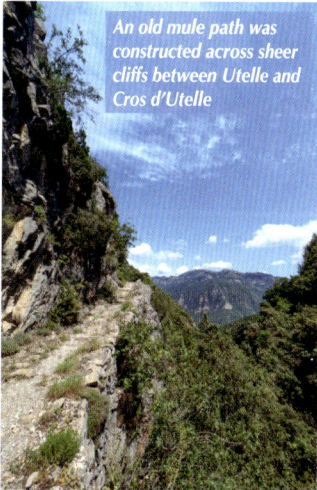

An old mule path was constructed across sheer cliffs between Utelle and Cros d'Utelle

Walk down from the main road to cross the graceful stone arch of **Pont du Cros** at 180m.

Climb a winding path and cross the Canal de la Vésubie where it runs through a tunnel. Zigzag uphill, among pines, junipers, box trees and guelder rose. Follow a concrete road uphill a little but leave it using a path on the left to reach a tarmac road. Cross over and follow a broken, concrete track up to a house. Keep left to walk along a terrace, passing above a small quarry, then follow a road to a junction in the lower part of the village of **Levens**, at 550m (nearby supermarket; hotels off route in the higher part of the village; Lignes d'Azur bus to Nice: www.lignesdazur.com).

Levens to Ste-Claire

1hr 30min, 5km, +160m -190m

Turn right, up Avenue Maréchal Foch, then fork left to walk up a road flanked by 'no entry' signs, passing close to the higher part of the village (shop and restaurants; tourist information office: tel 09 62 66 85 84 https://levens.fr). Turn left, down Chemin des Valettes, a road that becomes a zigzag stone-paved track, with olive millstones at the bottom. Go straight along Avenue Charles David, as

265

signposted for La Roquette. Turn left at the end and walk to a road bend behind an Aldi supermarket.

Follow a path on the right, which leads up to a main road. Turn right to follow the road between tall houses then drop down a concrete track on the right. Cross an old, stone bridge and turn left to follow a stony path uphill to **Le Vignal**. Turn left, along Chemin du Vignal, then right, along Route de St-Blaise, to walk beside the wide, grassy meadow of **Les Grands Prés** (hotels, restaurants and water; Lignes d'Azur bus to Nice: www.lignesdazur.com).

Towards the end of the meadow, watch for a gap on the right, beside house number 684. Follow a path up a slope bearing a few pines then turn left to cross a shoulder covered in oaks. Take care to follow the marked route, straight past old terraces, as there are other paths. Cross a gentle gap covered in pines at 584m, from where there is a view of the Mediterranean. Walk down past a stone ruin to

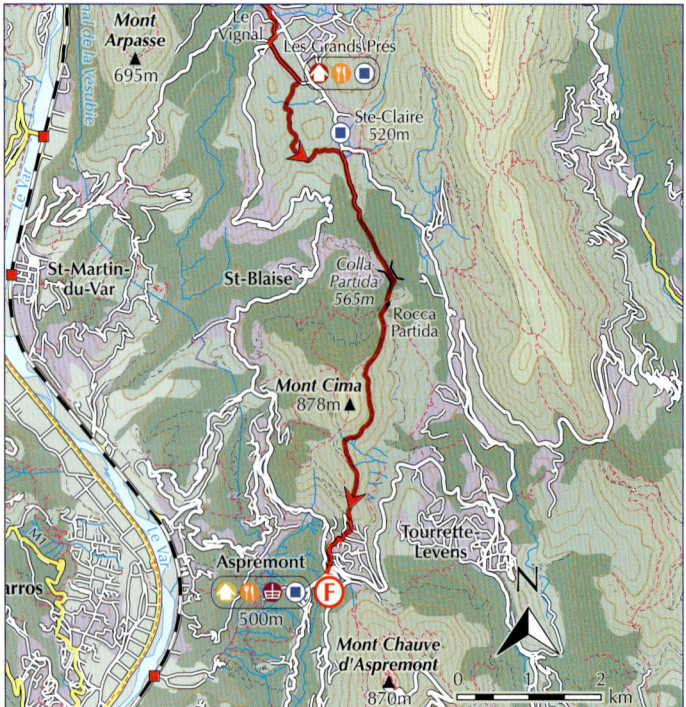

reach a path junction. Turn left and rise across a slope of pines, then walk down steps to reach a road beside the village of **Ste-Claire**, at 520m (Lignes d'Azur bus to Nice: www.lignesdazur.com).

Ste-Claire to Aspremont   2hr 15min, 7km, +235m -250m

Turn right to walk away from the village, keeping straight ahead at a road junction. The road rises, bends and falls gently, on a slope of oaks. Turn left, up a forest track, the Piste de Rocca Partida. Pass evergreen oaks and a few pines to reach a signpost on **Colla Partida** at 565m.

Turn right, along a path that heads into trees, taking care passing the split cliff of Rocca Partida, where the boulder conglomerate is unstable. If you are worried, stay on the forest track, since the path and the track meet at a complex junction on a gap at 609m. Climb as signposted, straight up a crest of conglomerate bearing pine trees. Cross a slight hump to reach a path junction at 708m, where the GR5 heads left. (Mont Cima is signposted to the right, where an optional detour offers fine views from the 878m summit.)

The path contours easily across slopes of pine and broom, with fine valley views. Turn left, along a battered road, the Piste du Mont Cima, to pass a barrier. Turn left, down a track, and quickly step up to the right. Follow a limestone path down past broom, juniper and evergreen oaks, with Aspremont in view below. Turn left a short way down a road then turn right, down steps, to another road, Route de la Cima. Walk down to a viewpoint at Place des Salettes. Turn right, down Montée du Commandant Gérome, passing a barrier at the bottom, then walk down Avenue Caravadossi into the village of **Aspremont**, at 500m (shop and restaurants; no accommodation apart from an Airbnb; Lignes d'Azur bus to nearby Nice: www.lignesdazur.com).

ASPREMONT

Around the year 900, many people took to the hills to avoid Saracen raiding parties along the coast. Aspremont, one of several easily defended sites, was known from 1062. Ludovic Macquesan fortified Aspremont in 1432 but Napoleon I burnt the defences in 1810. The Place du Château can be visited in the highest part of the village.

STAGE 28
Aspremont to Nice

Start	Aspremont
Finish	Nice
Time	4hr 15min
Distance	13.5km
Total Ascent	220m
Total Descent	720m
Terrain	A path crosses a final hill, then simple road-walking leads all the way through the city of Nice to finish on the shore of the Mediterranean.
Maps	3742 OT
Refreshments	Plenty of choice in Nice.
Accommodation	Plenty of choice in Nice.

This is an easy day but it can feel very hot after you've spent so long among high mountains. The arid slopes of Mont Chauve d'Aspremont are followed by a gradual descent. The city of Nice is full of attractions and distractions and is well worth exploring in detail. The GR5 is marked all the way through the city but it is necessary to keep your eyes open for waymarking. The long trail ends at a huge monument beside the Mediterranean.

Aspremont to Aire St-Michel   2hr, 6.5km, +210m -395m

Leave Aspremont by walking a short way down a road from a car park, as sign-posted for Nice. Steps down to the right reveal Chemin de la Vallière, which is a path that runs parallel to the road, joining it again on a bend. Walk up Chemin du Campoun, a narrow road climbing past a school. Turn right, as signposted for the GR5. Walk up a path on a slope of sparse pines. The way is stony as it climbs a slope covered in broom, passing a ruin at **Fondalin**. Roughly contour across the slopes of **Mont Chauve d'Aspremont**, reaching a wide track on a gentle gap at **Les Morgues**, at 670m.

The wide track ends abruptly, and a pleasant path runs easily along the broom-covered flanks of Crête de Graus, descending gently and passing beneath a pylon line to reach a gap at 499m. Cistus and broom grow on broken limestone,

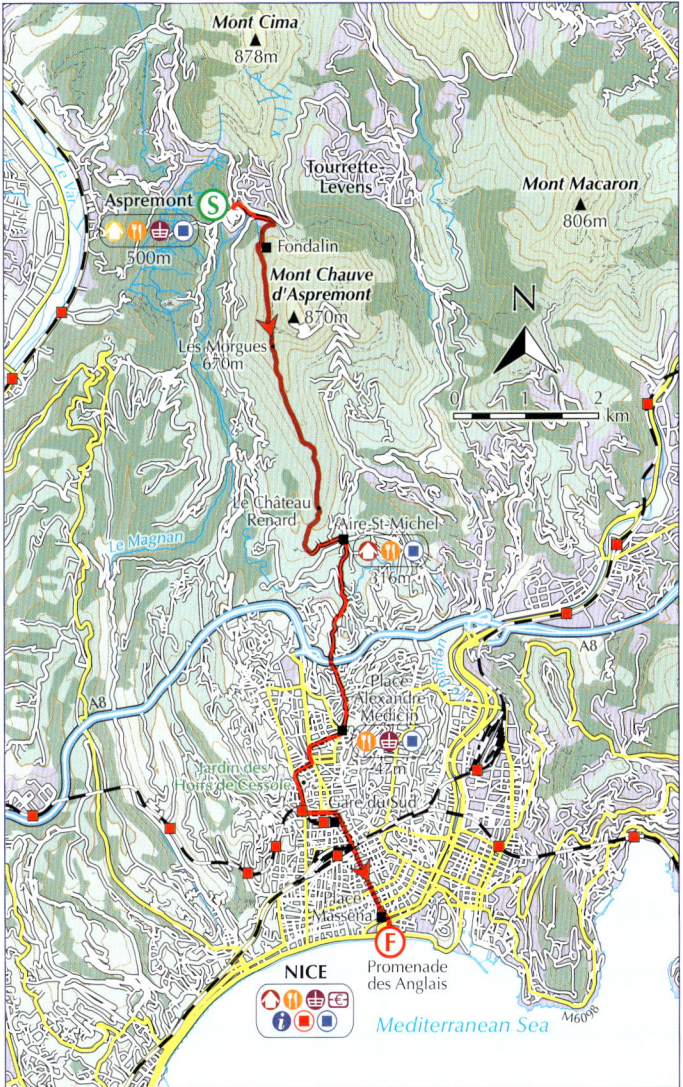

Mont Cima
878m

Tourrette-
Levens

Mont Macaron
806m

Aspremont
500m

Fondalin

Mont Chauve
d'Aspremont
870m

Les Morgues
670m

N

0   1   2
km

Le Château
Renard

Le Magnan

Aire-St-Michel
316m

A8

Place
Alexandre
Médicin
4 m

Jardin des
Hoirs de Cessole

Gare du Sud

Place
Masséna

NICE

Promenade
des Anglais

M6096

Mediterranean Sea

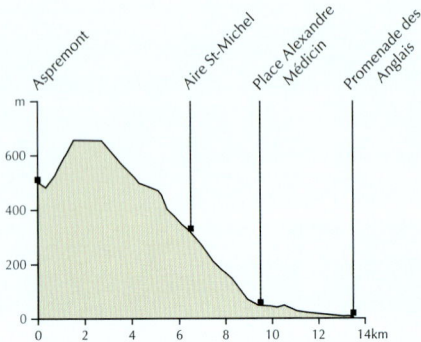

and the path passes another pylon line. A rough and rocky stretch passes the old stone ruin of **Le Château Renard** among deciduous and evergreen oaks.

Follow the path down to yet another pylon line and turn right, then later, turn left at a path junction. Walk down through scrub and pass evergreen oaks and a ruined building. The path continues downhill, turning right at a junction, leading to steps (water) and a road. Walk down the road to reach a mini-roundabout at **Aire St-Michel**, at 316m (hotel, restaurants, water; Lignes d'Azur bus into Nice: www.lignesdazur.com).

Aire St-Michel to Place Alexandre Médicin   1hr, 3km, +0m -265m
Walk straight down Vieux Chemin de Gairaut and turn left at a school at the bottom. Pass the entrance to the Domaine de Châteauneuf then cross the road and walk down steps and along a narrow lane to reach a road junction (restaurants; bus into Nice). Continue down Vieux Chemin de Gairaut and cross a bridge over the **A8** motorway, which slices through the Collines Niçoises. Pass a school and walk straight down across a busy road. Keep ahead at another junction with a busy road to follow Avenue Henry Dunant to **Place Alexandre Médicin** at 47m (shops, bars, restaurants; bus into Nice). This used to be the 'official' end of the GR5, commemorated by a long-vanished plaque on a wall.

Place Alexandre Médicin to Promenade des Anglais   1hr 15min, 4km, +10m -60m
Walk through the leafy Place Alexandre Médicin to reach a pharmacy and continue along Rue Paul Bourdin. At the end of the road, cross Boulevard Gorbella at the Gorbella tram stop and turn left to follow the road. The tramway was opened in 2007 at huge expense. Pass through the leafy Square Roger Boyer and turn right at a taxi stand, along Avenue Castellane. Turn left at the end of the road to follow

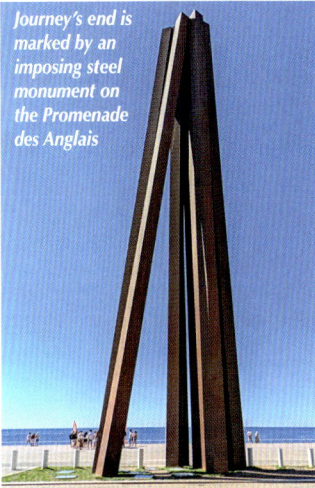

Journey's end is marked by an imposing steel monument on the Promenade des Anglais

the Boulevard de Cessole down past the **Jardin des Hoirs de Cessole**.

Turn left, along Boulevard Joseph Garnier, and follow it to the Place du Général de Gaulle. Turn right to pass the monumental **Gare du Sud**. Keep to the right-hand side of Avenue Jean Médicin to reach the spacious Place Masséna and its splendid ornamental fountain. Pass to the left of the fountain to walk along one final short street then walk through a small park to reach the **Promenade des Anglais**. The tall monument was inspired by the seven valleys that converge on the city of Nice. Dip your feet in the Mediterranean and you can declare your trek along the GR5 well and truly complete. Congratulations!

NICE

Nice (or 'Nissa' in the local dialect) is the fifth largest city in France, so no justice can be done to it in such limited space. The name derives from 'Nikaia', which was a Phocian/Greek trading post in the 3rd century BC. Start your explorations where the city was founded, on the **Colline du Château**. Celtic Ligurians occupied and fortified the hill, and their settlement was Romanised in early Christian times. A medieval town crowned the hill, where the ruins of the 11th-century **Cathedral de Ste-Marie** can be inspected. Nice was once under the authority of Provence but from 1388, it came under the authority of Savoie. It was a stoutly defended citadel in the 16th century, with a rampart protecting the lower part of town, now known as **Vieux-Nice**. Louis XIV had the defences dismantled in 1706, following the French occupation of the city during the War of the Spanish Succession. The hill was abandoned and used as a cemetery from 1783, then later converted into a park.

The Colline du Château and Vieux-Nice are flanked to the east by a bustling port, referred to as **Le Port**, from where ferries sail to Corsica. To the west, the new city sprawl is referred to as **Nice-Ville**, which contains the bulk of the services and facilities – easily the fullest range on the whole GR5.

The main bus station, or *gare routière*, is at Vauban, while the *gare SNCF*, or railway station, is centrally located in Nice-Ville. The tourist information office is next to the *gare SNCF*: tel 04 92 14 46 14 www.explore nicecotedazur.com.

Getting away from Nice

Anyone who has trekked across the Alps will have no problem with flat city pavements. The railway station, or *gare SNCF*, and bus station, or *gare routière*, are only a few minutes' walk from the Promenade des Anglais, and even the Aéroport Nice Côte d'Azur is little more than an hour or so on foot along the promenade, if you want to save the bus fare!

Local bus Lignes d'Azur (www.lignesdazur.com) operates bus services to and from the *gare SNCF* and *gare routière*, but few operate to both, so the easiest method is to change at the intermediate Station Jean-Claude Bermond. To reach the airport, use either the number 98 bus (every 20 minutes from the *gare SNCF*) or the number 99 bus (every 30 minutes from the *gare routière*). The best way to deal with bus travel is to buy a day pass, which offers cheap and unlimited transport on all Ligne d'Azur buses and the city tram.

Long-distance bus Flixbus (www.flixbus.com) offers services from Nice to London, with a couple of changes along the way, as well as serving other destinations all over Europe. Coaches operate to and from the *gare routière* at Vauban.

Train Check out timetables for the French railway system at www.sncf-connect.com or on the SNCF app. Services offer links between Nice and Geneva via Grenoble.

Air The Aéroport Nice Côte d'Azur has plenty of flights to and from Britain, as well as other destinations. Budget flights are available with operators such as Easyjet (www.easyjet.com) and Jet2.com (www.jet2.com). Air France (www.airfrance.com), the national carrier, offers scheduled flights, as do many other carriers. For airport information, see www.nice.aeroport.fr.

Ferry In the summer months, a leisurely departure by ferry is possible. Services operate to Monaco, for onward connections along the Rivièra. Adventurous walkers who wish to extend their experience beyond the GR5 can catch a ferry from Nice to Corsica and walk the celebrated GR20 through the mountains of Corsica! (See *Trekking the GR20 Corsica* by Paddy Dillon, Cicerone Press.)

GR52 ROUTE TO GARAVAN/MENTON

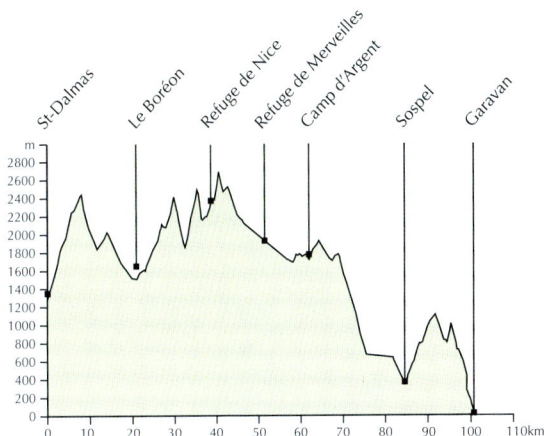

GR52 STAGE 1
St-Dalmas to Le Boréon

Start	St-Dalmas
Finish	Le Boréon
Time	9hr 15min
Distance	21km
Total Ascent	1365m
Total Descent	1150m
Terrain	A forested ascent leads to rugged slopes and a high col. A rough descent follows, then easier paths and tracks through forested valleys, ending with a long forest-road-walk.
Maps	3641 ET and 3741 OT
Refreshments	Roadside snack van before Col de Veillos. Restaurants at Le Boréon.
Accommodation	Hotel, *gîte d'étape* and bivouac at Le Boréon.

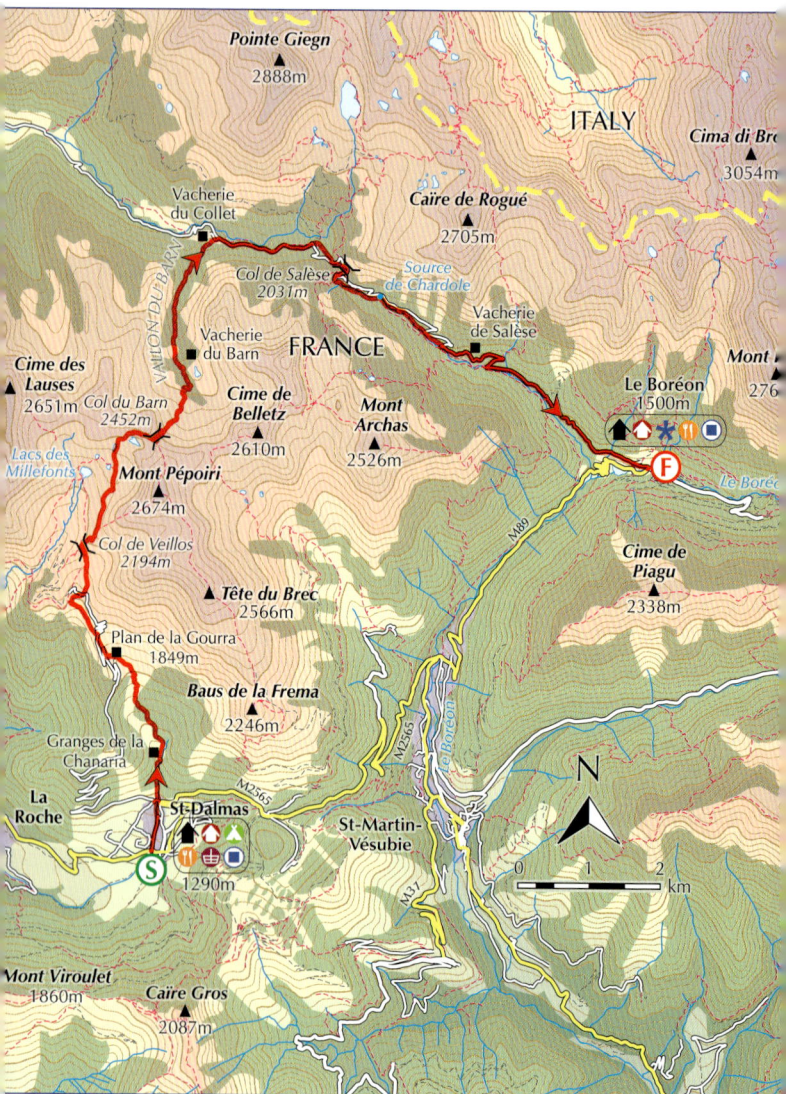

Pointe Giegn
2888m

ITALY

Cima di Bre
3054m

Vacherie
du Collet

Caire de Rogué
2705m

Col de Salèse
2031m

Source
de Chardole

Vacherie
de Salèse

FRANCE

Cime des
Lauses
2651m

Vacherie
du Barn

Le Boréon
1500m

Mont
276

VALLON DU BARN

Col du Barn
2452m

Cime de
Belletz
2610m

Mont
Archas
2526m

Lacs des
Millefonts

Mont Pépoiri
2674m

Le Bore

Col de Veillos
2194m

Cime de
Piagu
2338m

Tête du Brec
2566m

M89

Plan de la Gourra
1849m

Baus de la Frema
2246m

Granges de la
Chanaria

M2565

N

Le Boréon

La
Roche

St-Dalmas

M2565

St-Martin-
Vésubie

S

1290m

0   1   2 km

M37

Mont Viroulet
1860m

Caire Gros
2087m

The GR5/GR52 link route leaves St-Dalmas and climbs steadily north, which feels odd after spending weeks walking south. Crossing Col du Barn, the route enters the Parc National du Mercantour, and views of the mountains along the Franco-Italian border are stunning. The route runs from one forested valley to another, crossing Col de Salèse to reach the hamlet of Le Boréon. Detours have been in place ever since parts of the GR52 were destroyed during Storm Alex in 2020.

St-Dalmas to Col de Veillos   3hr 30min, 5.5km, +910m -5m

Leave St-Dalmas by following a road opposite Bar Le Millefonds called Route des Barches. This climbs past a car park and later bends right, so keep straight ahead instead, up a track and a path in a (hopefully) dry river-bed, until a left turn leads up to a road junction. Turn right and cross a bridge, then turn left to follow a path, Chemin de l'Intraou, up through Vallon de la Chanaria. The river-bed is usually dry and the valley sides are forested. Follow the path away from the river-bed, up a more open, sloping tongue of land, passing the ruined **Granges de la Chanaria** and a memorial. Pass a water trough, where the path levels out a bit, then it climbs a bouldery, forested slope. The path winds about as it crosses a couple of clear-felled slopes before crossing a track below a cabin on **Plan de la Gourra**, at 1849m.

Climb uphill to clip a road bend then climb again to cross the road at a higher level. Cross a shoulder offering fine views of a forested valley, with Rimplas visible in the distance. Pass beneath crumbling limestone cliffs then zigzag up to the

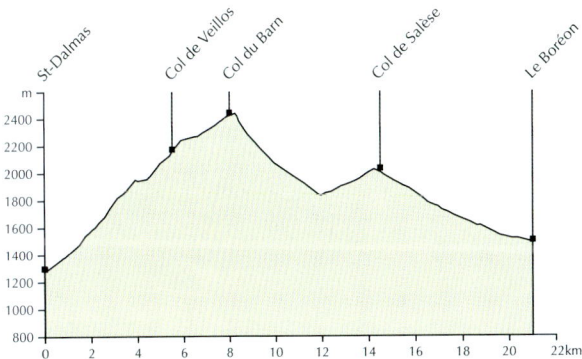

road again, near a car park. Don't go to the car park (snack cabin) but instead climb to join a well-worn path that zigzags up to **Col de Veillos** at 2194m.

Col de Veillos to Col du Barn   1hr 30min, 2.5km, +265m -0m

Don't drop down the other side of the col but instead turn right to continue up a crest. The path wanders around impressively bouldery slopes, later falling as well as climbing. The boulders are hard gneiss, with clumps of alpenrose and parsley fern growing between them. Lac Petit might be noticed off to the left, and as the path climbs, it passes closer to Lac Rond, Lac Long and Lac Gros. These small lakes are collectively known as the **Lacs des Millefonts**. Beyond the lakes lies the high **Col du Barn**, at 2452m. Enter the Parc National du Mercantour, enjoying splendid views of the mountains.

Col du Barn to Col de Salèse   2hr 15min, 6.5km, +190m -615m

The path down from the col is rough, stony and convoluted as it negotiates steep and bouldery slopes. Forest gradually becomes established, and the ground cover includes alpenrose, juniper and bilberry. Cross three footbridges and note the ruined **Vacherie du Barn** off to the right. Walk through a clearing in the forest then later, cross another footbridge to leave the **Vallon du Barn**. The path leads close to the **Vacherie du Collet** but turns right to reach a nearby road.

On the descent from Col du Barn deep into the Vallon du Barn

Turn right to follow the road uphill, walking alternately on tarmac, concrete and gravel. The road mostly runs through forest but there are views of nearby mountains. Turn right towards the top to follow a path up to where the road crosses **Col du Salèse** at 2031m.

Col de Salèse to Le Boréon   2hr, 6.5km, +0m -530m

Turn right to cross the col and walk down a stretch of tarmac-and-concrete road to reach a sharp bend. Either drop down to the right to follow a rough and bouldery, storm-damaged path through the forest or stay on the road for an easier walk, joining the path a little later, when it is much easier to follow. Clip the forest road further downhill but stay on the rugged path, unless water is required, in which case, stay on the road to reach the nearby **Source de Chardole**.

The path can be followed down through the forest as far as the **Vacherie de Salèse** but several stretches further down the valley were completely destroyed during Storm Alex and cannot be used. Switch to the forest road to complete the rest of the descent, passing a gîte d'étape on the way down to a bridge in the hamlet of **Le Boréon**, at 1500m (hotel, gîte d'étape, bivouac and restaurants; free bus, or navette gratuite, to St-Martin-Vésubie to link with Lignes d'Azur bus to Nice and St-Dalmas: www.lignesdazur.com).

VALLÉE DU BORÉON

Damage caused in the valley by Storm Alex in 2020 is still very evident and has resulted in the GR52 being diverted. The route described on these pages is the one that was in place in 2024. Follow the direction indicated by déviation temporaire notices, bearing in mind that some of these detours could become permanent where paths have been damaged beyond repair. Do not use any paths marked as sentier fermé or accès interdit.

The attraction of Le Parc Alpha offers an opportunity to view wolves at close quarters: see www.puremontagne.fr. There have been wolf packs in these mountains since 1992 but they are highly unlikely to be spotted by trekkers.

GR52 STAGE 2
Le Boréon to Refuge de Nice

Start	Le Boréon
Finish	Refuge de Nice
Time	11hr
Distance	18.5km
Total Ascent	1765m
Total Descent	1040m
Terrain	Forest tracks and paths at first, then a rough and stony path over Pas des Ladres. Very steep and bouldery over Pas de Mont Colomb.
Maps	3741 OT
Refreshments	Refuge de la Cougourde, La Madone de Fenestre and Refuge de Nice.
Accommodation	Refuge de la Cougourde, Refuge de la Madone de Fenestre and Refuge de Nice.

The GR52 climbs through a forested valley to a charming lake then reaches the rugged Pas des Ladres. The route runs so close to the Franco-Italian border that many trekkers make a detour in order to peep through the Col de Fenestre into the Parco Naturale Alpi Marittime in Italy. You can stop at the Refuge de la Madone de Fenestre, but if you continue over the Pas de Mont Colomb to the Refuge de Nice, note that the ground is very steep, bouldery and slow-going.

Le Boréon to Refuge de la Cougourde   2hr 30min, 6.5km, +600m -0m

Leave the bridge at Le Boréon and follow a road upstream. Turn right, up a forest track marked '*déviation temporaire*'. Shortcut up a path onto a higher track and turn right again. The track bends left; follow it across the forested slope until it descends through a car park. Follow a track and a path that climb past the Restaurant L'Alpage and **Vacherie du Boréon**. Reach another car park and keep to the left of it to find a signposted path and noticeboards.

Walk up a broad, stony path, further into the forest, and later, pass the **Chalet Vidron**, in a marshy area at 1770m. Cross a little footbridge before crossing the larger footbridge of **Pont de Peïrastrèche** at 1828m. Continue upstream through

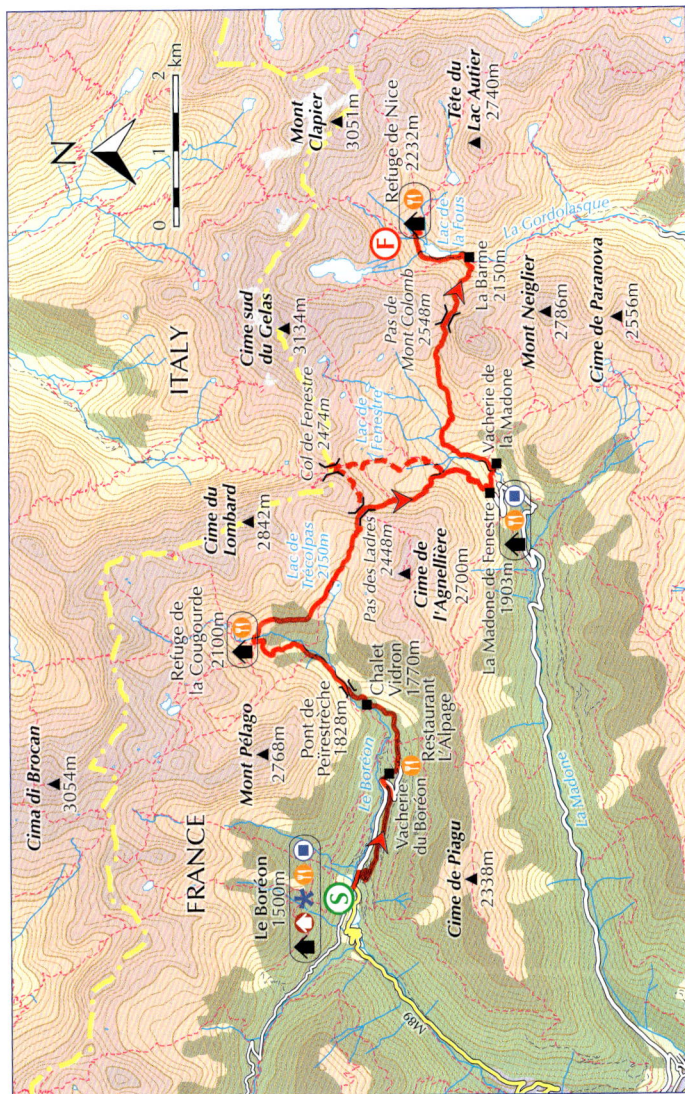

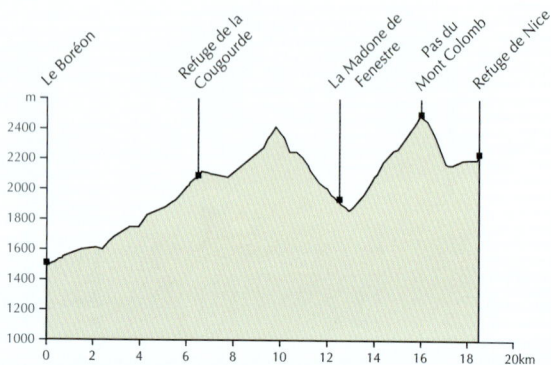

The view from a forest clearing on the climb from the Vacherie du Boréon to Pont de Peïrestrèche

the Val du Haut Boréon and enter a clearing surrounded by fine mountains. The GR52 used to turn right and cross a footbridge, and this can still be used as a shortcut; otherwise, keep left and follow the winding path up to the **Refuge de la Cougourde** at 2100m (refuge and restaurant).

Refuge de la Cougourde to La Madone de Fenestre 3hr 30min, 6km, +400m -600m

Cross a footbridge close to the refuge and follow a path, which generally descends before climbing across the mountainside. The path levels out as it approaches the lovely **Lac de Trécolpas**, at 2150m. Keep to the left side of the lake and climb again. The path is steep and zigzags up a bouldery slope to reach the high col of **Pas des Ladres**, at 2448m, where the main route turns right and a variant route to Col de Fenestre turns left (see below for details).

Turn right, crossing the col, to follow a steep and stony path winding downhill. The gradient eases for a while then the path steepens again. After roughly contouring across the slope, it zigzags down to a junction with the variant route and continues downhill to reach a group of buildings at **La Madone de Fenestre**, at 1903m (pilgrim church, refuge, restaurant; free bus, or *navette gratuite*, to St-Martin-Vésubie to link with Lignes d'Azur buses to Nice and St-Dalmas: www. lignesdazur.com).

La Madone de Fenestre to Pas du Mont Colomb   3hr 30min, 3.5km, +700m -50m

Walk down across a wet hillside to cross a wooden bridge over a river at the **Vacherie de la Madone**. Turn left to follow a path climbing steeply upstream, passing sparse pines and grazing cows. Swing right, towards the rugged slopes of Caïre de la Madone, then swing left to cross a bouldery slope. Watch for red/white markers, which show the easiest way, especially when a short 'hands-on' scramble is required. The route passes bouldery hollows, which may contain pools of water. Watch for chamois and bouquetin grazing grassy areas. The path climbs one last, loose, awkward slope of boulders to reach the narrow, rocky col of **Pas du Mont Colomb** at 2548m, which has a huge stump of rock, a gendarme, in the middle.

Pas du Mont Colomb to Refuge de Nice   1hr 30min, 2.5km, +65m -390m

Keep to the right of the gendarme (an equally steep and rocky path lies to the left). Note how the rock crumbles: this is the weakness that formed the col. A tightly winding path leads down onto a tongue of boulders. Watch carefully for markers and cairns. Another steep and rugged path continues downhill, reaching a junction with a path above a river at **La Barme**, at 2150m.

Turn left and follow the path uphill to join an old construction track beside **Lac de la Fous**, which is a reservoir. Walk beyond the head of the reservoir and

The GR52 climbs round the rocky slopes of Caïre de la Madone to reach Pas du Mont Colomb

cross a footbridge, then climb stone steps to reach the **Refuge de Nice** at 2232m (refuge and restaurant).

Variant route via Col de Fenestre   extra 45min, 1.5km, +140m -140m

Turn left as you cross **Pas des Ladres** to follow a path up a rocky slope then walk down a path hammered from the rock. Climb again, on boulder scree, to reach a junction then turn left and zigzag a short way uphill to reach the rugged **Col de Fenestre** at 2474m (Italian: Colle di Finestra). The col is on the Franco-Italian border and the boundary between the Parc National du Mercantour and Parco Naturale Alpi Marittime.

Drop back down to the path junction and keep left to descend, as signposted for La Madone de Fenestre. The convoluted path crosses bare rock and boulders, passing **Lac de Fenestre**. Continue downhill but look to the left to spot Pas de Mont Colomb, which will be crossed later. The path winds downhill, passing a junction with the main GR52 route and continuing downhill to reach a group of buildings at **La Madone de Fenestre**, at 1903m.

Start	Refuge de Nice
Finish	Refuge des Merveilles
Time	6hr
Distance	9.5km
Total Ascent	620m
Total Descent	720m
Terrain	Steep, rocky and bouldery slopes are traversed across two cols, followed by a descent through the bouldery Vallée des Merveilles.
Maps	3741 OT
Refreshments	Refuge des Merveilles.
Accommodation	Refuge des Merveilles.

This is a short day's walk but it takes time because the ground is so steep, rocky and bouldery. The scenery is astounding, and the mountains contain several small natural lakes, as well as reservoirs. If you arrive at the Refuge des Merveilles early, it is worth joining an archaeological tour to visit interesting Bronze Age rock carvings. There are over 36,000 of them, so only a small selection can be seen. It is forbidden to explore off the course of the GR52 without a guide as the area is very sensitive.

Refuge de Nice to Baisse du Basto   3hr, 3km, +465m -0m

A path leaves the Refuge de Nice and quickly climbs over a slight rise to reach a valley, where a footbridge spans a stream. Climb again, following a path that is steep at first but levels out and then becomes rough, rocky and bouldery as it climbs again. An easy stretch passes **Lac Niré**, at 2353m, in a bouldery hollow.

The way ahead passes a couple of small lakes, which can dry out in summer although patches of grass tend to remain green and offer good grazing for chamois and bouquetin. Slowly climb another rocky, bouldery slope, keeping an eye open for red/white markers revealing the best course. Pause and admire wonderful mountain views on the ascent. A crunchy, worn, stony path finally leads to the col of **Baisse du Basto** at 2693m.

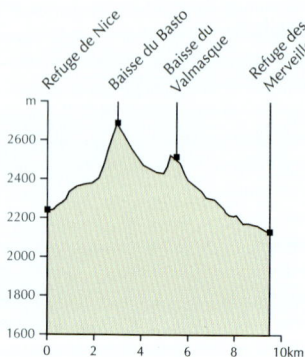

Baisse du Basto to Baisse de Valmasque
1hr 30min, 2.5km, +150m -300m

Cross the col and follow a path down a bouldery slope, passing well to the right of a little lake among rock and boulders. Watch carefully for red/white markers and cairns as the path crosses plenty more boulders. There are views down the valley to the dammed Lac du Basto, which looks pleasant when full but ugly when the water is low. A junction of paths is

reached, and the GR52 turns right to follow a well-trodden, zigzag path uphill. Huge boulders of gneiss are mixed with distinctive boulders of volcanic breccia, fallen from peaks on the right. The path crosses another col, **Baisse de Valmasque**, at 2549m, from where there is a splendid view down through the rugged Vallée des Merveilles.

Baisse de Valmasque to Refuge des Merveilles   1hr 30min, 4km, +5m -420m

A convoluted path leads down a steep and rugged slope littered with boulders of volcanic breccia and conglomerate. One stretch of path is level and easy, then there are plenty more boulders in the Vallée des Merveilles on the way to the little **Lac des Merveilles**. Note that the valley is a protected archaeological site, and trekking poles must not be used on the way through.

The valley is usually busy with visitors, many of them on guided tours around a series of rock carvings on glacially polished rocks. Trekkers must stay on the GR52, except where signposts allow visits to a small number of specific sites. The path later runs level and easy, passing within sight of little **Lac Mouton**. One final, zigzag path runs down smooth rocks above **Lac Long Supérieur**, leading to the **Refuge des Merveilles** at 2130m (refuge, restaurant, bivouac, information panels, and starting point for guided archaeological tours exploring Bronze Age petroglyphs).

Lac du Basto is seen to good effect on the way to Baisse de Valmasque

GR52 STAGE 4
Refuge des Merveilles to Camp d'Argent

Start	Refuge des Merveilles
Finish	Camp d'Argent
Time	6hr
Distance	13km
Total Ascent	595m
Total Descent	975m
Terrain	Rugged paths at first, giving way to easier paths and tracks.
Maps	3741 OT and 3741 ET
Refreshments	Restaurants at Camp d'Argent.
Accommodation	Hotel and *gîte d'étape* at Camp d'Argent.

The GR52 originally featured a long day's walk from the Vallée des Merveilles to Sospel, but in 2010, the route was altered to include Camp d'Argent. Once the Pas du Diable has been crossed and bouldery slopes left behind, easier paths cut across smoother slopes and prove easier to follow than those of previous days. After passing close to a fort on Pointe des Trois Communes, the route runs along a ridge and gradually descends from the Parc National du Mercantour to reach Camp d'Argent and its hotel/gîte.

Refuge des Merveilles to Pas du Diable   1hr 15min, 3km, +300m -0m
Leave the refuge by walking back up the smooth rocks then turn left, as marked and signposted. The GR52 climbs and keeps to the left of the dam of **Lac Fourca**. Follow only the marked path alongside the reservoir, avoiding others, weaving easily past outcrops and boulders. The path swings right to pass a cliff, exploiting a natural breach. Climb a little further then dip down to pass between **Lac du Trem** and the dam of **Lac de la Muta**. Climb alongside the latter, still weaving around outcrops and boulders. A grassy slope leads up to a signpost at the little **Lacs du Diable**. Turn left, and an easy climb leads to the col of **Pas du Diable** at 2430m.

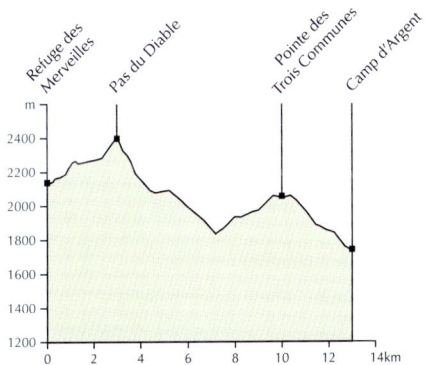

Descending from the Pas du Diable

Pas du Diable to Pointe des Trois Communes
3hr 30min, 7km, +290m -640m

Leave the Parc National du Mercantour and walk straight downhill to follow a rugged path across slopes of grass and boulders overlooking a combe full of boulders. The path descends and crosses a valley, so keep right at a path junction. Climb gently, across steep slopes covered in long grass, and note how the bedrock crumbles to gravel. Cross the grassy col of **Baisse Cavaline**, at 2107m. Dolomitic limestone is encountered here, and the path contours across the slopes of Cime de Raus, descending past a few pines, to reach **Col de Raus** at 1999m.

Turn left then quickly right to leave the col, following a clear and obvious path across the steep, grassy slopes of **Cime de Tour**. A gentle, downhill traverse leads to another col at **Baisse de St-Véran**, at 1836m. Follow a broad, sweeping, zigzag path up what appears to be a pyramidal peak, passing concrete ruins. The path becomes a track – an old military road – climbing gradually then steepening as it approaches a hill crowned with a fort. Turn left to make a short detour up to the fort at **Pointe des Trois Communes**, at 2080m. The Redoute de la Pointe des Trois Communes was an important site for the defence of the Alpes-Maritimes.

Pointe des Trois Communes to Camp d'Argent
1hr 15min, 3km, +5m -335m

Turn right, as marked, and follow a clear track towards a row of ruined barracks. Continue past these until the track swings round to the left. Watch for a narrow path signposted on the right, which crosses a grassy rise. Keep left to cross another rise then continue along and down a rounded crest. There are views southwards through the deep, forested valley of La Bevera.

The path drops down to a building at a road junction, car park and information boards at **Cabane de Tueis** at 1889m. Follow the road gently downhill from the junction, bending left, right and left as you leave the Parc National du Mercantour. Watch for a signposted path rising on the right, which crosses a slope and descends beside a ski lift. Rejoin the road on a broad col at **Camp d'Argent** at 1750m (hotel, gîte d'étape, hire tents, bivouac and restaurants).

Start	Camp d'Argent
Finish	Sospel
Time	9hr
Distance	22km
Total Ascent	470m
Total Descent	1870m
Terrain	Mostly good paths that traverse steep slopes or run along ridges, or close to them, finishing with a forested descent.
Maps	3741 ET
Refreshments	Plenty of choice at Sospel.
Accommodation	Plenty of choice at Sospel.

Today's fine walk involves contouring across steep slopes then walking along or beside ridges that offer good views. After walking from Mont Giagiabella to Mangiabo, a long and mostly forested descent leads to the interesting and historic little town of Sospel. The route crosses the ancient Vieux Pont, where tolls were once paid by traders carrying salt along the Route du Sel from the coast into the high mountains.

Camp d'Argent to Baisse de Ventabren   3hr, 8.5km, +350m -240m

Walk down the road from the hotel at Camp d'Argent and turn sharp left, along a forest track, as signposted. This descends gently, rises a little then ends suddenly. Keep left to continue along a narrow path, generally drifting down, across a steep, forested slope. Enter the Parc National du Mercantour and pass a couple of spring-fed troughs. The path climbs and drops a few times then reaches another water trough. A broader path runs parallel to a road and reaches it at a junction with a broad track at the **Cabanes Vieilles**, at 1779m (ruined barracks with an American Stuart tank and a nearby *vacherie* selling cheese).

Turn right, along the track, then immediately turn left, as if heading for the nearby *vacherie*. When the track turns sharp left, continue straight ahead, along a forest path, zigzagging down to a footbridge over a stream below the *vacherie*.

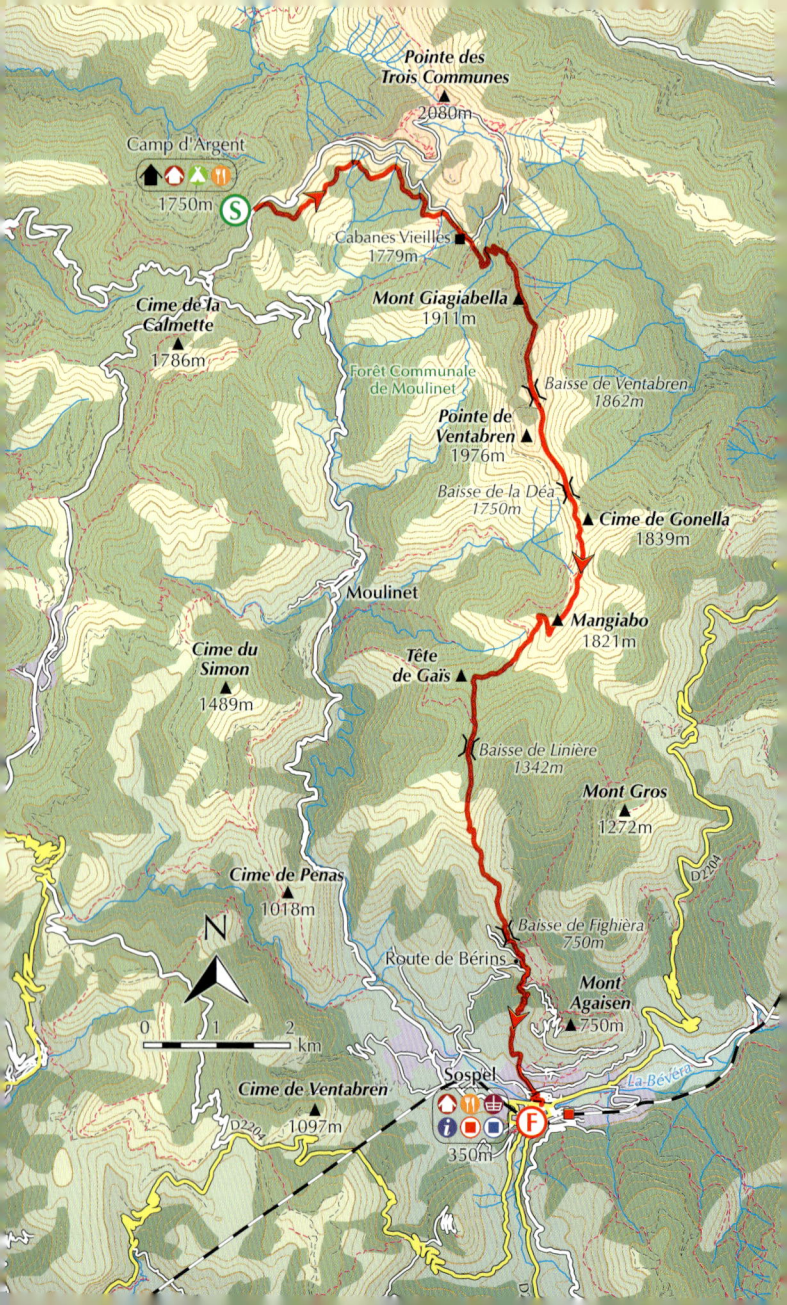

Pointe des
Trois Communes
2080m

Camp d'Argent
1750m
S

Cabanes Vieilles
1779m

Cime de la
Calmette
1786m

Mont Giagiabella
1911m

Forêt Communale
de Moulinet

Baisse de Ventabren
1862m

*Pointe de
Ventabren*
1976m

Baisse de la Déa
1750m

▲ *Cime de Gonella*
1839m

Moulinet

Cime du
Simon
1489m

*Tête
de Gaïs* ▲

▲ *Mangiabo*
1821m

Baisse de Linière
1342m

Mont Gros
1272m

N

0   1   2
km

Cime de Penas
1018m

Baisse de Fighièra
750m

Route de Bérins

*Mont
Agaisen*
▲ 750m

Sospel
350m
F

Cime de Ventabren
1097m

La Bévéra

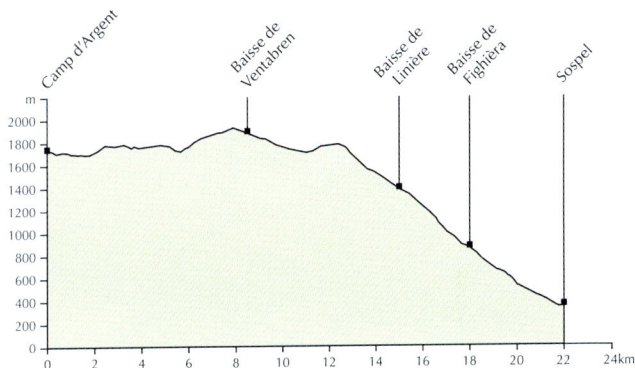

Zigzag up the other side of the valley and cross a track. Turn right, along a path that climbs and passes close to the top of **Mont Giagiabella**. The path rejoins the track at a higher level but is more pleasant underfoot. Follow a level stretch of track then take another path up to the left, which levels out on a grassy, flowery slope with only a few pines dotted around. The path joins the track again on the col of **Baisse de Ventabren** at 1862m.

Baisse de Ventabren to Baisse de Linière   2hr 45min, 6.5km, +125m -640m

Continue straight ahead, along a path cutting easily across the steep slope of **Pointe de Ventabren**, which is covered in clumps of long grass. A prominent track cuts across the next col, **Baisse de la Déa**, at 1750m. The path switches to the other flank of the ridge, becoming a little more rugged as it passes concrete bunkers on the steep, rugged slopes of **Cime de Gonella**. The path switches back across the ridge and climbs, then cuts across the slope to pass a memorial in a small patch of forest. Continue up the ridge to reach the summit of **Mangiabo**, at 1821m, from where there are fine views.

Watch carefully for marker posts to follow a narrow path off the summit, turning sharp right on a shoulder and later swinging left across a rocky patch, continuing down a steep, grassy slope and keeping straight ahead at a junction. Walk through forest and emerge on a pleasant, grassy shoulder on **Tête de Gaïs**, passing a cannon barrel. The path turns sharply left to descend through deciduous woodland and cross another col at **Baisse de Linière**, at 1342m.

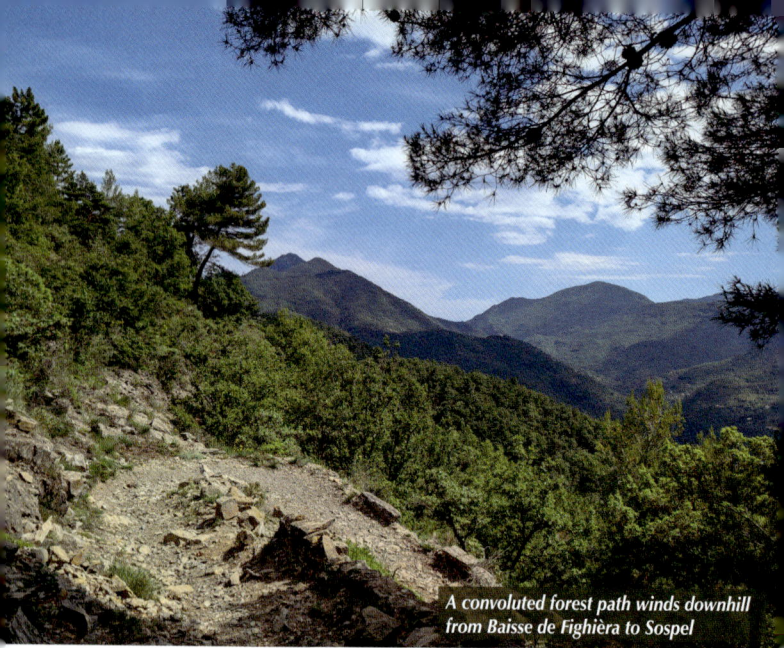

A convoluted forest path winds downhill from Baisse de Fighièra to Sospel

Baisse de Linière to Baisse de Fighièra   1hr 45min, 3km, +5m -590m

Walk down through woods, as marked, and continue along a broad path on a well-defined crest, where gaps in the pines and bushy scrub allow occasional views of the valleys alongside. Leave the Parc National du Mercantour for the last time. Drop down a winding, stony path through mixed woodland to reach a road at **Baisse de Fighièra** at 750m.

Baisse de Fighièra to Sospel   1hr 30min, 4km, +0m -400m

Cross the road and turn right, down a path featuring well-engineered zigzags leading to a lower part of the road, Route de Bérins. Turn left to reach a junction on a prominent road bend then step down, as signposted, onto a path cutting across a slope of oaks. Keep left at a path junction, and a convoluted path later winds downhill, among pines, and crosses a stone bridge. It then continues more directly down, through mixed woods. There are valley views throughout but the centre of Sospel remains hidden until the end. Walk straight down a road, Chemin de Cantamerlou, to reach a school. Go straight down 32 concrete steps called Montée du Serret then turn right, along a road, to reach a bridge called Pont de la Liberation, in **Sospel**. Don't cross it but instead turn left, along the riverside, and cross the ancient Vieux Pont instead, at 350m.

SOSPEL

Settled since Neolithic times, Sospel avoids the worst heat of Mediterranean summers and the cold of Alpine winters. It was a notable staging point on the Route du Sel, or Salt Route, from Nice to Piémont from the 13th century. Traders crossing the Vieux Pont paid a toll, and the peak trading period was the 18th century. Explorations reveal old ramparts and a *donjon* keep. The 16th-century church of Ste-Croix was associated with the Pénitents Blancs. The Cathedral de St-Michel, full of Baroque art, dates from 1762 and is one of the grandest in the Alpes-Maritimes. It is flanked by the Chapelle des Pénitents Rouges and the Chapelle des Pénitents Gris. Mont Agaisen looms over Sospel and is crowned with military structures dating from the 1930s, associated with border disputes with Italy.

There is a full range of services, including trains to Menton and Nice, and Zest buses to Menton: tel 04 93 35 93 60 www.zestbus.fr. Tourist information office: tel 04 83 93 95 70 www.menton-riviera-merveilles.fr.

The twin-arched Vieux Pont controlled trade along the Route du Sel as it passed through Sospel

GR52 STAGE 6
Sospel to Garavan/Menton

Start	Sospel
Finish	Garavan/Menton
Time	9hr 45min
Distance	17.5km
Total Ascent	1130m
Total Descent	1470m
Terrain	A forested ascent is followed by a fairly easy walk from col to col. After a final climb, a steep and stony descent ends on an urban coastline.
Maps	3741 ET and 3742 OT
Refreshments	Restaurant off route at Morga. Plenty of choice at Garavan and Menton.
Accommodation	Campsite and dormitory off route at Morga. Plenty of choice at Garavan and Menton.

This is the last day on the GR52. A long and well-wooded climb from Sospel gives way to an easy walk from one col to another, with glimpses of the Mediterranean. After you've climbed to a final col, a long and stony descent offers occasional views of Menton, but this last stage is very steep and requires careful route-finding through the suburbs of Garavan. All that remains is to ceremonially dip a boot in the Mediterranean then figure out how to get home.

Sospel to Col du Razet
2hr 45min, 6km, +695m -10m

Leave Sospel by following the road signposted 'Menton', then after a roundabout, take the road signposted 'Col de Castillon'. Cross a railway and later, just before you reach the Piscine Municipale Sospel, turn right, up a path with steps, to short-cut a road bend. Cross the road and climb up another road, Piste de l'Albaréa, which later becomes a track. A gentle ascent leads through mixed forest. Watch for a signpost on the right, where a rough, stone-paved path shortcuts to a higher bend on the track, near the ruins of **Castès**. Keep straight ahead then keep left at a later track junction. Almost immediately, a rugged path climbs to the right to reach a signposted junction at **L'Albaréa**, at 638m.

Sospel
Mont Agaisen
▲ 750m
350m

La Bévéra

Castès

L'Albaréa
638m

Mont Barbonnet
▲ 845m

D2204

Ravin de Roulabre

Ciucco di Gerri
▲ 1026m

ITALY

D2566a

Mont Razet
1286m

Col du Razet
1032m

Le Grand Mont
▲ 1379m

Colla Bassa
1107m

Mont Ours
▲ 1239m

Castillon

D2566

Morga
820m

Monte Grosso
▲ 909m

FRANCE

Vieux Castellar

Monte Fuga
▲ 786m

Col du Berceau
1050m

Cime de Baudon
▲ 1265m

Plan du Lion
720m

Mont Carpano
▲ 772m

Castellar

N

Granges St-Paul
460m

Moniéri
280m

0   1   2
└────┴────┴────┘
km

Garavan

Menton

A8

D6007

Mediterranean Sea

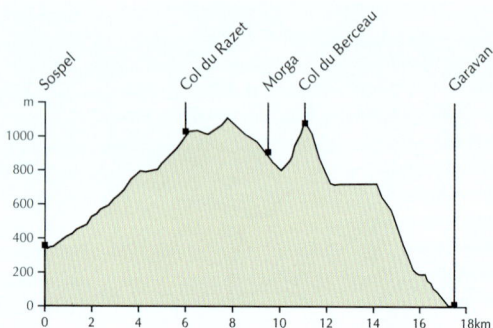

Fork right and follow a path past a ruin, heading further up through the forest and reaching a shoulder offering fine views (water). Follow the path to the left of a Franco-Italian memorial gently down into the well-wooded **Ravin de Roulabre** before climbing more and more steeply. Chestnut trees and holly give way to pines and holly as you reach a junction of paths and tracks on **Col du Razet**, at 1032m, from where there is a view of the Mediterranean.

Col du Razet to Morga   1hr 45min, 3.5km, +115m -330m

Cross the col before turning left as marked and signposted, walking gently through an old coppice wood. Pass the ruins of a house, with Le Grand Mont in view ahead. The path climbs through dense pines to reach a track and sheep pens on **Colla Bassa**, at 1107m. Nearby **Le Grand Mont** (Italian: Grammondo) is a fine viewpoint on the Franco-Italian border and can be climbed by way of a short detour.

Turn right to walk down a rough and stony track. There are open areas with views of the sea, then mixed woodland gives way to pines on a col at 969m. Turn right, along a path that runs down past a small building followed by a handy shelter (water), passing evergreen oaks to reach a ruin at **Morga**, at 820m (campsite, dormitory and restaurant off route at La Ferme St-Bernard).

Morga to Col du Berceau   1hr 30min, 2km, +290m -60m

Turn left to walk gently uphill, along a pleasant, grassy terrace, to reach a track. Turn right to walk down towards a large, modern byre near a pylon line, around 800m. Turn left, as signposted. A stone-paved path climbs past another farm, keeping to the right of its boundary fence then passing near a rocky outcrop bearing the ruins of **Vieux Castellar**. Climb further and keep right at a signposted

A path climbs through forest and clearings on the way to Col du Razet

junction, sometimes walking among pines and sometimes on a rocky, scrubby slope. Dense pines are passed on the final approach to **Col du Berceau**, at 1050m, from where there is a view of the twin harbours of Garavan and Menton.

Col du Berceau to Garavan   3hr 45min, 6km, +30m -1070m

Follow a path winding down a slope of scree and broom scrub. Further down are mixed woods, then pines dominate. The GR51, which traverses the Balcons de la Méditerranée, heads right, down to Castellar, so follow the GR52 straight ahead, climbing a little, to pass a couple of ruins on a level, grassy area at **Plan de Lion**, at 720m.

The path climbs a little, then a signpost points left to **Mont Carpano**: the 10min detour affords a fine view into Italy. Keep right to stay on the GR52, which runs downhill and steepens as it passes sparse pines, evergreen oaks, broom, guelder rose and aromatic scrub. At a track junction at **Granges St-Paul**, at 460m, step down from a ruin and go down a steep and rugged path on a slope of pines.

297

Dense parasol pines feature further downhill, before the path lands awkwardly on a road at **Moniéri** at 280m.

Take care with route-finding on the final descent to avoid being drawn onto lengthy loop roads. Cross the road and walk steeply down to another road. Turn right to walk down Chemin Bella Vista then turn sharp left to follow another road under the busy **A8** motorway. Climb for a while, later turning right, down a steep, concrete road, then turn left, down a path, to drop to a road end. Walk down the road, around a bend, then turn left after passing Villa Cristina to shortcut down a path.

GARAVAN/MENTON

These two settlements merge into one resort, and it is well worth strolling from Garavan to Menton. **Old Menton**, huddled on a hill once crowned with a *château*, was from 1346 until 1861 a possession of the Grimaldis of Monaco. The landmark **Basilica de St-Michel** dates from the 17th century. Visit the **Cimitière du Vieux Château**, marvelling at the variety interred there: princes and peasants, exiles and ex-pats – some from countries that no longer exist. Rugby fans should search for the grave of William Webb-Ellis, founder of the sport.

'*Menton – ma Ville est un Jardin*' proclaims the local tourism authority, and the area abounds in exotic gardens, while the main streets are planted with palms and oranges. The **Musée Jean Cocteau** is housed in a bastion on the sea wall, and the **Promenade du Soleil** can be followed, as can shady shopping streets.

A full range of services are available, mostly in the new town. Tourist information office: tel 04 83 93 70 20 www.menton-riviera-merveilles.fr. When the time comes to leave, head inland from the casino for the rail and bus stations.

Cross the road and drop down a nearby path. Turn right, down a road, and pass beneath two arches. Do not pass the house called Bethsaïda but instead turn right, down steps. Cross a road and continue down more steps, passing under a railway bridge at the bottom. Officially, the GR52 turns right, along Rue Webb-Ellis, to finish at the **railway station** in **Garavan**, but you should walk down Avenue Katherine Mansfield and turn left to finish beside the Mediterranean. A tiny scrap of a beach can be found to the left of the harbour, with a couple of free showers for sweaty bodies. Walking any further in that direction quickly leads into Italy. The long Alpine trek is over. Congratulations!

Getting away from Garavan/Menton

Local bus Zest is the local bus operator: tel 04 93 35 93 60 www.zestbus.fr. Several buses link Garavan and Menton, the latter having the main bus station, or *gare routière*. This is located close to the *gare SNCF*, or railway station.

Long-distance bus Zou bus 600 runs from Menton to Nice every 15 minutes, taking approximately 1hr 45min to complete the journey. The train is faster but the bus offers many more stops along the way.

Train Trains depart hourly from Garavan SNCF station, running to Menton and stopping at all stations on the way to Nice, taking less than an hour for the full journey. Speedier half-hourly services can be caught at Menton SNCF station. Connections at Nice link with the airport and the rest of the French rail network. Those who prefer to leave via Italy can take a train across the border to Ventimiglia (French: Vintimille). Timetables and information are easily obtained at stations or can be checked at www.sncf-connect.com, or use the SNCF app.

Air The Aéroport Nice Côte d'Azur has plenty of flights to and from Britain, as well as other destinations. Budget flights are available with operators such as Easyjet (www.easyjet.com) and Jet2.com (www.jet2.com). Air France (www.air-france.com), the national carrier, offers scheduled flights, as do many other carriers. For airport information, see www.nice.aeroport.fr.

Ferry In the summer months, a leisurely departure by ferry is possible from Menton. Services operate to Monaco and St-Jean-Cap Ferrat. Ferries from Monaco operate to Nice. Check details with tourist information centres along the Rivièra.

Nice If you intend to visit Nice before returning home, basic information about the city and its services can be found at the end of Stage 28.

A tiny beach on the shore of the Mediterranean at the port of Menton-Garavan

APPENDIX A

Accommodation listings

Stage	Location	Name	Type
Stage 1	St-Gingolph	Hôtel Le Rivage	⭕
Stage 1	Novel	Hôtel Les Chemins du Léman	⭕ ▲
Stage 1, Stage 1b	La Chapelle-d'Abondance	Plenty of choice	⭕
Stage 1a	Thonon-les-Bains	Plenty of choice	⭕
		Camping le Lac Noir	🟢
Stage 1a	Armoy	Entre Montagnes et Lac	⭕
		L'Echo des Montagnes	⭕
Stage 1a	Vinzier	*Hébergement GR5*	▲
		Camping Municipal de Vinzier	🟢
Stage 1b	Dent d'Oche	*Refuge de la Dent d'Oche*	▲
Stage 1b	Chalets de Bise	Refuge de Bise	▲
Stage 2	Trébentaz	*Refuge de Trébentaz*	▲ ✱
Stage 2	Chésery	Refuge de Chésery	▲
Stage 3	Chaux Palin	Gîte Chaux Palin	▲
Stage 3	Lapisa	Gîte d'Alpage Lapisa	▲
Stage 3	Col de Coux	Cabane du Col de Cou	▲
Stage 3	Chardonnière	*Refuge de Chardonnière*	▲
Stage 3	Col de la Golèse	Refuge de la Golèse	▲
Stage 3	Samoëns	Plenty of choice	⭕
Stage 4	Sixt-Fer-à-Cheval	Plenty of choice	⭕

🔴 hotel/*chambres d'hôte* 🟢 self-catering/glamping 🟡 home stay
🔺 hostel/bunkhouse/hut/refuge/*gîte d'étape* △ unmanned hut 🔵 campsite
✳ bivouac/wild camp

Tel	Web/email	Comments
+41 244 827 032	www.rivage.ch	
+33 4 50 72 10 77	www.les-chemins-du-leman.com	
	www.leman-mountains-explore.com	
+33 4 50 71 55 55	www.thononlesbains.com	Contact tourist information for details
+33 6 68 70 74 74	www.camping-lelacnoir.fr	
+33 6 74 96 01 26	https://entre montagnesetlac.fr	
+33 4 50 73 94 55	www.facebook.com/echoarmoy	
+33 6 83 03 77 85	https://vinzier.com/heberge-ment-gr5-ancienne-cure-/contenu_1541.html	
+33 4 50 73 61 19	https://vinzier.com/camping-municipal/contenu_1542.html	
+33 6 48 90 57 41	https://refugeladentdoche.ffcam.fr	
+33 6 70 95 17 06	www.refugedebise.com	
+33 6 07 14 49 34	http://refugetrebentaz.canalblog.com	
+41 797 256 820	www.lacvert.ch	
+41 772 698 848		Under reconstruction 2024
+41 244 793 643	www.lapisa.ch	
	www.cabane-col-de-cou.net	Under reconstruction 2024
+33 4 50 90 11 40		
+33 4 50 90 59 53	www.refuge-golese.com	
+33 4 50 34 40 28	www.samoens.com	Contact tourist information for details
+33 4 50 34 49 36	www.haut-giffre.fr	Contact tourist information for details

Stage	Location	Name	Type
Stage 4	Chalets d'Anterne	Refuge Alfred Wills	▲
Stage 4	Moëde Anterne	Refuge Moëde Anterne	▲ ✶
Stage 5	Le Brévent	Refuge de Bellachat	▲
Stage 5	Les Houches	Plenty of choice	⬡
		Camping Bellevue	◉
Stage 6, Stage 6a	Col de Voza	Refuge du Fioux	▲
Stage 6	Bionnassay	Auberge de Bionnassay	▲
Stage 6, Stage 6a	Les Contamines-Montjoie	Plenty of choice	⬡
Stage 6a	Chalets de Miage	Refuge de Miage	▲ ✶
Stage 6a	Chalets du Truc	Auberge du Truc	▲
Stage 7	Le Pontet	Camping et Gîte le Pontet	▲ ◉
Stage 7	Nant Borrant	Refuge de Nant Borrant	▲
Stage 7	La Rollaz	Aire de Bivouac de la Rollaz	✶
Stage 7	La Balme	Aire de Bivouac de la Balme	✶
		Refuge de la Balme	▲
Stage 7	Croix du Bonhomme	Refuge du Col de la Croix du Bonhomme	▲
Stage 7	Plan de la Lai	Le Chalet du Berger	▲
		Refuge du Plan de la Lai (and yurt)	▲
		Gîte d'Alpage Plan Mya	▲
Stage 8	Presset	*Refuge de Presset*	▲
Stage 8	La Balme	Refuge de la Balme Tarentaise	▲ ✶
Stage 8	Valezan	Auberge le Valezan	▲
Stage 8	Landry	Hôtel L'Alpin	⬡
		Maison Caramel	⬡
		Camping Canopee	◉

Tel	Web/email	Comments
+33 6 70 63 12 45	www.monrefugepaysdumont-blanc.com	
+33 4 50 93 60 43	www.monrefugepaysdumont-blanc.com	
+33 7 75 83 02 70	www.refuge-bellachat.com	
+33 4 50 55 50 62	www.chamonix.com/la-vallee/les-stations-villages/les-houches	Contact tourist information for details
+33 6 33 50 34 12	https://camping-bellevue-leshouches.com	
+33 4 50 93 52 43	www.montourdumontblanc.com	
+33 4 50 93 45 23	www.auberge-bionnassay.com	
+33 4 50 47 01 58	www.lescontamines.com	Contact tourist information for details
+33 4 50 93 22 91	www.refugemiage.com	
+33 4 50 93 12 48	www.monrefugepaysdumont-blanc.com	
+33 4 75 04 63 07	www.campinglepontet.com	
+33 4 50 47 03 57	www.montourdumontblanc.com	
+33 4 50 47 03 54	www.montourdumontblanc.com	
+33 4 79 07 05 28	https://refugecroixdubonhomme.ffcam.fr	
+33 6 36 47 03 48	www.lechaletduberger.com	
+33 4 79 89 07 78	https://chaletplandelalai.ffcam.fr	
+33 9 88 99 32 03	www.refuge-mya.com	
+33 6 87 54 09 18	https://refugedepresset.ffcam.fr	
+33 6 84 35 07 41	www.refuge-balme-tarentaise.fr	
+33 6 98 10 03 19	www.auberge-valezan.com	
+33 4 79 55 33 00	www.hotel-lalpin.com	
+33 6 15 81 70 26	www.maisoncaramel.com	
+33 6 73 90 18 05	https://canopee-camping.eu	

Stage	Location	Name	Type
Stage 9	Peisey-Nancroix	Plenty of choice	⬡
Stage 9	Les Lanches	Camping Les Lanchettes	⬢
		Le P'tit Refuge	▲
Stage 9	Rosuel	Chalet-Refuge de Rosuel	▲
Stage 9	Lac de la Plagne	Refuge d'Entre le Lac	▲ ✳
Stage 10	Col du Palet	Refuge du Col du Palet	▲ ✳
Stage 10	Tignes le Lac	Plenty of choice	⬡
Stage 10	Val d'Isère	Plenty of choice	⬡
Stage 11, Stage 11a, GR5E Stage 1	Le Villaron	Gîte de la Bâtisse	▲
Stage 11, Stage 11a, GR5E Stage 1	Bessans	Plenty of choice	⬡
Stage 11a	Fond des Fours	Refuge du Fond des Fours	▲ ✳
Stage 12, GR5E Stage 1	L'Illaz	Camping de l'Illaz	⬢
Stage 12	Vallonbrun	Refuge de Vallonbrun	▲ ✳
		Refuge du Cuchet	△
Stage 12	Bellecombe	Refuge-l'Auberge de Bellecombe	▲
Stage 12	Plan du Lac	Refuge du Plan du Lac	▲ ✳
Stage 13	Arpont	Refuge de l'Arpont	▲ ✳
Stage 13	Le Montana	*Chalet Le Montana*	⬡ ▲
Stage 14	Plan Sec	Refuge de Plan Sec	▲ ✳
Stage 14	Fournache	Refuge de la Fournache	▲ ✳
Stage 14, GR55 Stage 3	Chalets de l'Orgère	*Refuge de l'Orgère*	▲ ✳

Tel	Web/email	Comments
+33 4 79 07 94 28	www.peisey-vallandry.com	Contact tourist information for details
+33 4 79 07 93 07	www.campinglanchettes.com	
+33 4 79 07 97 16	https://ptitrefugerosuel.fr	
+33 6 50 21 91 37	https://refuge-rosuel.vanoise.com	
+33 6 14 11 54 65	https://refugeentrelelac.fr	
+33 6 68 28 52 47	https://refuge-coldupalet.vanoise.com	
+33 4 79 40 04 40	www.tignes.net	Contact tourist information for details
+33 4 79 06 06 60	www.valdisere.com	Contact tourist information for details
+33 4 79 83 14 51	www.gitedelabatisse.com	
+33 4 79 05 96 52	www.haute-maurienne-vanoise.com	Contact tourist information for details
+33 6 03 54 50 55	https://refuge-fonddesfours.vanoise.com	
+33 6 45 89 02 32	www.camping-bessans.com	
+33 6 31 79 38 16	https://refuge-vallonbrun.vanoise.com	
+33 6 82 24 18 17	www.aubergedebellecombe.com	
+33 4 79 20 50 85	https://refuge-plandulac.vanoise.com	
+33 7 83 48 42 27	https://refuge-arpont.vanoise.com	
+33 4 79 20 31 47	https://chalet-montana.com	
+33 4 79 20 31 31	www.refuges-vanoise.com	
+33 6 09 38 72 38	www.refuges-vanoise.com	
+33 7 61 71 68 47	www.refuges-vanoise.com	

305

Stage	Location	Name	Type
Stage 14, GR55 Stage 3, GR5E Stage 2	Fourneaux	Plenty of choice	⌂
GR55 Stage 1	Val Claret	Plenty of choice	⌂
GR55 Stage 1	La Leisse	Refuge de la Leisse	▲ *
GR55 Stage 1	Entre Deux Eaux	*Refuge d'Entre Deux Eaux*	▲ *
GR55 Stage 2	Col de la Vanoise	Refuge du Col de la Vanoise	▲ *
GR55 Stage 2	Les Barmettes	Refuge des Barmettes	▲
GR55 Stage 2	Pralognan	Plenty of choice	⌂
GR55 Stage 2	Les Prioux	Refuge le Repoju	▲
GR55 Stage 2	Roc de la Pêche	Refuge du Roc de la Pêche	▲
GR55 Stage 3	Péclet-Polset	Refuge de Péclet-Polset	▲
GR5E Stage 1	Bonneval-sur-Arc	Plenty of choice	⌂
GR5E Stage 1	Lanslevillard	Plenty of choice	⌂
GR5E Stage 1	Lanslebourg-Mont-Cenis	Plenty of choice	⌂
GR5E Stage 1	Termignon	Plenty of choice	⌂
GR5E Stage 2	Sollières L'Envers	Camping Le Chenantier	⬤
GR5E Stage 2	Le Verney	Camping Le Val d'Ambin	⬤
GR5E Stage 2	Bramans	Chalet Les Glaciers	⌂
GR5E Stage 2	Avrieux	*Auberge La Cascade*	⌂
GR5E Stage 2	La Norma	Plenty of choice	⌂
Stage 15	Valfréjus	Plenty of choice	⌂
Stage 15	Mont Thabor	Refuge du Mont Thabor	▲

Tel	Web/email	Comments
+33 4 79 05 26 67	www.haute-maurienne-vanoise.com	Contact tourist information for details
+33 4 79 40 04 40	www.tignes.net	Contact tourist information for details
+33 9 72 40 03 23	https://refuge-leisse.vanoise.com	
+33 4 79 05 27 13	www.refuges-vanoise.com	
+33 4 79 08 25 23	https://refugecoldelavanoise.ffcam.fr	
+33 4 79 08 75 64	www.lesbarmettes-refuge.com	
+33 4 79 08 79 08	www.pralognan.com	Contact tourist information for details
+33 6 83 58 21 73	www.refuge-repoju.com	
+33 4 79 08 79 75	www.lerocdelapeche.com	
+33 6 63 68 46 92	https://refugepecletpolset.ffcam.fr	
+33 4 79 05 95 95	www.bonneval-sur-arc.com	Contact tourist information for details
+33 4 79 05 99 06	www.valcenis.com	Contact tourist information for details
+33 4 79 05 99 06	www.valcenis.com	Contact tourist information for details
+33 4 79 05 99 06	www.valcenis.com	Contact tourist information for details
+33 6 86 85 76 98	www.camping-lechenantier.com	
+33 4 79 05 03 05	www.camping-bramansvanoise.com	
+33 6 11 90 57 06	https://chalet-les-glaciers.rhone-alps-hotels.com	
+33 6 81 01 45 59	www.facebook.com/aubergeavrieux	
+33 4 79 05 99 16	www.la-norma.fr	Contact tourist information for details
+33 4 79 05 99 16	www.valfrejus.com	Contact tourist information for details
+33 6 77 49 92 07	https://refugedumontthabor.ffcam.fr	

Stage	Location	Name	Type
Stage 16	Les Granges de la Vallée Étroite	Rifugio i Re Magi	▲
		Regure Terzo Alpini	▲ ✱
Stage 16	Roubion	La Joie de Vivre	⟳
		Gîte des Mélézets	▲
Stage 17	Briançon	Plenty of choice	⟳
Stage 18	Villard St-Pancrace	Le Toit de l'Europe	⟳
		Gîte Le Bois de Barracan	▲
Stage 18	L'Izoard	Camping de l'Izoard	⬗
Stage 18	Brunissard	Le Chalet Bazan	⟳
		Gîte d'étape Les Bons Enfants	▲
Stage 19	La Chalp	Hôtel La Ferme de l'Izoard	⟳
		Gîte d'étape La Teppio	▲
		Le Chalet Viso	⟳
Stage 19	Arvieux	*Les Escoyères*	⟳
Stage 19	Château Ville-Vieille	*Hôtel Le Guilazur*	⟳
		Gîte Les Astragales	▲
Stage 19	Ceillac	Gîte Le Matefaim	▲
		Gîte Les Baladins	▲
		Camping Municipal Les Moutets	⬗
Stage 20	Pied de Mélézet	Camping Les Mélèzes	⬗
		Logis Hôtel La Cascade	⟳
Stage 20	Maljasset	Refuge de Maljasset	▲
		Auberge de la Cure	⟳
		Maison d'hôtes Les Zélés	⟳
Stage 21	St-Paul-sur-Ubaye	*Plenty of choice*	⟳
Stage 21	Fouillouse	Gîte Les Granges	▲
		Chez Bourillon	⟳ ✱

Tel	Web/email	Comments
+39 349 611 29 20	www.rifugio.iremagi.it	
+39 012 290 20 71	www.terzoalpini.com	
+33 4 92 21 30 96	www.la-joie-de-vivre.fr	
+33 4 92 20 08 34	www.les-melezets.fr	
+33 4 92 24 98 98	www.serre-chevalier.com	Contact tourist information for details
+33 6 10 98 62 35		
+33 4 92 21 27 79	https://leboisdebarracan.fr	
+33 6 33 33 98 12	www.campingdelizoard.com	
+33 6 10 73 72 65	https://lechaletbazan.com	
+33 4 92 46 73 85	https://lesbonsenfants.eu	
+33 6 63 44 57 02	www.laferme.fr	
+33 4 92 46 73 90	www.teppio.com	
+33 4 92 46 85 77	https://chaletviso.com	
+33 6 08 30 06 23	www.lequeyras.com/offres/les-escoyeres-1967-arvieux-fr-3258943	
+33 4 92 46 74 09	https://queyrashotelguilazur.com	
+33 4 92 46 70 82	https://gitelesastragales.fr	
+33 6 64 80 02 16	www.lematefaim.com	
+33 4 92 45 00 23	www.lesbaladins.com	
+33 4 92 45 17 89	https://ceillac.fr/pratique/campings	
+33 7 49 77 58 32	www.campingdeceillac.com	
+33 4 92 45 05 92	www.logishotels.com/fr/hotel/logis-hotel-la-cascade-1962	
+33 7 44 85 28 55	www.chaletmaljasset.ffcam.fr	
+33 4 92 84 31 15	https://maljasset.fr	
+33 9 88 18 84 16	www.leszeles.com	
+33 4 92 81 04 71	www.ubaye.com	Contact tourist information for details
+33 4 92 84 31 16	www.gite-les-granges.com	
+33 4 92 84 34 74	https://chezbourillon.fr	

Stage	Location	Name	Type
Stage 21	Larche	Gîte d'étape GTA Le Refuge	⌂
		Auberge du Lauzanier	⌂
		Les Marmottes	⊗
Stage 22	Bousieyas	Gîte de Bousieyas	⌂
		Le Café à Marius	⌂ *
Stage 23	St-Dalmas le Selvage	Gîte d'étape Chez Philippe	⌂
		Chambres d'hôte Chez Olga	⊘
		Les Gîtes du Presbytère	⊘
Stage 23	St-Étienne de Tinée	Plenty of choice	⊘
Stage 23	Auron	Plenty of choice	⊘
Stage 24	Roya	Gîte d'étape de Roya	⌂ *
Stage 24	Longon	Refuge de Longon	⌂
Stage 25	Roure	Gîte d'étape Communal	⌂
		Les 3 Flocons	⊘
Stage 25	St-Sauveur sur Tinée	Gîte d'étape (GR5 walkers only)	⌂
		Hôtel Le St-Sauveur	⊘
Stage 25	Rimplas	L'Hostellerie de Rimplas	⊘
Stage 25	La Bolline	Hôtel de Valdeblore	⊘
		Chambres d'Hôtes à la Belle Époque	⊘
Stage 25	St-Dalmas	Camping de la Ferme	⊗
		Gîte d'étape Les Marmottes	⌂
		Le Presbytère du Val	⊘
Stage 26	Les Granges de la Brasque	Les Granges de la Brasque	⌂
Stage 26	Utelle	Gîte d'étape Communal	⌂
		Ferme Le Mérinos	⊘

Tel	Web/email	Comments
+33 4 92 84 30 80	www.gite-etape-larche.com	
+33 4 92 84 35 93	www.gite-le-lauzanier-larche.com	
+33 9 88 18 46 40	www.camping-marmottes.fr	
+33 4 93 02 69 73	www.gitedebousieyas.fr	
+33 4 93 03 53 30	www.chambres-d-hotes-bous-ieyas.fr	
+33 4 93 02 44 61	www.gite-chez-philippe-06.fr	
+33 6 12 89 54 71		
+33 4 93 02 48 40	www.gitesdupresbytere.com	
+33 4 93 02 46 40	www.saintetiennedetinee.fr	Contact tourist information for details
+33 4 93 23 02 66	https://ete.auron.com	Contact tourist information for details
+33 4 93 03 43 05	www.gitederoya-tinee.fr	
+33 4 93 02 83 99	https://refugedelongon.fr	
+33 4 93 02 00 70	https://roure.fr/hebergements	
+33 6 73 34 41 16	www.les3flocons.fr	
+33 6 75 21 13 55	www.saintsauveursurtinee.fr/tourismeethebergement	
+33 4 93 02 00 03		
+33 4 93 02 01 45	www.hostellerie-rimplas.fr	
+33 4 93 03 28 53	www.hotel-valdeblore.fr	
+33 6 07 31 30 63	https://katestravelexperience.eu/a-la-belle-epoque-france	
+33 4 93 02 83 30	https://campingleduff.wixsite.com/camping-la-ferme-val	
+33 4 93 02 89 04	www.gite-marmottes.fr	
+33 6 58 49 63 26	www.chambrespresbytereduval.com	
+33 7 69 68 12 02		
+33 6 31 67 01 27		
+33 6 88 26 94 83	www.fermelemerinos.fr	

Stage	Location	Name	Type
Stage 27	Levens	Hôtel La Vigneraie	⬡
		Les Bambous	⬡
		Akwaba Chez Ouli	⬡
Stage 27	Aspremont	Airbnb only	⬡
Stage 28	Nice	Plenty of choice	⬡
GR52 Stage 1	Le Boréon	Gîte du Boréon	⬆ ✳
		Le Grand Chalet du Lac du Boréon	⬡
GR52 Stage 2	Val du Haut Boréon	Refuge de la Cougourde	⬆
GR52 Stage 2	La Madone de Fenestre	Chalet de la Madone de Fenestre	⬆
GR52 Stage 2	La Barme	Refuge de Nice	⬆
GR52 Stage 3	Vallée des Merveilles	Refuge des Merveilles	⬆ ✳
GR52 Stage 4	Camp d'Argent	L'Estive du Mercantour	⬡
GR52 Stage 5	Sospel	Plenty of choice	⬡
GR52 Stage 6	Garavan/Menton	Plenty of choice	⬡

Tel	Web/email	Comments
+33 4 93 79 77 60	https://lavigneraielevens.com	
+33 6 49 39 56 98	https://katestravelexperience.eu/les-bambous-b-b-france	
+33 7 62 89 86 41	www.akwabachezouli.com	
	www.airbnb.com	
+33 4 92 14 46 14	www.explorenicecotedazur.com	Contact tourist information for details
+33 7 86 18 66 59	https://giteduboreon.com	
+33 7 84 64 27 56	www.legrandchaletdu-lacduboreon.com	
+33 9 78 23 31 59	https://refugelacougourde.ffcam.fr	
+33 6 09 17 89 58	https://chaletmadonedefenestre.ffcam.fr	
+33 6 61 97 59 38	https://refugedenice.ffcam.fr	
+33 4 93 04 64 64	https://refugedesmerveilles.ffcam.fr	
+33 6 87 80 53 93	www.estive-mercantour.fr	
+33 4 83 93 95 70	www.menton-riviera-merveilles.fr	Contact tourist information for details
+33 4 83 93 70 20	www.menton-riviera-merveilles.fr	Contact tourist information for details

APPENDIX B
Basic French for the GR5

Arrival in France

Hello!/Good evening/How are you?	*Bonjour!/Bonsoir/Ça va?*
Where can I get a taxi?	*Où puis-je trouver un taxi?*
Take me to…	*Conduisez-moi à…*
…the railway station/the hotel/this address	*…la gare/l'hôtel/cette adresse*
How much is it?	*Combien est-ce?*
Where is the bus stop/train station?	*Où se trouve l'arrêt du bus/la gare?*
the tourist information office	*l'office de tourisme/le syndicat d'initiative*
the post office/the grocery store	*la poste/l'alimentation*
I'd like a single/return ticket to…	*Je voudrais un billet aller simple/aller-retour à…*
Can I have a timetable?	*Puis-je avoir un horaire?*
information/open/closed	*reseignements/ouvert/fermé*

Staying the night

Rooms available/No vacancies	*Chambres libres/Complet*
I'd like a single/double room	*Je voudrais une chambre pour une personne/deux personnes*
How much does it cost per night?	*Quel est le prix par nuit?*
How much does it cost for bed and breakfast?	*Quel est le prix avec petit déjeuner?*
Is there hot water/a toilet/a shower?	*Y a-t-il l'eau chaude/une toilette/un douche?*
Where is the dining room/bar?	*Où est la salle à manger/bar?*

Walking the GR5

Where is the GR5?	*Où est le GR5?* (pronounced 'jair sank')
the path/the waymarks/rucksack	*le sentier/les balises/sac à dos*
Where are you going?	*Vous allez où?*
I'm going to…	*Je vais à…*
right/left/straight ahead	*à droit/à gauche/tout droit*
Can you show me on the map?	*Est-ce que vous pouver me le montrer sur la carte?*

Camping/Fire prohibited

Camping/Feu interdit

At the refuge
guardian

gardien (male)/gardienne (female)

Can I stay in the refuge?
dormitory/bed/sleeping bag
Can I camp here?
tent/camping space/campsite

Puis-je rester dans le refuge?
dortoir/lit/sac à couchage
Puis-je camper ici?
tente/emplacement/aire de bivouac

Where are the toilets/showers?
Can I have a meal/a beer/breakfast?

Où sont les toilettes/douches?
Puis-je avoir un repas/une bière/petit déjeuner?

What is the weather forecast for tomorrow?
hot/cold/rain/snow/storm/mist

Quel est le météo demain?
chaud/froid/pluie/neige/orage/brouillard

If it all goes wrong
Help me!
I feel sick
There has been an accident

Aidez-moi!
Je suis malade
Il y a eu un accident

Last resort
I don't understand
Do you speak English?

Je ne comprends pas
Parlez-vous anglais?

Lazy walker's French
Bonjour, merci and *s'il vous plaît* will get you a long way!
Bonjour! (hello) is standard greeting and useful everywhere you go. For instance, on entering a refuge or bar, greet all present with this single word.
S'il vous plaît, un lit/un repas/une bière (please, a bed/a meal/a beer) is the simplest and politest way of dealing with requests and needs.
Combien? (how much?), *Merci!* (thank you) – keep it polite and simple!
Au revoir (goodbye), *A tout à l'heure* (see you later – as English 'toodle-loo!').
NB The bigger the word in English, the more likely the French word will be similar!

PRICE LIST SEEN OUTSIDE THE CAFÉ LA PETIT SYRAH IN NICE

'Un café' €7

'Un café, s'il vous plaît'   €4.25

'Bonjour, un café, s'il vous plaît' €1.40

Food, drink and menus

French	English
abricot	apricot
agneau	lamb
ail	garlic
amandes	almonds
anchois	anchovies
banane	banana
beaucoup	a lot
beurre	butter
bière	beer
biftek	steak
boeuf	beef
boissons	drinks
(froid/chaud)	(cold/hot)
bombe	ice-cream
bon appétit!	enjoy! (say this to anyone eating)
bonbons	sweets
café/café au lait	black/white coffee
champignons	mushrooms
charcuterie	cured meats served cold
châtaigne	chestnut, used in main courses and desserts
chocolat	chocolate
citron	lemon
confiture	jam
crème	cream
crème fraîche	thick cream
crêpe	pancake
croque madame	ham and cheese toastie topped with egg
croque monsieur	ham and cheese toastie
crudités	chopped raw vegetables or salad
déjeuner	lunch
dîner	dinner
flan	an egg-custard dessert
fraise	strawberry
fromage	cheese
gâteau	cake
glace	ice

French	English
haricots	beans
huile	oil
jambon	ham
J'aime	I like
Je n'aime pas	I don't like
jus d'orange	orange juice
legumes	vegetables
lentilles	lentils
miel	honey
myrtille	blueberry
oeufs	eggs
omelette	omelette
pain (chaud)	(hot) bread
panini	filled bread rolls, often toasted
pâté	paté
pâtes	pasta
petit déjeuner	breakfast
pique-nique	picnic/packed lunch
poivre	pepper
pomme de terre	potato
porc	pork
poulet	chicken
riz	rice
rosbif	roast beef
rôti	roast
salade	salad
sandwich	sandwich
saucisson	sausage
sel	salt
sucre	sugar
tarte	tart/pie
thé/thé au lait	black/white tea
thon	tuna
tranche	slice
un peu	a little
viande	meat
vin blanc/rouge	white/red wine
yaourt	yoghurt

Trekking and travel (French–English)

French	English
aiguille	needle-like peak
aire du bivouac	camping area
alimentation	grocery
alp	summer farm
arête	ridge/crest
auberge	inn
balise	waymark
balme	cave
baraquements	barracks
blanc/blanche	white
bois	wood
cabane	cabin/hut
cascade	waterfall
chambres d'hôte	guesthouse
chapelle	chapel
chemin	track
chemin du fer	railway
clap/clapier	boulders
col	gap/saddle
combe	high, dry valley
couloir	gully
crête	ridge/crest
croix	cross/crucifix
église	church
estive	summer pasture
forêt	forest
gare	railway station
gare routière	bus station
gendarme	rock pinnacle (literally, policeman)
gîte d'étape	equivalent to a youth hostel
grand/grande	large/big
Grande Randonnée (GR)	hiking trail
haut/haute	high
heure	hour
hôtel de ville	town hall
jour	day
lac	lake
mairie	mayor's office/town hall
malpas/mauvais pas	bad step

French	English
mont/montagne	mountain
navette	shuttle bus
neige	snow
noir/noire	black
parc	park
parc national	national park
parc naturel	natural park
pas	steep-sided gap
pastou	sheepdog
petit/petite	little/small
piste	dirt road/ski route
plagne/plan	plain
plateau	plateau
pointe	peak
pont	bridge
porte	door/gateway
puits	pools
raid	mountain race
refuge	hiking-trail hut
rivière	river
roc/rocher	rock
rouge	red
route	road
ruisseau	stream
sentier	path
sentier nature	nature trail
serre	jagged mountain ridge
sommet	summit
source	spring
téléphérique	cable car
téléski	ski lift
télésiège	chair lift
tête	head
troupeau	herd of sheep
vacherie	cowshed/dairy
val/vallée	valley
velos tous terrain (VTT)	mountain bikes
vert/verte	green

NOTES

NOTES

CICERONE

Trust Cicerone to guide your next adventure, wherever it may be around the world...

Discover guides for hiking, mountain walking, backpacking, trekking, trail running, cycling and mountain biking, ski touring, climbing and scrambling in Britain, Europe and worldwide.

Connect with Cicerone online and find inspiration.

- buy books and ebooks
- articles, advice and trip reports
- GPX files and updates
- regular newsletter

cicerone.co.uk